THE POLITICS OF POETIC FORM

The POLITICS of POETIC FORM

Poetry and Public Policy

Charles Bernstein, Editor

ROOF

Testimony by Charles Reznikoff is quoted with the generous permission of Black Sparrow Press and the Estate of Charles Reznikoff.
ISBN: 0-937804-35-5 (paper)
          0-937804-36-3 (cloth)

Library of Congress Catalog Card Number: 89-063639 (cloth)
                                                89-063640 (paper)

This book was made possible, in part, by a grant from the New York State Council on the Arts.

Design by Susan Bee.
Typography by Telos Press.
Cover by Susan Bee.

ROOF Books are published by
The Segue Foundation
303 East Eighth Street
New York, NY 10009

CONTENTS

Preface

The relation of poetry to public policy is usually assumed to be tenuous, at most secondary.

Poems are imagined primarily to express personal emotions; if political, they are seen as articulating positions already expounded elsewhere.

In contrast, poetry can be conceived as an active arena for exploring basic questions about political thought and action.

In these essays, the poets assembled extend Shelley's dictum that poets are the unacknowledged legislators of the world and George Oppen's revision: that poets are the legislators of the unacknowledged world. The particular focus of this collection is on the ways that the formal dynamics of a poem shape its ideology; more specifically, how radically innovative poetic styles can have political meanings. In what way do choices of grammar, vocabulary, syntax, and narrative reflect ideology? How do the dominant *styles* of oppositional — left and liberal — political writing affect or limit what can be articulated in these forms?

The relation of aesthetics to politics needs to be explored anew to answer to the shifting aesthetic and political climates we find ourselves in, whoever *we* find ourselves to be. In this series of encounters with that relation, there is a fundamental value in the fact that the interrogators are artists. In that sense, this book represents a continuation of a dialogue begun in $L=A=N=G=U=A=G=E$.

Roger Horrocks usefully pointed out to me a constellation of five approaches to the issue that often get interwoven, or multitracked, into these essays: the politics of the writing process, the politics of the reading process, the politics of poetic form, the politics of the market (publication, distribution), and the social politics of poetry (group/scene/community/individual and the relation of these to other institutions).

Most of these talks were originally presented in a Friday night series at The Wolfson Center for National Affairs at the New School for Social Research in New York in October, November and early December of

vii

1988. Edited transcripts of some of the discussion after the talks follow the essays. Nathaniel Mackey, Jackson Mac Low, and P. Inman presented versions of their contributions at St. Mark's Talks, in a series I had earlier curated at The Poetry Project in New York. Mac Low and Inman, along with Erica Hunt and Bruce Boone, were part of a "Politics and Language" forum presented October 25, 1984. Nathaniel Mackey's St. Mark's Talk was April 26, 1985 and his essay was first published in *Callaloo* (10:1, 1987) and is reprinted with the permission of the author and thanks to *Callaloo*.

This series could only have taken place at the New School because a committed group of poets, among others, in New York were willing to buy subscriptions for it; they are the real underwriters of the book. Nor would the program have been possible without the support of Jerry Heeger, John Major, and Lewis Falb of the New School for Social Research. Thanks also to Jeffrey Jullich, James Sherry, and Susan Bee for their work on the book's production. Some trouble has been taken to avoid standardization of style, punctuation, and reference from essay to essay in order to respect the individual authors' preferences.

With more than a couple of happy exceptions, the poets presented here are not affiliated with any university and their investigation of poetics and politics continue to be conducted without much institutional support. I find this encouraging; and it shows up the narrow frame of reference of those, like Russell Jacoby, who would insist that there are no longer "public intellectuals" in America. Perhaps the problem is that there is no public for its intellectuals, which means that a *republic* (of letters? of, as we now say, discourses?) needs to be found(ed), which is to say, *made*. That task requires poetic acts, but not just by poets.

The decline of public discourse in the United States is an urgent matter best not left to politicians and academics, especially since the conception of public space and of public discourse will have to be radically contested if this situation is to change for the better. Poetry remains an unrivaled arena for social research into the (re)constitution of the public and the (re)construction of discourse.

Charles Bernstein
Bethel, New York
July 18, 1989

Ethnopoetics & Politics /
The Politics of Ethnopoetics

Jerome Rothenberg

I did not know — at the opening — how old the work was. Like others
my age then — & others before & after us — I was looking for what in
my own time would make a difference to that time. What is easily for-
gotten is the condition of the time itself that should make us want to go
in that direction: to pull down & to transform. As a young child I heard
people still talking about the *world* war (even the *great* war) in the singu-
lar, but by adolescence the *second* war had come & with it a crisis in the
human capacity to reduce & stifle life. Auschwitz & Hiroshima came to
be the two events by which we speak of it — signs of an enormity that
turned myth into history, metaphor into fact. The horror of those events
encompassed hundreds and thousands of like disasters, joined (as we
began to realize) to other, not unrelated violence against the environ-
ment/the earth & the other-than-human world. By the mid-twentieth
century, in Charles Olson's words, "man" had been "reduced to so
much fat for soap, superphosphate for soil, fillings and shoes for sale,"
an enormity that had robbed language (one of our "proudest acts" he
said) of the power to meaningfully respond, had thus created a crisis of
expression (no, of *meaning*, of *reality*), for which a poetics must be de-
vised if we were to rise, again, beyond the level of a scream or of a si-
lence more terrible than any scream.

It is in this sense that I would speak of poetry & politics. The poets
who live with language & remember the need to resist & remake feel
whatever moves they make to be political & charged with meaning in
the political sense. Time will determine if the politics are good or bad —
if (as I would see it) they contribute to our liberation or our deeper
entrapment, but that they are a politics is something I would choose
never to deny. As a poet I am most interested in the work of those other
poets & artists for whom such questions have clearly played a central

1

role — & for whom the politics has played itself out not only (or even principally) as a subject matter but in the language & structure of the poem itself. (Whether such a politics of language, such a political poetics, is finally viable is a further question from which we often turn aside, but one that we may need sooner or later to confront.)

It's the poets then who have had it bad — this revolution of the word that's a revolution of the mind & (consistently or not) a revolution in the (political, material, & social) world itself. The first one to decisively link it all was William Blake, who proclaimed (circa 1800) a liberation through — & *from* — the poem, as an instrument of vision & of a new politics of revolution. "Poetry fetterd fetters the human race!" was the quintessential Blake — along with its corollary, that poetry liberated/set free (of inherited, legislated meaning & reality) would set *us* free in turn. Over a half-century later, a similar concatenation of language & reality marked what Walt Whitman called "the language experiment" of his *Leaves of Grass* — a radical poetics more immediately influential than Blake's, & whose opening/liberation of the verse line was tied by Whitman to a still potent (& often dangerous) American idea of revolution ("democratic & heretical" he called it).

There is a whole history of poetics informed by this language-&-reality / art-&-life configuration. Arthur Rimbaud, in shadow of the Paris commune (1870), declared that "one must be absolutely modern," and to bring it off (& here's the Rimbaud clincher) "new ideas demand new *forms*." From there it was a short jump to Apollinaire's calligrams & "new spirit," coming hand in hand with the (1909) Futurist proclamation by Marinetti (whose politics veered rightward into fascism) of not only *verse* but *words* freed up or liberated. (Yet here the totalitarian potential weighs heavy & should not be simply disregarded.) Ezra Pound, like the Italian Futurists, was also to embrace fascism, but not without creating a kind of archival/historical collage ("the epic as a poem including history") that was to encompass (in his Cantos) the "tale of the tribe" newly told.

From its left side / its Russian variant, Futurism took aim at a language trap that had to be smashed toward the emergence of new & revolutionary forms of human discourse & expression. Mayakovsky, a major poet & lesser experimenter (though an experimenter for sure), moved into mainstream bolshevism, while Khlebnikov tried for a futurian fusion of poetry, mathematics, & science, that included the creation of a new language (a mix of metaphor & soundplay) that he named *za-um*, "beyondsense." If Khlebnikov was a modernist system-maker, his Dada contemporaries in World War One Zurich come across (still) as systemdestroyers, but with as strong a sense as with the Russians that the changes in their poetry (& beyond that in their strategies of representation/signification) are acts of a political & social nature. In Tristan Tzara's 1918 Dada manifesto — like the blueprint for a hygienic act of deconstruction — he wrote: "There is a great negative work of destruction to be done. Cleaning. Sweeping. The cleanliness of the individual asserts itself after the state of madness — the aggressive complete madness of a world left in the hands of bandits, who vandalize & destroy the centuries." And Hugo Ball, who constructed "sound-poems" in a wordless language, wrote of that effort: "A line of poetry is a chance to get rid of all the filth that clings to language, to get rid of language itself. I want the word where it ends and begins. Dada is the heart of words."

Erupting from Dada, Surrealism [circa 1924] proclaimed a "surrealist revolution" & subsequently a "surrealism at the service of the [Russian] revolution" — thus accepting, in André Breton's formulation, the postponement of its own desires for a revolution of the word through a recovered language of dream & "unconscious" mental process on the one hand, systematic chance operations on the other, until the victory of the working class, the Russian state, etc. had come to pass. But something like the Dada/constructivist sense of a language destruction & reconstruction entered (differently but unmistakably) into William Carlos Williams' description of Gertrude Stein's work: "going systematically to work smashing every connotation that words ever had, in order to get them back clean." His (and hers as he interpreted it) was a program for poetry / for language that Williams would often repeat and would tie, in context of world war & of cold war, to a sense of poetry as that kind of language for the lack of which men were everyday / miserably / dying. As in his 1950 letter to the young Robert Creeley, where he wrote (in much the manner of Tzara's hygienic Dada streetcleaner): "Bad art is then that which does not serve in the continual service of cleansing the language of all fixations upon dead, stinking dead, usages of the past. Sanitation and hygiene or sanitation that we may have hygienic writing."

(It is a curious responsibility for language as a thing to be purified and/or invigorated for the public good — not, let me stress, as a conservative matter of prescriptive style & grammar, but as a radical rethinking & reinvention of expression & meaning. I don't know if anything like this exists today at anywhere near the cutting edge of poetry, though I can think of many & various claims to certain aspects of it. But presumably that's what this series is here to discuss.)

Still, in American poetry from Williams until now, the language & reality connection (along with what Williams in Paterson contrasts as "a false language" & "a true") has continued to be a central issue. (It is like a vital force, a public plasma that still keeps us going — away from the pitfalls of the merely new, the thereby trivial.) Charles Olson was one of those who brought it early into my own generation, going from first suggestion of an already existing "open" or "projective" verse (with its exploration of "the elements & minims of language") to the question of how said verse alters & is altered by one's "stance toward reality."

If Olson's projectivist manifesto was early & germinal, it was in no way singular. Robert Duncan, with a more detailed grip on the modernist inheritance (& what came before it), presented it not as the work of "we moderns" (he wrote), not as the components of a modernist fashion, "but as links in a spiritual tradition," going back into the near romantic & distant gnostic past. Jackson Mac Low, like his fellow-poet & -composer John Cage, connected his precise experiments with systematic chance operations to a basis in buddhist and anarchist thought — among many & diverse sources, both political & religious in nature. Allen Ginsberg (whose political & moral conscience grows more impressive with the years) quoted as a title for one of his manifesto-essays, "When the Mode of the Music Changes, the Walls of the City Shake," & Gary Snyder, who remains a leading activist in American ecological politics, defined the "real work of modern man" as "uncover[ing] the inner structure and actual boundaries of the mind." A sense of the political dimension of poetic acts (the connection of politics, metaphysics, & language) is also a key part of those recent works that have been variously presented as "language poetry" or "language-centered writing" [and so on], as when Ron Silliman (poet & editor of the California-based *Socialist Review*) wrote in a 1977 essay, "Disappearance of the Word, Appearance of the World": "The work of each poet, each poem, is a response to a determinate coordinate of language and history," & several years later attempted to substitute "realism" for "language" as the designation for this kind of (rigorously experimental) poetry.

* * *

The instances are many & they continue into the very present moment. I am citing them here to indicate that there is in modernism (& *post*modernism) an honorable formalist tradition that is in no sense a *mere* formalism. It is in the context of this inherently political, problematically public tradition — of a language-centered & formally experimental poetry aimed at social, political, & personal transformation — that I would

like to address the idea of an ethnopoetics as it has arisen among us —
as a way of exploring/considering the strategies of language/reality etc.
in a range of human circumstances & places "other" & often (histori-
cally & culturally) wiser, more grounded, than our own. The still larger,
still more political context for all of this is the struggle with imperialism,
racism, chauvinism, etc., to which such an exploration might still contri-
bute as resistance & as provocation.

Ethnopoetics — my coinage, in a fairly obvious way, circa 1967 — re-
fers to an attempt to investigate on a transcultural scale the range of
possible poetries that had not only been imagined but put into practice
by other human beings. It was premised on the perception that western
definitions of poetry & art were no longer, indeed had never been,
sufficient & that our continued reliance on them was distorting our view
both of the larger human experience & of our own possibilities within it.
The focus was not so much inter*national* as inter*cultural*, with a stress (for
reasons that I hope to get into later) on those stateless & classless
societies that an earlier ethnology had classified as "primitive." That the
poetry & art of those cultures were complex in themselves & in their
interconnections with each other was a first point that I found it neces-
sary to assert when, circa 1968, I assembled a series of instances in *Tech-
nicians of the Sacred* (subtitled: *A Range of Poetries from Africa, America, Asia, &
Oceania*). I began the pre-face there as follows:

> That there are no primitive languages is an axiom of contemporary linguis-
> tics where it turns its attention to the remote languages of the world. There
> are no half-formed languages, no underdeveloped or inferior languages.
> Everywhere a development has taken place into structures of great com-
> plexity. People who have failed to achieve the wheel will not have failed to
> invent & develop a highly wrought grammar. Hunters & gatherers innocent
> of all agriculture will have vocabularies that distinguish the things of their
> world down to the finest details. The language of snow among the Eskimos
> is awesome. The aspect system of Hopi verbs can, by a flick of the tongue,
> make the most subtle kinds of distinction between different types of mo-
> tion. What is true of language in general is equally true of poetry & of the
> ritual-systems of which so much poetry is a part. It is a question of energy &
> intelligence as universal constants &, in any specific case, the direction that
> the energy & intelligence (= imagination) have been given. No people today
> is newly born. No people has sat in sloth for the thousands of years of its
> history. Measure everything by the Titan rocket & the transistor radio, & the
> world is full of primitive peoples. But once change the unit of value to the
> poem or the dance-event or the dream (all clearly artifactual situations) & it
> becomes apparent what all those people have been doing all those years
> with all that time on their hands.

That was in the middle to late 1960s, and I've tried at various times
since then to explain what the situation was vis à vis a possible ethno-
poetics when I & a number of fellow poets & artists began (not for the
first time in this century) to place a value on it. It was already clear by
then that 20th-century art was a powerful enough force to demand a
reconsideration of its own history & prehistory, though the parameters
of that reconsideration were (as they are today) still open to question.
The where and when of it, in brief, was whether a still largely western
movement should claim a linkage to what was historically & culturally
outside it, or, even where looking within, whether it should or could
break the hierarchical dichotomies between high & low art, elitist &
popular. How significant, on the one hand, was the turn to Africa in
cubist or expressionist painting? how significant, on the other, was the
attraction in these and related movements to folk & popular images, &
so on? that Picasso had elevated an African sculpture over the Venus de
Milo as Marinetti had a racing car over the Victory of Samothrace was
well enough known, but was the gesture central, crucial, viable, even al-
lowable? was it (on Picasso's part) merely exploitative, another example
of neo-imperialistic expropriation? was there a western turning toward
the culture of the third world as a kind of countermovement to the third
world's gravitation (intellectual & economic) toward the west?

I was at that point in time already coming at the poetry — the verbal
aspect of the work in contrast to the visual — & had been doing so in a
concerned but not a very concentrated way since sometime in the early
1950s. While there was nothing like the proliferation of materials that
had accumulated around the primitive or neo-primitive aesthetics that
permeated the other, non-verbal, non-translatative arts, what came im-
mediately to hand was in no sense insignificant. Translation was of
course the great problematic in all of this, & that meant (as it does today)
a reliance on several generations of ethnographers & linguists (Boas &
the Boasians, Malinowski & the Malinowskians, etc.), who not only gave
us translated "myths & texts," but attempted by accompanying commen-
taries to place them into a culturally specific, social & religious context.
(That context — often ritualistic & imaginal — might be, often was, as in-
teresting & germinal as the [translated] texts themselves.) It should be not-
ed too that the public translation work in general was & has largely contin-
ued to be the activity not of native poets but of cultural outsiders.

I was also aware at the time (& increasingly thereafter) of those earlier
poets — often "movement" connected — who had themselves made
stabs at assembling & (sometimes) retranslating what ethnographers &
others had originally gathered. Tristan Tzara, who did an unpublished

"anthologie nègre" at the time of Zurich Dada was one; Blaise Cendrars, who published an anthology of African myths & texts (largely translated as prose) was another. Khlebnikov, as a third great name of early modernism, both gathered & commented on Slavic oral & folk poetry as a kind of popular/magical basis for the new *za-um* language he was creating circa 1914. (Russian Futurism was in fact permeated by folk art, shamanism, etc.) The Surrealist poet, Benjamin Peret, did an equivalent for the Indian Americas of Cendrars' African book. Langston Hughes included traditional segments in larger gatherings of African & Afro-American poetry & folklore. And there were also regional & interregional anthologies by lesser known figures — poets & non-poets alike. (I know of no major poet, then or now, who was also an *extensive* fieldworker, directly gathering & translating rather than compiling & reworking. Possibly Michel Leiris, though I don't think his work went toward a working with or making up of texts. My own sporadic efforts in that direction — I did get into a kind of fieldwork for a while — would probably not qualify.)

By the middle 1960s also, what Donald Allen had called "the new American poetry" was giving evidence of a series of poetic but non-literary influences from sources like those I've been describing. Sometimes these acted as content & referent, sometimes as model for formal, procedural or visionary moves in our own work. Blues — as language, as structure, as tone — would be an obvious example, & with that (for the new Black poets particularly but *not* exclusively) a whole range of procedures drawn from African-American folk sources. Traditional American Indian poetry (& the great mythic & ritual worlds for which it was the verbal/vocal expression) would be the other great instance — in a specifically American (bioregional or ecological) sense, or as related to other tribal & specifically shamanistic poetries through-out human time & space. If this was related in any sense to the old western/romantic "search for the primitive" — or, as Stanley Diamond had more accurately described it, "the attempt to define a primary human potential" — then the feeling for origins & potentials (as for sur-vivals & realizations) could be seen in a whole range of concurrent ex-plorations: the Mesopotamian & Sumerian probings in the work of Olson or Schwerner; the Chinese inventions of Ezra Pound & the later reinventions (from a Buddhist perspective) by Gary Snyder or by Cage & Mac Low in their discovery of the systematic chance operations per-meating the Confucian *I Ching*; the gnostic concerns & investigations of poets like Robert Duncan & Diane di Prima; the delving into Egyptian texts by someone like Ed Sanders; the probing of Hebrew kabbala

(both language & myth) by David Meltzer & others, myself included.
[And so on.] Hieratic civilizations here as well as stateless & classless
ones, but all that reading, delving, dedicated to a new & expanded con-
cept of what we ever had achieved or might again achieve as languaged
beings. (This I came to think of as the ethnopoetics project in the widest
sense.)

   As a poetry project — a project involving the interaction of poets,
scholars, & others — the work probably peaked circa 1980 with the de-
mise of *Alcheringa*, the magazine of ethnopoetics that I co-founded with
Dennis Tedlock in 1970 & from which I separated in 1976 to publish
(with Charlie Morrow) & edit (with Barbara Einzig and David Guss,
then with Jed Rasula and Donald Byrd in the terminal issues) the *New
Wilderness Letter*. (It was in *Alcheringa*, by the way, that Ron Silliman's first
mini-anthology of "language poetry" appeared in the early 1970s.) I
would like at this juncture to acknowledge some of those I've continued
to think of as directly a part of, or indirectly contributors to, the ethno-
poetics project. Among the poets, ethnologists & critics (many of them
previously involved), who entered directly into the discourse, circa 1970
& after, were David Antin, Paula Gunn Allen, Kofi Awoonor, Ulli Beier,
Michel Benamou, James Clifford, Stanley Diamond, Diane di Prima,
Robert Duncan, George Economou, Clayton Eshleman, Jean Pierre
Faye, Robert Filliou, Anselm Hollo, Dell Hymes, David McAllester,
Steve McCaffery, Michael McClure, W.S. Merwin, Barbara Myerhoff, bp
Nichol, Simon Ortiz, Rochelle Owens, George Quasha, Ishmael Reed,
Diane Rothenberg, Richard Schechner, Armand Schwerner, Gary
Snyder, William Spanos, Dennis Tedlock, Nathaniel Tarn, Victor Turn-
er, and Anne Waldman.

   Some of these were also active as translators (technical & precise or
experimental & precise or both), & from their individual & collective ef-
forts came a series of significant, often astonishing translatative works,
which I can do no more (again) than catalog for you at present. Among
the principal ones since 1968 — & discounting my own anthologies &
experimental translations — were Dennis Tedlock's *Finding the Center*
(traditional Zuni oral narratives by Andrew Peynetsa & others) and *Popol
Vuh* (the surviving "epic" poem of the pre-Columbian Mayas); Howard
Norman's *Wishing Bone Cycle* & other Cree Indian oral narratives (in
which Samuel Makidemewabe figures as the principal narrative artist);
Nathaniel Tarn's translation of the Mayan ritual drama, *Rabinal Achi*;
David Guss's prose translation of the Makiritare [Yekuana] Indian
Watunna cycle [from Venezuela]; Judith Gleason's *A Recitation of Ifa*, a
Yoruba (Nigerian) divination cycle; Kofi Awoonor's direct translations of

Ewe (Ghanaian) abuse poetry; John Bierhorst's translation of the 16th-century Aztec [Nahuatl] *Cantares Mexicanos*; the oral autobiography & chanted poems of the Mazatec shamaness Maria Sabina, as translated by Alvaro Estrada & (into English) by Henry Munn; Allen F. Burns's *Epoch of Miracles*, translations from the contemporary Yucatec Mayan oral poet, Alonzo Gonzales Mó; Simon Ortiz's or Peter Blue Cloud's revisionings of Coyote narratives from (their own) Native American traditions; Donald Phillipi's *Songs of Gods, Songs of Humans: The Epic* [& shamanistic] *Poems of the Ainus*; A.K. Ramanujan's translations from 8th and 9th-century Bakhti poet-saints in books of his like *Hymns for the Drowning* [from the Tamil] and *Speaking of Shiva* [from the Kannada]; and the often hieratic chanted poetry of the Peruvian curandero Eduardo Calderón Palomino.

[I could go on . . . with these . . . with others where the energy enters directly into the new work, the poem or book as such. And there would be an overlapping too — not always simple — with the new ethnic poetries & the traditional powers they have sometimes brought to light.]

* * *

". . . There is a politics in all of this," I wrote with Diane Rothenberg in the Pre-Face to *Symposium of the Whole* (an anthology of basic writings by myself & others on ethnopoetics), "& an importance, clearly, beyond the work of poets & artists. The old 'primitive' models in particular — of small & integrated, stateless & classless societies — reflect a concern over the last two centuries with new communalistic & anti-authoritarian forms of social life & with alternatives to the environmental disasters accompanying [a growing & centralized state and] an increasingly abstract relation to what was once a living universe. Our belief in this regard is that a re-viewing of 'primitive' ideas of the 'sacred' represents an attempt — by poets & others — to preserve & enhance primary values against a mindless mechanization that has run past any uses it may once have had. (This, rather than the advocacy of some particular system, seems to us the contribution of the 'primitive' [the traditional tribal] to whatever world we may yet hope to bring about.) As a matter of history, we would place the model in question both in the surviving, still rapidly vanishing stateless cultures & in a long subterranean tradition of resistance to the twin authorities of state & organized religion."

[To which I would add: (1) That the multiple poetries revealed by an *ethno*poetics lead inevitably to the conclusion that *there is no one way*; thus, they contribute to the desire/need already felt, to undermine authority, program, & system, so as not to be done in by them in turn. (2) That we bridge history by placing the poem back into history; that if the poem's social/historical dimension is thereby tricky to describe (& it is), it does not diminish the poem (its interest & usefulness at present) if we so describe it. And (3) that the models in question are all instances in which the communal/poetic/public are in conjunction, not in conflict: a situation of communitas (V. Turner) — as both a hope & threat deferred.]

To continue, then. [Adapting the next three paragraphs from the Preface to *Symposium of the Whole*.]

Along with the political model (which seems increasingly elusive as we inch toward the millennium), there are other modalities to be noted. One involves the paradigm/the dream of a total art — & of a life made whole — that has meant different things & been given different names throughout this century. "Intermedia" was a word for it in its 1960s manifestation — also "total theater" & "happenings" — behind which was the sense of what the 19th-century Wagnerian consciousness had called *Gesamtkunstwerk* & had placed — prefigured — at the imagined beginnings of the human enterprise. The difference in our own time was to smash that imperial & swollen mold — to shift the primary scene from Greece, say, to the barbaric or paleolithic past, or to the larger, often still existing tribal world, & to see in that world (however "outcast & vagabond" — in Robert Duncan's words again — it had been made to look) a complexity of act & vision practiced by proto-poets/proto-artists who were true "technicians of the sacred." And along with this shift came the invention *and* revival of *specific* means: new materials & instruments (plastic and neon, film and tape) alongside old or foreign ones (stones, bone, and skin; drums, didjeridoos, and gamelans); ancient roles & modes of thought that had survived at the Western margins (sacred clowns & dancers, shamanistic ecstasies, old & new works of dream & chance); & a tilt toward ritual, not as "an obsessional concern with repetitive acts" but, as Victor Turner further described it for the tribal world, "an immense orchestration of genres in all available sensory codes: speech, music, singing; the presentation of elaborately worked objects, such as masks; wall-paintings, body-paintings; sculptured forms; complex, many-tiered shrines; costumes; dance forms with complex grammars & vocabularies of bodily movements, gestures, & facial expressions."

Turner's description, which fits both "them" and "us," holds equally true in the language arts (the work of poetry as such), though by the nature of language itself (& the need to translate ourselves in — always — partial forms) the complexity & the interplay of new & old haven't been as clear there. Taken as a whole, then, the human species presents an extraordinary richness of verbal means — both of languages & of poetries — largely closed to us until now by an unwillingness to think beyond the conventions & boundaries of Western literature. As an attempt to break those boundaries, ethnopoetics has involved both a new consideration of the non-literate & oral [its bestknown side] & a simultaneous expansion of the idea of writing & the text, wherever & whenever found. To summarize rapidly, the oral recovery involves a poetics deeply rooted in the powers of song & speech, breath & body, as brought forward across time by the living presence of poet-performers, with or without the existence of a visible/literal text. The range of such poetries is the range of human culture itself (that ours is also, largely, an oral culture is here worth noting); & the forms those poetries take (different for each culture) run from wordless songs & mantras to the intricacies (imagistic & symbolic) of multileveled oral narratives; from the stand-up performances of individual shamans & bards to the choreographies of massed singers & dancers, extended sometimes over protracted periods of time. From the side of visual & written language — which may, like the oral, be as old as the species itself — a fully human poetics would include all forms of what Jacques Derrida calls archécriture (which I translate here, however loosely, as primal writing): pictographs & hieroglyphs, aboriginal forms of visual & concrete poetry, sand paintings & earth mappings, gestural & sign languages, counting systems & numerologies, divinational signs made by man or read (as a poetics of natural forms) in the tracks of animals or of stars through the night sky.

That practices like these correspond — both superficially & profoundly — to experimental moves in our own time isn't needed to justify them, but it indicates why we're now able to see them & to begin to understand as well the ways they differ from our own work. Other areas in which such correspondences hold true may be more involved with "idea" than with "structure," though the distinction isn't always easy (or useful) to maintain. Traditional divination work, for example-the Ifa Oracles of Africa, say, or the Chinese I Ching — rests on the recognition of a world revealed moment by moment through processes of chance & synchronicity (i.e., the interrelatedness of simultaneous events), & these processes in turn inform one major segment of our avantgarde. Similarly, the widespread practice of exploring the "unknown" through the creation of new languages shows a strong sense of the virtual nature of reality (what Léopold Sédar Senghor speaks of in African terms as the traditional surreal) & the linguistic means to get it said.

I have been speaking here of acts both of vision & of speech — of vision & of language; & it is those two [vision, language] that I take to be the twin centers of the poetics that I'm presenting. In this sense I would have had no hesitancy in my own terms to call myself a "language" poet [or half a language poet . . . or a language poet & a half] . . . did in fact respond with some feelings of deprivation to the use of the term by poets outside of my own immediate cohort, & would not have surrendered that designation as easily as some seem to have done. So, since we're in something like that context here tonight, I'd like to call special attention to it: to the centrality of language, not only in our own poetry but in those "other" forms of poetry to which an ethnopoetics can direct us. On the one hand this would bring us into the domain of that kind of artifice that Charles Bernstein describes elsewhere as central to the poetic act, but seen now as a spectrum of means available/developed in different ways in different cultures. In any given instance of a shamanistic poetry, say, this would involve the use of particular forms of verbal/linguistic artifice (many foregrounded, prominent, opaque, &/or [as Bernstein puts it] *non*-absorptive) towards a heightened involvement, *absorption*, in the magical, visionary act of the moment. On the other hand, in so far as we're dealing with languages as such, what the diversity reveals to us is the specific way in which any language (our own included) is a system of both special possibilities & special traps. (Thus, in Benjamin Whorf's now well-known example, Indo-European languages lead "us" to a linear sense of time [past, present, future], while Uto-Aztecan languages like Hopi lead "them" to a cyclical sense [potential, actual] — either of which I would see as functional or dysfunctional, dependent on the circumstances.) Any language poetry [language-centered poetry] among us would, it seems to me, be advanced by a heightened awareness of the ways in which language (as our principal culture-bearing instrument) shapes reality in divergent times & places. What has happened, what may happen, in the telling.]

In her oral autobiography the Mazatec shamaness María Sabina speaks of her work as being, in effect, a poetics of healing based on a poetics of language. Unlettered herself she reads the Book of Language & she cures through Language. That means that her "I," like that of Rimbaud's seer, is other; that in the act of chanting, making poetry, "she" is being thought by "someone else." For the new poet — the poet of the new — to come to such a realization Rimbaud proposed not only a derangement of the senses but the reconstitution of a language / of language itself. "A new language must be found," he wrote. Not only for the sake of speaking but of seeing, knowing. Therefore — for him &

her — the hypothesis would be: I *see* through language. And its corollary: without language, I am blind.

For us too it would raise a question, among many, that we should be careful not too easily to dismiss — that of a language poetics [a language poetry] as a way of life. An instrument (if I can use that word) of *liberation*. A private/public healing.

* * *

I have spoken before of how we have been able to use our own expanded ideas of the poem to identify a fuller range of poetries in the cultural areas under question; how in turn, by focusing on the life situations in which the traditional poetries functioned, we can see if such a new understanding might show us new or alternative ways to integrate art & life. In a *personal* sense I have found much of this to be transformative, regarding how I see myself as a poet & a man in this world. The same, I know, can be said for others. Yet on the whole the ethnopoetic project has not been successful in the world at large & is today mostly carried on (assuming it's even the same project) within a segment of the academic world in which the relation to contemporary praxis (as analog or paradigm) becomes dimmer & dimmer. Still, there is now some activity along these lines, although one may still be caught up, as I was a dozen or so years ago, by Ron Silliman's words, referring to the kind of poetry I had been presenting in *Technicians of the Sacred*: "The fact that there have been as yet few attempts to incorporate such materials into 'comparative literature' curricula is not simply attributable to racism, though racism inevitably plays a role. Rather, it is that in the reality of capitalism (or of any society well down the road toward capitalist modes of production) there is no meaning here."

The implications of this (& there are more implications here than at first may meet the ear), I will leave for discussion elsewhere & will go on now to do what I most like to do: present some of that range of poetries that I was tracking down in *Technicians of the Sacred* & thereafter, with a particular emphasis on those language works that a new/experimental poetics first allowed us to perceive as such.

DISCUSSION

CHARLES MORROW: Since Jerry mentions that the recovery of "wordless" oral poetries is one of the goals of ethnopoetics, I thought that Paul Anders Simma, who is an artist visiting from Lapland, might say a few words about "yoiking" — a form of poetry-without-words from his culture.

PAUL ANDERS SIMMA: What I could say is that what we have is a kind of portraying people, places, and also feelings without words, just with the use of rhythm. Every person, at least in our area, has kind of their own rhythm-picture, and it's also a rhythm-picture that is belonging to your family. So, if someone yoiks my song, they can tell me from what area I am, from what family, and also something about my personality — by listening to that song. And that song has no words whatever.

CHARLES BERNSTEIN: Could you be more specific about the types of personalities or family distinctions that would be made, with respect to a given sound, say?

SIMMA: First of all, all the areas have their own special type of yoiking. A person that comes from the tundra or a specific river valley has their own type of singing; so that's the main form. Then you also can hear if you know that valley, you know also what people are living in that area, and you could say very roughly to which family this person belongs, if this person is someone who is involved in reindeer herding or if it's a farmer, because there are different kinds of yoikings that belong to different kinds of ways of living. Then there is also very important part in a yoik that tells about how a person's personality is.

It's very difficult for me to describe this in English.

One of our most popular artists is a professional yoiker. I think he must know thousands of different rhythms and different musicians. He has a kind of signature that tells everyone who this guy is, and it's like

 HEY ELLO HEY ELLO HEY ELLO HEY ELLO HEY LUHA
 SAY HELLO LAY LELLO HEY ELLO LO LELAH HEY ELLO
 LO LELAH HEY ELLO LO LELAH

And this goes on. And in this yoik the very rough cuts in the end tells that this person is a really powerful man and, for the person who knows the aesthetics of this way of telling, when he meets this man, can, even if he has not met him before, maybe tell that.

ROTHENBERG: Are all yoiks without words? I wouldn't think so.

SIMMA: No. There are also yoiks with words, with a lot of words, but the types of yoiks I'm talking about that are describing a person or a place or a feeling or an animal, they are very often without words.

STEPHEN LOWEY: Do all the people share in yoiking or is there one yoiker amongst the people?

SIMMA: All people share, but it's also kind of like gossip. If you like a person, you can create a very beautiful yoik about that person, but you can also create a yoik that is teasing the person or even telling that this man is a thief or he is a coward, or whatever you want, you can picture the person through that yoik.

LYNN CRAWFORD: On what occasions would you use this? Is it primarily in a formal setting or is it just that you meet someone and you kind of sing a little bit of a tune as a greeting or something like that?

SIMMA: Often it is used when you come to a new area, where you don't know people, or if you meet someone that you haven't seen for a very long time, then you use the song as a kind of start of oral dialogue. But I've also heard in my home area a husband and a wife nagging by yoiking, not by shouting but by yoiking [laughter]. So there are very many uses of yoik. But mostly it's just a kind of a way of telling that this is me and I come from this area and this is our tradition and it gives a picture of who I am and it is also a kind of invitation for a dialogue.

CRAWFORD: Is it something that is still alive? Do people still do it? It's not considered something old fashioned, or a tradition that's dying?

SIMMA: It's very much alive, but it's also threatened. The first thing colonialists did when they came to Lapland in the beginning of the thirteenth century was to ban the yoik. To have a shaman's drum and to yoik was forbidden in law, so a lot of people were burned or hanged or their heads were cut off because of this yoiking tradition, and still today we have in Lapland, in the most Lappish areas, there are still laws forbidding teachers to teach the students how to yoik.

BERNSTEIN: So here's a clear example of the relation of poetry to "public policy," in the most literal sense: the colonizers redefining, by force of arms, what the "public" is and a residual, deeply rooted resistance to that redefinition. And what could be more a matter of "national affairs": no matter how odd it may first seem to talk about poetry in this way. These issues are in no way "settled" for North American cultures, no matter how much the settlers keep trying to put an end to them. The near-religious allegiance to Standard English and the xeno-phobic attempts to suppress linguistic difference in the English First movement are two manifestations that are all too current.

SIMMA: I have been traveling around the Indian reserves and been meeting Indians here in the USA and Canada. I have been almost shocked by the fact that the Indians were not allowed to use their own religion until very recently.

ROTHENBERG: Yes, there have been many attempts to restrict the traditional religious practices.

BERNSTEIN: And the President of the United States just recently said that "we" made a mistake to let native Americans go on with their own practices. Speaking in the Soviet Union, President Reagan said that we should not have permitted the Indians to have their reservations and to be a separate culture, we should have insisted that they assimilate into our culture.

ROTHENBERG: Meanwhile, the Soviets are part of the problem for the Sumis, for the Lapps. Soviet policy is no great shakes in this area.

SIMMA: An American anthropologist, Michael Harner, went to the So-viet Union, to Siberia, and met people from the highest Soviet. And they were very interested in using his shamanistic technique, his shamanistic songs, for curing alcoholism. They didn't call it shamanistic song, they called it rhythmo-therapy [laughter]. So, Michael is traveling to Siberia to learn [teach?] the Indian techniques. But it has to be a white man to get the Russians to listen to them. And it has to come from the U.S.

ROTHENBERG: He comes from the New School for Social Research!

Q: I was wondering if yoiking developed because there were many dia-lects and people couldn't understand each other, and through this there was a way of non-verbal communication?

SIMMA: I really don't know what the reasons are, how yoiks started, but I believe that it's also the mistrust against words again. You know that there are other more important ways of communicating than talk-ing, so I think our cultures are in a way very non-verbal cultures. Of course, this can be a reason, that there are many different dialects, and there might be difficulties to communicate.

ROTHENBERG: It's a very tricky question, and there can be many answers to it. My observation has been that in cultures where there are many of these wordless songs, say with the Seneca Indians, whom I know fairly well, there's also a great tradition of oratory, and people, men and women, will under public circumstances certainly go on talking at great length. A traditional Seneca speech in the longhouse can go on for hours. So there is no reluctance about using language. People say now, as in many other places, "In the old days they really did the florid language and we have sort of cut it down and simplified it now." Though the people were given to excessive overspeaking and high rhetoric and all of that, still most of the songs fall into the wordless mode; others have words, and this extends from secular songs into the most religious of songs. There are also suggestions that the wordless songs may represent the language of gods or animals or the language (no longer understood) of an earlier people that preceded us to this place. Many different explanations.

BERNSTEIN: I want to curve back to something you were saying before, in relation to the "unsuccess" of ethnopoetics, and ask you something from the perspective of what's sometimes called "vulgar Marxism." Assuming that there are these cultural differences which have sometimes been suppressed brutally, assuming that there are various forms of expression and language which are not centralized and can't be translated, why, from a point of view of social progress, from the point of view of trying to make people aware of imperialism, of capitalist global economic systems, isn't it better to discourage these forms of primitive and backward-looking folk behaviors? Don't we do better to give up the romanticism attached to this and understand the need for instrumental language that can deal with the global economy? That while it may be a sacrifice, we can't go back to a pre-feudal kind of existence, because the world, whether we like it or not, is a post-industrial, global economic system in which there are languages of power, and that it's those languages that have to be confronted in their own terms, and that these untranslatable things are a kind of nostalgia for a world that we can't recapture.

ROTHENBERG: And this is true [laughter]. And therefore we are caught in a split between our poetry, often, and our other writing, in which the poetry represents a critique of the current language, if we take it to be that. But it's something that we don't carry into the instrumental language that accompanies the poetry. In other words we still need that instrumental language to underscore the poem, we can't simply go there, and then we realize of course that peoples who make poetry in those terms are not without the discursive language to accompany it, that poetry has its circumstances, that discourse has its circumstances, and that they sometimes overlap. It's not a clear distinction between them. There are points of confusion.

BERNSTEIN: But what do you suppose is lost? You talked about, quoting Silliman, the perception that, within capitalist (not to exempt state socialist) societies that "there is no meaning here." What is the political value of this non-instrumental form of cultural particularity? Why is that important?

RALPH STAVINS: Because it's primary to our own experience. The child in us. We have to begin somewhere, don't we?

JAMES SHERRY: Also, to the extent that we're creating or homogenizing a monoculture, we want to be sure that we get as much into the mix as we can, so we have to be aware of all the different parts of human experience that are going to go into this world culture that we idealize.

ROTHENBERG: I think this is a serious question. I think it goes to the heart. It's not just a question of the ethnopoetics, it's a question about most of what we do as poets under cultural, public, social circumstances, in which that poetry we make has very little impact on the surrounding community. So in a way the ethnopoetic does point to circumstances in which we assume that the public/poetic dichotomy did not exist, was not as intense as it is now. I think the problem is not just along the lines of the ethnopoetic. I think in a certain sense that it's not simply the ethnopoetic that is endangered, that poetry is in itself an endangered species. Why do we do it at all, why do we do any of it, when there are other forms of what seems to be more immediate communication, if that's what we're involved with? It's certainly not the easiest way, if we're into a 'reach out' program, it's not the easiest way to accomplish that. And when we want to come into some larger discourse, we don't use those methods, by and large. We modify them in some way, or we discard them. Like right now.

NICK LAWRENCE: We've heard testimony to the power that language has and that powerful language-users have in their respective societies. You mentioned the word 'shaman' a lot and also 'technicians of the sacred.' Technicians, *techne*, people skilled in a particular craft. What are the implications of a caste of language-users per se, those whose job it is simply to exercise their skill in language? Is that a division of labor we want to get away from? Wouldn't we want instead to move language play into the rationalizing discourses that are a direct product of our economic system? Or do we want to continue to siphon it off into a small circumscribed area separate from the rest of the use of language in general?

ROTHENBERG: In the best of all possible worlds, I would prefer the democratization of language and of poetry, so that we all become poets in the process. What steps can be taken in that direction at this time I don't know. I have felt more encouraged at other times that perhaps we might be moving back in that direction. I don't feel particularly encouraged that it's right around the corner.

LAWRENCE: One thing that might be done is to isolate those tendencies in ordinary language use that tend toward the non-instrumental, perhaps, or what's been called "the poetry of everyday life," to isolate that, to bring that out, to make people self-conscious about their own use of language.

ROTHENBERG: My impression is that there is a lot of difficulty with language! Not simply an alienation from, an inability to approach the languages of poetry, but that language with any degree of complication seems to be in trouble at present, as in the ongoing political discourse, such as it is, where I think we have pretty much accepted it as a given that the complexities cannot be presented in a public forum. Partially the rationale is that the public will turn off to them, the public will turn away. I don't know if the politicians are capable of doing it, but . . .

JACKSON MAC LOW: We used to have real debates, and very complex discourse. The people came to little towns to hear Lincoln and Douglas debate. Now we can't even have a debate. It's depressing.

I wanted to go back to something you said earlier, which is politically relevant to the attitude we might take toward these cultures. You said they were stateless, classless, and not totalitarian. I don't think any of these things is true. I remember at one point in our anarchist group in the 40s and 50s we idealized the Hopi and the Zuni, and then I came across the work of Karl Wittfogel and Esther Goldfrank, who showed that it's nothing of the kind, that you have secret masters, sometimes people disappear, children are scared to death by the kachina at a specific point in their lives to make them submissive to the mores, and so on. I think it is best, while understanding the many virtues of these societies, not to idealize them politically in any way. They didn't have states in our modern sense, but they had hierarchy.

ROTHENBERG: It's hard looking at these from the outside, and you don't want to say simply, across the board, "they are all stateless, classless, egalitarian," and so on. But I would be careful, talking out here in public, not to casually introduce possibly inaccurate terms like "secret master," or vague memory flicks about people disappearing, or assumptions about kachinas being instruments to make children submissive — all of which sounds very ominous when put like that. What it tends to do, again, is to cover over the "many virtues" you mention in favor of a poorly defined image of what was stereotypically described as "savagery." I don't think that's being particularly objective in response, although I recognize that what we've been talking about (as other-than-western or pre-industrial or some other broad term) covers a wide range of cultures, some of which were really hierarchical and hieratic. The Aztecs, say, were not an egalitarian, easy-going society [laughter], but there are societies without that kind of ranking.

Q: What societies are not hierarchical?

ROTHENBERG: Most American Indian societies weren't . . . not in any way that makes much sense to talk about a hierarchy . . . like a fixed or a hereditary ranking system . . . recognizable social groupings with a differentiated access to power. Charismatic leaders would be something else.

Q: There was the chief with all the feathers.

ROTHENBERG: Very few chiefs in a hierarchic sense . . . and very few feathers. That's an image out of western movies and a confusion of chiefs with kings or with despots or something like that. Arbitrary power, hereditary positions, a real state to back it up and pass it on — that simply wasn't the dominant pattern in North America; maybe in the southeastern (so-called) "kingdoms" and at a late point in the northwest. Otherwise there wasn't anything like the degree of vested authority or social ranking. But there were people appointed to positions . . .

MORROW: But weren't the elders and the concept of age . . .

ROTHENBERG: Age and experience, yes, but there are a lot of accounts of very young people who excelled, who were successful leaders: men in their twenties and thirties, some even younger. But, sure, it would be fair to say that there was a certain prestige or authority that went with age; and there are also questions of inequality with regard to sex or gender — to what degree the men, say, formed a kind of ruling group. But precisely here many of the Indian cultures give us the best examples we have of societies with shared power among men and women. Like the Senecas, if we want to go into it, where woman controlled both the food supply (the fields) and the households, and where they elected the men who served as "leaders" at their will.

And there's also the question of those we call the shamans — of whether they formed a power elite or a special caste, even prior to what was formally called a priesthood. In some societies — South America in particular — most adult males were shamans, although I don't know if you'd count that as an equalization or as an example of a specially empowered caste. But these are not (from our point of view) the most attractive cultures, since generally the women were without the numinous powers attributed to the men. These are obviously judgmental questions, and our ignorance and distance (maybe, even, our imperial distance) makes the rush to judgment even worse. What I would say, to keep it short, is that by their sheer very existence, these small stateless cultures may be so strikingly and significantly contrastive with our own, that they can exercise a disruptive power over the hegemony of that other discourse, the one about the nature of the human that engages us; so that it is enough to simply point to that, the "many virtues" and the differences — that it may help to shake us up, to reconsider who we are.

MAC LOW: That's just what I was pointing to: that disruptive power is more important to us than idealizing the social forms.

ROTHENBERG: It may indeed be.

Poetry as Explanation, Poetry as Praxis

Bruce Andrews

> *O, the vilest are destined for rewards*
> *and the best stand gaping*
> *mouths wide before an empty simalcrum,*
> *The narrative alone makes me gloomy,*
> *and the rich conduct their business on their heads.*
> — Marcabru, Provencal 12th century, tr. Blackburn

I'll use as the fulcrum of my remarks on politics & radicalism in recent literary work the two book-length anthologies of the kind of poetry Charles Bernstein & I focussed on in editing $L=A=N=G=U=A=G=E$ and *The* $L=A=N=G=U=A=G=E$ *Book* (Southern Illinois University Press, 1984): Douglas Messerli, ed., *"Language" Poetries* (New Directions, 1987) & Ron Silliman, ed., *In the American Tree* (National Poetry Foundation, 1986).

I'm always trying to reorganize my life. And I'm always trying to reorganize the world — words writing writing politics. Incomprehension is the subtitle.

I GET IMPATIENT
Conventionally, radical dissent & 'politics' in writing would be measured in terms of communication & concrete effects on an audience. Which means either a direct effort at empowering or mobilizing — aimed at existing identities — or at the representation of outside conditions, usually in an issue-oriented way. So-called 'progressive lit'. The usual assumptions about unmediated communication, giving 'voice' to 'individual' 'experience', the transparency of the medium (language), the instrumentalizing of language, pluralism, etc. bedevil this project. But more basically: such conventionally progressive literature fails to self-examine writing & its medium, language. Yet in an era where the

23

reproduction of the social status quo is more & more dependent upon ideology & language (language in ideology & ideology in language), that means that it can't really make claims to comprehend and/or challenge the nature of the social whole; it can't be political in that crucial way.

A desire for a social, political dimension in writing — embracing concern for a public, for community goods, for overall comprehension & transformation — intersects an overall concern for language as a medium: for the conditions of its makings of meaning, significance or value, & sense. Technicians of the Social — the need to see society as a whole. That has meant, in recent years with this work, a conception of writing *as* politics, not writing *about* politics. Asking: what is the *politics* inside the work, inside *its* work? Instead of instrumentalized or instrumentalizing, this is a poetic writing more actively *explanatory*. One that explores the *possibilities* of meaning, of 'seeing through': works that foreground the process by which language 'works', implicating the history & context that are needed to allow the writing to be more comprehensively understood, bringing those building blocks & limits of meaning & sense back *inside* the writing, giving you greater distance by putting them within the internal circuitry.

Explanation embeds itself in the writing itself — *locating* work in relation to its social materials: to what it handles, resists, characterizes. It reads the outside, it doesn't just read itself. It doesn't try to be self-explanatory in a formalist, process-oriented way, enclosed within its own separate realm. It is itself an interpretation. It is a response, a production that takes place within a larger context of reproduction. And this is the reflexivity which we should be on the look-out for — a social kind, that comes through *method* (of writing & of reading) — not (just) 'content'. Method as Prescription — posing problems, eliciting reading.

Nothing passes unalarmed. Limits aren't located until they're pushed. Rewriting the social body — as a body to body transaction: to write *into operation* a 'reading body' which is more & more self-avowedly *social*. Lay bare the device, spurn the facts as not self-evident. A V-effect, to combat the obvious; to stand out = to rebel; counter-embodiment, with our "paper bullets of the brain". All this points to a look at language as medium — in two respects: first, as a sign system; second, as discourse or ideology. Concentric circles, one inside the other. In both cases, though, the same concern: stop repressing the active construction, the *making* of meaning, the *making* of sense — social sense.

What we face first is the language seen in formal terms: the *sign*. There is no 'direct treatment' of the thing possible, except of the 'things' of language. Crystalline purity — or transparency — will not be found in words. That classical ideal is an illusion — one which recommends that we repress the process of production or cast our glance away from it. An alternative would face the medium of language — through which we might get a poetry that is a reading which acknowledges, or faces up to, its material base as a rewriting of the language. To cast doubt on each & every 'natural' construction of reality. Not just by articulating the gap between the sign & the referent — or theatricalizing that gap by avoiding meaning altogether — but to show off a more systematic idea of language as a system & play of differences, with its own rules of functioning. Radical praxis — at this level, at this level, or within this first concentric circle — here involves the rigors of formal celebration, a playful infidelity, a certain illegibility *within* the legible: an infinitizing, a wide-open exuberance, a perpetual motion machine, a transgression.

OVERALL OVER US ALL

It's time to get our hands dirty. Valorizing form has its limits — & so does ontologizing the arbitrary. Or taking items out of context to privilege them. Moving so thoroughly within — or getting lost in — the *surface*, we may become too easily separated from a more social grasp of the body of words & associations & addresses. The differences that count are not just those of signification, of semiotics alone — (but *certainly those* are made to count in this kind of poetry — unlike all non-radical modes of literary work today). So work *toward* the outside, through & beyond the internal processes of the sign — going beyond the project of constantly pulling it apart, & waiting for Humpty-Dumpty . . . — (after all, society puts a halt to endless free play, whether we do or not). And also moving beyond the conventional readymade vehicle of the subject. Ecstatic, in the root sense: to find yourself *standing outside yourself*. The site of the body is social, set in time — socially saturated: the body of the reader (the potential body of a potential reader) & the body of meaning, of the timely materials we make significance out of. There's an Outside = Context. 'Outside authorities' might be ignored; but they can't be understood by being ignored. Even autonomy is not autonomous. So we can take our well-developed attention to signs & our desire for their dishevelment & expose it to a social dialogue, to networks of meaning understood as thoroughly socialized, to questions about the making of the subject (Reading as Writing & Writing as Reading): the making of Americans — the making of me, myself & I — of you, yourself & *us*.

Our medium is not a warehouse of styles; it's the way signs are already ordered into social codes, into meaning making & mediating.

(or surplus), the social codes that bind & mediate. To argue: the way meaning is regulated is the way the social body is written — locally, nationally, globally (& even intergalactically?). And as the backdrop: meaning has become relocated in fixed modes — migrating into containment & social governance, obedient to policing / discipline / State / stability / force / self-regulation. (That makes it easier to work with what more orthodox Marxist critics would scorn as the "exorbitation of language" — as long as language is seen as a network of 'sense' *as well as*, & not just, of the play of signifiers. Besides, any enduring social change & social value transformation takes place both 'within sense' & 'over sense' at the same time.)

To *face* — or recognize the face of — a social *horizon*, a border condition or 'scope of operations' & scope of sovereignty. An overall body of sense: not a 'deeper' but a *wider* meaning, within a more nearly total context for it or patterning of it — bound up with the coercive social limits of the possible, the acceptably possible & proper. (After all, the social field itself seems more & more pumped up, or shot up, with ambitions aimed at a total arrangement, & social propriety, at the national & even global level — subjects & groups more & more mortgaged by an outside 'system', a socially constructed horizon — *darkening*.)

Language carries everyone's context, or imprint. In the midst of the personified impersonal, a personality stands here. And so do charged bits of meaning. But to comprehend their shape — the trajectory & shuffle-step of signs & subjects — we'll have to recast & reposition them: as functions of the field of sense in which they're operating. Rather than sit back & watch helplessly as they contribute to the governance & stability of that context, this is framing frenzy — making the form that's truly in question the form of society itself.

Beyond whatever autonomy we'd like to imagine for language, there's an outside: an organized & powered network; a set of priorities & practices, of exclusions & slightings, of promotions & publicizing — which power relations in society organize in a certain way. The process by which sense occurs, in other words, is *socially ruled* — staged into discourse & harnessed into ideology. Where the flurries of signs & aberrant individualities become processed: as mannered acts, recognizably normal performances, reassuringly typical maneuvers. The set of power relations behind ideology has practicality, heft, & machinery; its investments have 'set down roots'. Its apparatus anchors & orients meaning. It doles & shapes utility. And this leverage of the dominant social forms back onto the individual interposes itself within any dialogue we foster between reading & writing.

Free play meets its nemesis: one that had been crouching behind it in the shadows all along. The system of signs (our raw material) is choreographed *by* utterances & discourse — a regularizing anonymity. An outer context limits & disciplines & naturalizes; it pins meanings down; it positions identities, setting limits to the scope of content & address — so that a text, whatever formal autonomy we animate it with, also embodies & implicates a social saturation. The content gives orders to make order content.

This containment doesn't determine all the details. 'Meaning' seems to govern itself, according to certain rules & within certain limits — not so coercive-looking, not so blatantly 'unfree'. But the usual romantic view of the weightlessness & self-policing of the subject has disturbing parallels with a supposedly self-policing & weightless formalism of the sign. *Both* ignore the outer social context & its network of power relations.

This body of sense & ideology works to socialize. It acts on meanings the way it acts on individuals: it makes whatever you took to be your meaning into a 'subject', a control center. It constructs what is celebrated as the individual as a support system for itself: that's interpellation, subjection, enrollment, or recruitment — the offering of incentives — where society sells itself to its own products, constituting & reconstituting its vehicles, its (purportedly free) receivers. Socialization works by means of such a naming — & reading — society *reading* its subjects into light, into action: an incorporation, an inwardization, surveillance & digestion. According to the rules, *they* write our bodies — *when* we talk, according to the rules. And I can't hear 'dominated' without hearing 'denominated'.

But the testimony is always incomplete, always over-reaching. The commonplaces are like marshlands you want to step back away from; or, as spectators, to do the same thing to get a better view. Not rubbernecking, but contextualizing. Not celebrating identity, but recognizing its stereotyping & containment: how it's set up & positioned within a so-called 'bad whole'. Because if the system *accounts* for individuals & individual embodiments of meaning, the writing (as reading) can account for the system & help put the *social* self in question. Sense & the subject can be jiggled, recast — the reading subject & the writer as a reader — in light of the largest possible social whole in which action can occur. And so the reading might solicit a different future: by getting distance on the sign & getting distance on identity, on how they're produced; by *rereading* the reading that a social status quo puts us through.

WRITING AS READING

Things don't change rapidly enough. We're suffocating in the limits we're so involved with, so blind: not only to the limits of signifying but to social limits as well. Assertion is not enough; assertion fails. However much it celebrates the so-called 'productivity of meaning', certainly it fails to articulate the process by which sense (or expectations about sense & ideology) get produced. And that articulation needs to be present — & politicizing as well. A politics — at the same time — of both the Sign & the Social Context.

Writing can recognize its social ground by contesting its establishment, its institutionalization. — Radicalism as analytic. And if radical writing implies a self-questioning, a "hermeneusis of itself and its own activity," this needs to reach as far as the workings of the social sphere itself. Not just to contest the linear aggressiveness & overcertainties of 'regular' language by means of symbols & double meanings; but to contest the processes or the vehicles that deliver *both* meanings (of every doubling, & of all those swooning ironies & ambiguities). Not just to take as a given the existing apparatus, in order to push for the priority of group interest, or self-expression. Instead, to make as visible as possible the limits & norms & operations of the machinery. To show the *possibilities* of sense & meaning being constructed; to foreground the limits of the possible — & our possible lives; to create impossibility.

Define comprehension as something other than consumption. (*Other then.*) So it's politicizing: a radical *reading* embodied in writing. A writing which is itself a 'wild reading' *solicits* wild reading.. The reading is a response, is a *dialogue with* the paradigms of sense — with *rhetoric* (which is a misreading in the writing itself): 'We've been misread!' The job is to go beyond these norms & limits, to *read them backwards*, to offer up a different refraction of the circumstances. Let's let the status quo *read itself* being quarantined, scolded, frag'd & interrupted.

Writing doesn't answer charges. But circumstances elicit a response.

Radical writing explains. There is nothing to explain about the words. Writing makes explanation superfluous because it *is* explanation. It positions words carefully within the horizon of some outer social world. How to create an *adequacy*; how to be 'true to form'? By eliciting praxis — to carry out language's demand for prescriptions; for the Anti-Obvious. By actively pressing the 'the network of differentials' in the writing itself. How to disclose & unclothe the social world: moving outward through these broader & broader layers & concentric circles of intelligibility. By a writing that counter-occludes, or counter-disguises; that politicizes by repositioning its involvement in, its intersection with, a nexus of historical relations — that is, contingent social relations, an edifice of power — which otherwise 'ceaselessly governs' it. It rewrites its material — in this case: the raw materials of a society, a collection of practices & avowals & disavowals, governed by discourse. By *exciting*, by a more encyclopedic *mapping* — of *social limits*, circling around the limits of signification. Not by going 'deeper' than anyone else — (that personalized vanity) — but by fitting, outfitting, refitting, and de-outfitting the *context*. To make social processes visible; to revoke licenses; to ignite unimaginability. This writing is to Social Context as Prescription is to Explanation.

HORIZON

To be reflexive is to imagine: to imagine where the details might lead. And writing can be self-reflexive — but at a social level, where the scale & the context are total. Contextualizing as totalizing: as concentric encircling, sounding or noising, horizoning. To 'horizon' — as a verb, an infinitive — that is, to grasp what the animating pressures (or constructions & arrangements) of intention & desire are *given*, are *up against*, are faced with. (This is the hidden 'face' of desire.) The scope of this embraces the overall social body, the contested hegemonies on the map, the whole that needs altering, a total which is close to the 'false': not 'everything', not statistics, not the 'thousand points of light', but a system.

In its own workings, writing can offer a more intimate grasp of this totality: expanding to the limit the contextual horizon within which you can imagine meaning & sense being produced & realized. Even if the horizon celebrates itself as openness, I doubt we can locate its limits without challenging them, without attempting to set up something outside. The horizon is *sense* & how its organized: a normative system, ideological frames for experience, a social scaffolding of consciousness and action, of wish & will. And we can recognize that by probing its boundaries: the perimeter, not the 'margins'; the 'brink'. Test the horizons — to make an *agitated* totality, not a rested one. Context needs a Contest: & so writing contextualizes as it contests the limits — which are bonds & bounds of allegiance, of worth, of normal comprehensibility. 'Incomprehensible' — beyond bounds.

The play of language as action may suggest an infinity, an essential openness; but closure does occur outside it — in settled frameworks of perception & cognition & feeling. Poetic work can take on that establishment: of a paradigm of discourse & ideology, of meaningfulness which is organized socially, or socially coded, just like a sign: as a social body of what is *unsaid*, which carries (like a membrane) all that *is* said — the establishment's strategic project of already appropriating sense & already making use of it.

We do face competing ideologies; it's not all that monolithic outside. But within all this messiness there is a dominant constellation of values — winning teams & losing teams; a dominant hegemony backing up the status quo. Probing it down to the level of its construction — the basement, where the handlers are — writing finds openings, leaks, soft spots. It offers an *internal* site — within discourse, within ideology — for backlighting the limits & blindnesses of our own programs, our own forms of life. So that, faced with the differences of writing, the autonomy of discourse & language doesn't threaten to look so much like self-enclosure. What dissolves that autonomy is *use*. And if sense is use, our rearrangement of established meaning is a rechoreographing of use & of naturalness & of normative or ideological authority.

The system outside isn't all structure, with no room for praxis. It's criss-crossed by struggle, by matters that can't be systematized. It's unstable. It's open to change, to shifts. The context is a social body & so it can *move*. Yet it often moves in a totalizing way: to constantly vampirize more & more areas of social life — shaping them up, putting on the clampdown, putting them to work in an overall project of reproducing the status quo & making it seem *natural, inevitable*. We weren't asked & we weren't told.

Ideology & Discourse form a Machinery, an Apparatus with regular rules; a collective reference system made up of social practices which form a body or social structure of meaning, an empowered configuration of forces with its own impositions. Pointing outward, poetry can work or serve as an explanation *inside* this body of constraints & directives: by deviating from constraints by refashioning the directives. The social rules it confronts are both Negative (rules of constraint, rules that say 'no', that restrict) as well as Positive (constitutive or constructive rules, rules that define the very nature of identity & desire — like official rules of a game that make us what we are before we ever get to noticing constraints: rules that socialize). Desire has rules like these — & rules like to fill themselves up with desire.

METHOD
In editing $L=A=N=G=U=A=G=E$, we said we were "emphasizing a spectrum of writing that places attention primarily on language and ways of making meaning, that takes for granted neither vocabulary, grammar, process, shape, syntax, program, or subject matter." And that

refusal to take things for granted can in turn pose a direct challenge to *social norms* about vocabulary, grammar, process, shape, syntax, program & subject-matter.

The method of the writing confronts the *scale & method* by which established sense & meaning reign: an allegory — (or will we be called 'the Methodist Poets' now?). Form & content unfold within — that is to say, are choices within — *method*, on a total scale. And writing's (social) method is its politics, its explanation, since 'the future' is implicated one way or another by how reading reconvenes conventions. By obedience or disobedience to authority. By the way writing might be prefigurative in its *constructedness* at different levels, within different arenas: semiosis, dialogue, hegemonic struggles. To widen the realm of social possibility: not just by embodying dreams but by mapping limits — the possible rerouted through the impossible — by disruptiveness, by restaging the methods of how significance & value in language do rest upon the *arbitrary* workings of the sign yet also on the *systematic* shaping work of ideology & power. An encompassing method.

Faced with rules or patterns of constraint — the negative face of ideology — writing can respond with a drastic openness. Here, an open horizon gets defined, dynamically, by failures of immediate sense — surrenders, even — which are failures in the workings of this *negative power*. To look for — & make — problems. To open up new relationships by crazed collision — laying bare the device, but this time it's a more social device, the Emperor wearing no clothes.

It's as if the established order tries to sew itself up — into permanent stability — & to sew us & our meanings up inside it. Yet if the social order both constructs & disrupts us, we both construct & disrupt that social order. And if there was romanticism in celebrating the barely sustained cohesion of the sign, the same may be true socially. Writing's method, in other words, can suggest a *social* undecidability, a lack of successful *suture*. Tiny cuts: syntacted glare, facts *en bloc*, circuit breaking in which a break *renders*, syntax as demolition derby. This displacement or social unbalancing has more than nuisance value. It's more than an invitation to an ego trip for righteous poets. Instead, it offers a guide by which matters outside *do not* hang together — an unsuturable condition: where norms are contradicted & where you can recognize that therefore they *can* be contradicted, the space for reading blossoms.

But ideology also works in a positive way, as a form of *positive power*: constructing our identities, soliciting our identification, our pledges of allegiance. If identification is built into the subject form — so that its positive meanings are already overproduced — then 'subjects speaking

their minds' 'authentically' will not be enough. The overall shape of
making sense needs to be reframed, restaged, put back into a context of
'pre-sense' — to reveal its constructed character; to reveal by critique,
by demythologizing. Otherwise, its apparent immediacy dupes us: the
lack of distance is a kind of closure.

An active dramatizing of this socialization — by what the writing does
with its own reading & its own readability — shows off this process. By
detonating this identifying impulse, we get closer to a full social
reflexiveness. Questions & doubt subvert an exterior which has now in-
sinuated itself inside. For the only immediacy possible is an immediacy
of address, of *readers* 'talking back', where the distances writing creates
appear as hospitality.

What is called for is writing as a *counter*-reading — that is, as a counter-
socialization. To put in motion this *social* productivity: the process by
which significance is constructed for others (& for ourselves as others).
To remotivate & politicize, for the reader, the identity-making process;
to make it possible to become *less* of an exile in our own words — the
words we read by writing. Both negatively (confronting the restrictions
of constraining rules) — & positively (by remotivating the desires prod-
uced by positive or constitutive rules). [Provisionally — if we use the dis-
tinction between metonymy & metaphor — it looks like surprises of
constraint & the skirting of negative power would be most visible at the
metonymic level; while excitements of desire — 'deep content', verti-
cality, metaphor — would appear as recastings of *motive*, of the 'why for'
of positive power. A notion of an *allegory of method* would offer a way to
think about radical poetry's work *on this* positive, metaphoric front.]

Not only the workings of the sign but also the workings of sense & id-
eology are part of the social order's way of defining itself. And these can
both be questioned — within a counterculture or counter-hegemony
embracing reader & writer — so that a different & more global mode of
address is suggested: by poetry's social scale & social method as it
rematerializes & reconstructs the language (both as sign & context).
Writing that in this way public-izes, publicizing its way into the public
sphere, can foster this recognition of the system, of what we're up
against: a recognition that's at the basis of *social literacy*; a social compre-
hension or total encompassing & *maximizing* that we need to orient our
praxis & re-envision the social contract. This is the method of 'intelli-
gence', as Bakhtin defined it: "a dialog with one's own future and an ad-
dress to the external world." And if writing can imply such a future, that
future will serve as its radical prescription.

DISCUSSION

JAMES SHERRY: Could you expand on how we get from competing to a dominant constellation of values?

BRUCE ANDREWS: They don't all lead into the dominant constellation. I think an alternative reading of the social order from mine would see a great deal more indeterminacy, more pluralism, a more variegated field of operation — where all these different groups or individual possibilities are being articulated and come together in some overall pluralist whole. Now, that view would give you a sense that all you would need to do is identify with one of those groups or positions and try to advance it; often that's the criterion for judging political work . . . certainly political work in the arts. But to me it no longer seems sufficient to promote those specific identities or specific group interests. I don't think that that pluralism really has the kind of effectiveness that it might have had maybe a century ago — before things got so centralized, before things got so elaborately controlled, bleaching dry the energy that still exists residually in those groups. So that's a distinction I'm making: between two different ways of looking at the same thing as well as these two different elements that are both present in the same thing. Do you emphasize the underlying principles and total, controlling devices within this overall social machinery, or do you emphasize the openness and the pluralism of the situation?

SHERRY: Would it be fair to say that the methods of power unite these competing groups? So to the extent that there is a dominant constellation of values, it arises from the competing groups as a result of their common methodology, not as a result of their common ideology?

ANDREWS: There is a common boundary around those units. I don't know that they are that homogenized, though, or that they reproduce themselves through the same method that the whole reproduces itself. That would suggest something even more monolithic than what I'm seeing — as if somehow the outer limit had managed to homogenize everything inside of it and gotten it all on the same methodological tract. I don't think we've gotten there yet.

BARRETT WATTEN: Sartre in his essay "What Is Literature?" was investigating [the polarities between] a poetics involved in the substantiation of language as opposed to a prose which would be explanatory, which involved the transparency of language. I would think that would be something you would object to: Sartre's conclusion that what a

politically informed writing needs is a transparency, so that you get peo-
ple to see the world through language by initiating their reading. And it
seems to me that there's another position here which is that you're
more or less positing a substantiality of language, what Sartre hated in
the poetics process, right? . . . But still: through this resistance or
through this engagement with the substantial segments — which is what
I'm seeing in the way you work — there is an act of reading which
doesn't open up to a transparency of the world; it opens back into a
kind of subjectivity and a kind of criticality and so forth. Now the ques-
tion is: that posits a totality that can be read in a particular way. And yet
there are these competing tendencies within the social totality. I think
James's question is: How do you get from the competition or conflict to
this . . . subjective totality, or a linguistic totality. How do you deal with
this question of that conflict ending up in this kind of totalization that
you seem to be interested in?

ANDREWS: As I was saying in answer to James, the significance of
those internal conflicts is no longer as interesting. If you try to adopt
them as your position, and if they are in fact bounded in some compre-
hensive way by those outer limits, then those outer limits cannot very
easily be perceived, because you're not working with them. I'm clearly
making the claim that the way limits get acknowledged and articulated
in this writing is through some form of challenge. I haven't been able to
see another easy route to apprehension of those limits other than
through some kind of disruption or constant reframing of them. The is-
sue is not about getting bogged down in those internal conflicts and
then having a hard time reaching beyond them, because what I'm inter-
ested in having mapped out would be the outer limits themselves —
what those internal chunks and those internal conflicts never really con-
front. Instead they are, in that sense, more self-absorbed, tending their
own garden and developing their own internal substantiality without
having to confront the question of what's tying them all down or hold-
ing them all together.

ERICA HUNT: I found this discussion very interesting because I take
the point of view that there exist several distinct projects of opposition
and resistance that are every bit as serious and intent as those that take
the ground of textuality of language as the stake and the prize, or as the
critical lever for change. And I would say that the seriousness of these
projects can't be measured only by their use of normative language or
genre. It has to be measured by the kinds of oppositional strategies used
within the forms of writing those groups believe are the best vehicles

for reaching readers. I would say that remaking identity and uncovering suppressed histories are important projects that are analagous to a more textual project.

ANDREWS: Why would the project that they would set for themselves be less textual?

HUNT: When you identify group interests by their tactics without considering their goals, each group interest appears to be very distinct, with its own particular and idiosyncratic aesthetic politics of opposition, and this begins to diminish the majority power that a coalition of oppositional interests represents. It's like when the Democratic or Republican parties dismiss 65% of the electorate as competing 'special' interests.

ANDREWS: Wasn't it the press that did that?

HUNT: Yes, and reinforced by the parties: that so-called special interests are these cranky gremlins in the political and social life of the nation manipulating against the public interest on their own behalf. Special interest politics tend to trivialize and render invisible the bigger picture, the points of connection and critique that can be made of how social life, and art, is defined and organized. I raise this flag because you come back to the point of what are effective means of making change through art and art making change, and it's implicit in what James asked: What exactly is the status of special interests?

ANDREWS: Well, the status of group interests is not very prominent in my way of talking about these matters. In contrast, this issue that I'm raising doesn't seem to get raised all that frontally that often in literary and artistic discussions. It's raised all the time in radical politics. It's a crucial battleground on the Left: deciding between what I would call a more group or pluralist-oriented interest in empowerment and mobilization, on the one hand, and this other more totalizing, perspectival approach that I'm trying to work out. It's certainly not fixed doctrine at this point in my thinking, but this interest in exploring what the alternative to group empowerment or mobilization might look like in writing definitely comes from my unhappiness with that being always trumped up, trumpeted as the be-all-end-all of radical politics outside the literary and artistic realm. It doesn't seem to work satisfactorily in politics and, given the centrality of language even within the way the social order reproduces itself, it seems even less likely to be satisfying to me within writing. . . . The commonest tendency in addressing local projects or

local differences as to *not* route that project through what I emphasized
in the beginning of this presentation, which is an unveiling of the funda-
mental signification system, the nature of the sign in language. So if we
go back to what Barrett was talking about with respect to Sartre — trans-
parency — this always strikes me as a problem. Because if the funda-
mental building blocks of sense reside at a lower level in the fundamen-
tal structure of the sign, and how that functions systematically, then if
that's not addressed first, the power of the work to address the nature of
the social order evaporates. If it takes that earlier structure for granted
and tries to move on to mobilize or empower around a certain already-
existing identity, and already existing sense of how meaning occurs,
then I think it derails itself.

ANDREW LEVY: Is the kind of practice you've developed going to be
meaningful anywhere outside of your social class and intellectual back-
ground?

ANDREWS: Unanswerable question. If you're attempting to prefigure
the constructedness and reconstructedness of things at various levels, it
seems to me that that's going to be perceivable, that's going to be able to
be part of the reading process; so that you could see how things appear
to have been levitated to a certain degree — out of the general frame-
work. On the other hand, there may be a certain kind of apprehension
of the way the system works at all these levels that isn't going to be readi-
ly available to larger groups and categories of readers. I think that's
something that we all recognize. I mean, just the basic literacy problem
is forbidding enough. Limitations in readability, in readership-ability,
or however you want to characterize it, may make it impossible for the
kind of systematic apprehension I'm talking about to become clear in
people's lives; for them to be able to see that at all, whether they're see-
ing it through something they're reading or something somebody's tell-
ing them — it would be hard for them to have any direct daily experi-
ence with it, in that unencumbered way. That's why I said I thought the
question was unanswerable, because it's of course the most common
way of dismissing *all* experimental or avant-garde or modernist writing
or art of the last century, in political terms. When everything is framed
in terms of efficacy, the work that gets promoted as efficacious is work
that simply, to me, reinforces the very blindnesses that I think are so
central to the way the system holds itself together.

SHERRY: By giving what is easiest to digest.

ANDREWS: And by reinforcing a certain conception of identity, by re-inforcing a certain conception of dialogue, or a certain conception of communication, a certain understanding of the codes and the media that govern our lives.

LEVY: So in the context in which you operate, you see those efficacious modes of operating as just being cop-outs.

ANDREWS: Well, worse; I'm suggesting worse than a cop-out. It may simply make things more reinforced, more solidified; so that an overall perspective on what the social world consists of becomes even more fu-gitive, even harder to get a grasp on. That's why I think it's so troubling, because I don't think it's so easy — as many people, certainly on the Left, seem to think — just to reject whole categories of writing which are aiming at a certain mapping and disruption of the social whole and just say "well, our people can't read that" or "our people don't understand that, and they want something else, and you're not providing it," there-fore "you're 'objectively reactionary'" or "how dare you call yourself progressively minded," etc. etc. So that's hovering somewhere in the background of everything I've thought about the politics of (or in) writ-ing: that, to me, insoluble problem about readership (a), and (b), this very-well entrenched sense of confidence and certainty about another kind of mobilizing and empowering writing — which I just can't bear [laughter]. It seems to be actively promoting things that reinforce the things I'm troubled by. So it's very hard for me, these days, to even take that complaint — not that you're offering it, but that does fly around — with the kind of concern that it used to hit me with. . . . Personally, one thing I feel is that my own sense of helplessness in the face of these structures, edifices, these patterns, is consoled or reduced by my sense of comprehension — my sense that I have some understanding of how they work, and what they're doing to me on a day-to-day level. And that is quite a bit 'linguistic' or textual, in the sense mentioned earlier. Some of that has to do with the relative privilege of my position in this social order — where other types of just more blunt and brutal things that happen to me don't happen more often; so that if I'm talking about my feelings, my values, my attitudes, my hopes and visions, as different from just being able to avoid getting killed on a day-to-day basis, those things might be more central to my life than they would be to someone else's. They also seem very linguistic, in that sense: very much tied up with how things come to me in certain ways rather than others, and how things come to make sense and other things don't make sense. I feel that that's being orchestrated all the time in a way that I can partly perceive.

And to the extent that I feel I can do anything to get the leverage of all that lifted off of me by understanding how it works, then I am consoled to some degree. I also feel, politically, that this kind of understanding is something that could potentially bring diverse groups together around some larger project of reconstructing a public sphere which can then take on, at some point in the future, greater and greater importance — and maybe even be able to contest the dominant way that that's organized, or the dominant way that other possibilities are marginalized.

NICK LAWRENCE: At the end of Jerome Rothenberg's talk last week, we seem to arrive at a dichotomy between so-called instrumental power in language and disruptive power, which I take to be the "dishevelment of signs." And you also appear to propose a third linguistic power which you could perhaps call *constructive* — that is, in some sense, a meeting or confrontation between disruptive and instrumental discourses. You said that there is a necessity for exposing the dishevelment of signs to social dialogue. You also speak of a method. But the method obviously has to be strategic because social dialogue is changing, always, and so one has to reorient one's position vis-a-vis 'it.'

ANDREWS: When I used the phrase 'social dialogue,' it was more along the lines of a dialogue *with* the social.

LAWRENCE: The social body.

ANDREWS: Which I may have a much more fixed and unfluid sense of than you do.

LAWRENCE: O.K., you consider it more of a static and totalizing and immobile force rather than . . .

ANDREWS: I've been widely accused of that, yeah [laughter].

LAWRENCE: O.K., and yet dialogue with the social body does imply a two-way street. Perhaps you could say whether there's responsibility on the part of your project to take into account the economic bases or context of producing this dialogue; in other words, the methods of physically producing it and putting it before a public, any readership. Do you believe that this kind of constructive power should go out and meet, to some extent, the responsibility of publicizing; in other words, getting this project available to more people. Is there some way you think that it's not really germane to the project — as if we should just be monk-like and . . .

ANDREWS: This is the point where Charles is supposed to pass out the Segue catalogs [laughter]. I have tended to think about this social machinery being confronted more as a methodological issue, more as something where challenge is prefigurative or parallels what other kinds of larger challenges would look like or could look like in society. As different from thinking of it in terms of chipping away at the margin, or having certain commodities operate with a more prominent profile within that machinery. That goes on too, and I think a lot of us are involved in some of that, just to avoid drying up out on the margins. But I haven't felt, in myself and with people I'm most closely associated with, that the politics of *that* have seemed so central, or have been able to carry the political thrust of what people thought they were doing in their actual writing. On the other hand, there is some parallelism between that work going on in the writing and at least the desire in having it go out and impinge upon the established structures of reading and distribution and product-making and all the rest. I would think, actually, that the people who are the most self-preening about their marginality are the ones that have been somewhat less interested in this social and political dimension in the writing itself. There's some exceptions, but a parallelism does come to mind there.

JACKSON MAC LOW: I've been thinking of an analogy and metaphor — for the project of what such a writer who would confront the social body and its limitations might do. The analogy is that of the radical who's disgusted with all of the established groupings, the parties, and yet who feels it's necessary to put that little bit of power on one side or another — i.e., that anarchists should vote, etc. Now the analogy in writing would be a tandem project of social writing, not one that scorns either side. One might make works that might be, if not efficacious, at least understandable to a wider audience without the background, etc. Now you might say, as some anarchists say, for example: Don't vote, it just encourages them. Or don't write in the transparent modes, even if in directly critical and negating ways apprehensible to anyone who could read the language, because that only encourages the hegemony. But I question very strongly that that all should be abandoned as part of the writer's work. Even if you associate the Left with a rejection of radical disruptive writing, you don't have to buy into that and say "only do this" or, with ordinary Leftist rhetorics, "only do that." What do you think of a tandem project of this sort? — that it does encourage the bastards?

ANDREWS: I feel that it only encourages the bastards *in me* [laughter]. That it only makes me worse — to do it; forget whatever effect it might have on other people, because I'm the main reader of what I write. It's designed for me. And I'm making that link pretty strongly in this presentation between reading and writing. So if I notice that I'm being made to feel more accepting, more identified, more locked-in, more filled with embrace of convention in my writing, I'm unhappy. And I don't seem to do that kind of writing, as a result.

MAC LOW: But isn't there a usefulness to such direct, negating writing? — writing that questions the positions of, say, government or hegemonic groups.

LEVY: Jackson, would your poem "Central America" be an example?

MAC LOW: Yeah, that's an example of that kind of writing, for me.

ANDREWS: Well, I'm trying not to offend generalities by the intensities of my particularities, which is mostly what I'm talking about. What I'm arguing is what I'm interested in and what I think is useful; I'm not on record as sneering dismissively about all those other forms of writing for other people.

MAC LOW: So you're only saying that for yourself, not as a general program for writing.

ANDREWS: I'm easily provoked on that [laughter]. I'm just on the cusp of lashing out at this whole alternative project. I can't see an adequate defense of it . . . it doesn't to me seem to get at the heart of the matter.

MAC LOW: Just as voting doesn't seem to get at the heart of the matter. Right? But it might have a marginal efficacy.

ANDREWS: I don't deny it [laughter]. If you mean mobilizing people to take issue with the government's position, for instance? Yeah, it could have that efficacy.

Q: But do you see it as a switch that goes on and off — you're either transparent or you're not? Transparency versus non-transparency?

ANDREWS: That almost was what I felt was implied by what Jackson was saying.

MAC LOW: No, I was taking those as extremes.

ANDREWS: As if you have the two drawers; you open one drawer and you take those works out and you write the speeches or you write the

the mobilizing, transparent works . . . ? I've generally felt, even when I've appreciated that kind of work, that it was speaking to the converted, by and large.

WATTEN: Less so than what you just read? That I can't really believe, I really can't.

ANDREWS: No, but I'm not making an argument for this kind of direct efficacy. If I were, that would be a logical and perfectly appropriate attack. So I'm suspicious about the efficacy here.

MAC LOW: So am I. But nevertheless, I feel sometimes I ought to speak in a way that a larger number of people here and there might be interested in; you might not just have the converted, but those on the line, etc. — by bringing in a lot of things that are efficacious, in the sense of a rhetorical poetry . . . a more basic poetry.

JEFFREY JULLICH: It seemed that I had one thing to add which was a lot like the issue about publishing that came up, but leads into a question that bothers me more. The first thing that I get a sense of is that somehow by working in the genre of poetry, it's already defeating the political outreach. In other words, to put something onto the shelf, in Barnes & Noble, in which certain books are funneled into this delimitation called poetry, is already part of the problem. That by becoming a book it's the very defusing of the political activism.

ANDREWS: A "book" as different from . . .

JULLICH: A billboard, or electric lead-board like Jenny Holzer works on. This project repeatedly comes up in the 20th century — the Stein project, or Hugo Ball's project — in other words, the pushing of the limits, pushing the limits of the system of signs. And yet what I've been wondering is whether the actual social constraint is not linguistic and not grammatical but is in fact a non-verbal one that happens on a plane below language, and if that isn't the reason why these efforts seem to go just so far. It's that they could go infinitely far, but that that is not the binding or the dominant pressure. So the first question is whether poetry is an arena that has been set aside by the powers that be, for a type of linguistic misbehaving with no spill-over effect.

ANDREWS: Speaking of Barnes & Noble, I notice they have their poetry shelf, alphabetized, and then, not far from it, they have a large shelf on Marxist theory. I would see this problem that you're posing with respect to poetry in somewhat similar light. That there's a range of types of activity which seem to be able to take on, or think through, the nature of the social order that are marginalized in that world out there, and examples of that marginalization are there in Barnes & Noble. And it may be that there's some parallel between the kinds of activity that can claim, inside themselves, to sustain this ambition of understanding and thinking through what's going on, and those activities which are going to be marginalized in a way that seems unfortunate. I don't think it's just that literary misbehavior is shunted aside, as a little bauble that's not going to bother anybody; it's also whole ranges of theoretical discourse trying to come to grips with history, the world system, the nature of America's political economy, etc. etc. that equally don't have the ability, like those excruciating banalities of Jenny Holzer, to get up on Times Square and broadcast to thousands of people. It's not just poetry that suffers from that kind of marginalization. But there may be a curious parallel between the kinds of activities that carry, in themselves, as part of their own kind of identity, that reach, and the ones that are specifically denied that kind of reach by the mainstream culture.

SALLY SILVERS: You talked about 'totalizing'. Or a process of horizoning, and of 'going wide' with an understanding of the social order which is something 'out there' instead of 'in here' where you exist and where you do something in arrangements with it. I was wondering whether there was also a way of somehow not contrasting *wide* with *deep*, but having both of those happen at the same time, in the sense of understanding. Whether that automatically compartmentalizes the information, by thinking that it needs to go deep or whether that's just an illusion that comes from emphasizing the subject?

ANDREWS: I was using 'deep' in the conventional sense of personalized depth. You can also use 'surface' and 'depth' to talk about the structure of the sign, so that surface/depth metaphor pops up in a range of places. Lately I've gotten more attracted to a kind of spatialized, concentric circular mapping metaphor to try to figure out what you do next. So 'further,' instead of meaning 'deeper,' I now think of more in wider terms. But how to square that circle, that is to say, between personal depth and social extent, social extension — because it seems clear that the social order does hold itself together by creating and shaping subjectivity in a certain way, and that to drop out of that whole struggle, that whole question of how the subject gets built, I now find *not* satisfying as a way of trying to come to grips with the whole social field. It's an absolutely crucial arena, but I've become convinced that you can only get to it by seeing how ideology works to put certain things in the

foreground and hide others, rather than to get to it directly or imme-
diately by starting with self-expression.

SILVERS: I kept getting the sense of 'out there' without seeing whether
that comes back the other way. I mean of course the subject is formu-
lated by that, but the interaction seems one-directional.

ANDREWS: I wasn't thinking about how these things are located spe-
cifically in personal depths so much as orienting the attention of the
reader toward the outside. There's something about that process of al-
ways thinking about what's social and important as what's inside you,
inside that particular person, which seems so specialized. A certain so-
cial material is going to be in a single person, and there's a tremendous
attraction to exploring just that realm of social material that's in you,
that's in me, that's in one person.

SILVERS: The arbitrary structure of the individual.

ANDREWS: Right. As if when your discoveries start to get extended
outward into the social horizon that's determined them, there's a pull-
ing back, as if: wait a minute, I don't know that I want to go all the way
out that far; I kind of enjoy reliving or reprocessing these experiences
that happened to me and I'm going to keep repeating my attachment to
them, my identification with them. But there is also this other agenda
that might be explorable, that doesn't have so much to do with what
you could dredge up out of yourself, personally, as feeling the impact
on not just you but on others that you can see occurring, feel occurring,
and map out the occurrence of it, socially. ·

Alarms & Excursions

Rosmarie Waldrop

"Alarums and excursions" is an Elizabethan stage term for off-stage noise and commotion which interrupts the main action. This phrase kept running through my head while I tried to think about our topic because all that occurred were doubts, complications and distractions. So I decided to circle around this mysterious interaction of private and public that is poetry with theses (things I believe or *would like* to believe), alarms (doubts), and excursions into quotes, examples, etc. I numbered the theses to give an illusion of progression which will only make their contradictions more obvious.

Let me start with some of the assumptions of this seminar.

THESIS 1

Shelley: "Poets are the unacknowledged legislators of the world."
Oppen: "Poets are the legislators of the unacknowledged world."

EXCURSION

This astonishing kind of importance is often ascribed to poets and writers (mostly by writers?). Sartre, for instance, held Flaubert responsible for the failure of the Commune of 1870 because he never wrote about it.

In the recent French discussion on whether Heidegger's Nazism invalidates his philosophical work, Edmond Jabès assigned a responsibility to writers which is commensurate with this kind of importance:

> I believe a writer is responsible even for what he does not write.
> To write means to answer to all the insistent voices of the past and
> to one's own: profound voice, intimate, calling to the future.

What I believe, hear, feel is in my texts which say it, *without some-times altogether saying it.*

But what do we *not altogether say* in what we say? Is it what we try to keep silent, what we cannot or will not say or precisely what we do want to say and what all we say hides, saying it differently?

For these un-said things we are gravely responsible.[1]

ALARM

But I am not only astonished, but uneasy with our two quotes, with the poet as legislator, no matter of which world. It sounds to me like a hang-over from the times when the poet occupied a priestly position. But in our time, poetry has no such institutionalized function, and I must say I am not sorry. Or is it a male aspiration? I certainly have no desire to lay down the law. To my mind writing has to do with uncovering possibilities rather than with codification. My key words would be exploring and maintain-ing: exploring a forest not for the timber that might be sold, but to under-stand it as a world and to keep this world alive.

COUNTER ALARM

My uneasiness means perhaps only that I prefer a different image while I grant poetry the same importance. After all, poets work on the language, and language thinks for us or, as Valéry puts it more cautiously:

> I am almost inclined to believe that certain profound ideas have owed their origin to the presence or near-presence in a man's mind of certain forms of language, of certain empty verbal figures whose particular tone called for a particular content.[2]

EXCURSION

When Confucius was asked what he would do first if he were ruler he said: improve the use of language:

> if the words are not right, what is said is not what is meant. If what is said is not meant, work cannot flourish. If work does not flourish, then customs and arts degenerate. If customs and arts degenerate, then justice is not just. If justice is not just, the people do not know what to do. Hence the importance that words be right.

Bertold Brecht also tells how Confucius practiced this by changing just a few words in an old patriotic history, so that "The ruler of Kun had the philosopher Wan killed because he said . . ." became "The ruler of Kun had the philosopher Wan murdered"; "the tyrant X was assassinated" became "the tyrant X was executed by assassination." This brought about a new view of history.[3]

ALARM

The two decades before Hitler came to power were a period of incredible literary flowering, upheaval, exploration in Germany. All the dadaists and expressionists had been questioning, challenging, exploring, changing the language, limbering up its joints. So the German language should have been in very good condition, yet the Nazis had no trouble putting it to work for their purposes, perverting it to where what was said was light-years from what was meant. So, while language thinks for us, there is no guarantee that it will be in a direction we like.[4]

THESIS 2

The main thesis of this whole seminar is that a) poetry has social relevance. It is not just an ornament or just private, an expression of personal emotions. b) Its relation to society is not just reflective or mimetic, not just articulating what oft was thought, but never so well expressed. It can make the culture aware of itself, unveil hidden structures. It questions, resists. Hence it can at least potentially anticipate structures that might lead to social change.

EXCURSION

It is difficult to be aware of our own social and historical position, let alone to know how far our works are expressing the explicit or implicit givens of our society and how far they make them conscious and possibly contribute to their changing. The borderline between private and public is very elusive. On the one hand, there seems to be a fairly high *quantitative* threshold for something to have effect. On the other hand, I suspect that nearly everything we do has some social effect, simply because we are members of a society. (What could be more private than making love — but if you are not careful, and the couple is heterosexual, it may produce a citizen.)

So even if poetry were just expressing personal emotions, it would have a social function, namely acknowledging the importance of the emotions even though (or because) they often hinder our smooth functioning within a social order.

In contrast, literature as ornament or entertainment brings up a conservative function which poetry can have and which our initial thesis does not consider.

I once got a rejection slip which said: "I do not find your poems comfortable." I was comforted by this statement. There are poems which are comfortable, immediately recognizable as poems. When they moreover celebrate unquestionable values like love or nature, they make people feel good and give them the illusion of being in touch with something "higher," some transcendental poetic essence. It gives them what Roland Barthes calls "the good conscience of realized significance." [5]

I might want to argue that even these poems for all their reinforcing the status quo still present a small challenge by stepping out of the frame of what is useful. But I am willing to bracket these poems and believe with our THESIS 2 that poetry's function is critical, questioning. Georges Bataille sees *transgression* as literature's essential quality. Edmond Jabès calls it subversive:

Subversion is the very movement of writing: that of death.[6]

ALARM

Jabès takes this subversion immediately to a level where it is seen as the very principle of change, hence of life, rather than directed against a particular social order:

Did I already know that opening and closing my eyes, lying down, moving, thinking, dreaming, talking, being silent, writing and reading are all gestures and manifestations of subversion?
Waking upsets the order of sleep, thinking hounds the void to get the better of it, speech in unfolding breaks the silence, and reading challenges every sentence written.

There is much support for art's social function as a conscious-making counter-projection. For instance Adorno says:

art does not recognize reality by reproducing it photographically, but by voicing that which is veiled by the empirical forms of reality.[7]

Writing becomes action through this unveiling.

ALARM

While part of me wants this social function, I must admit that any such consideration is far from my mind when I am writing and that George Bataille's notion of art as a glorious waste of excess energy seems to me much closer to what is going on.

THESIS 3

The function of poetry is to waste excess energy.

EXCURSION

Let me summarize briefly the main tenet of Bataille's "general economy" which should really be called "economy on the scale of the universe," as given in *The Accursed Share*.

He starts from a given of excess energy derived from the sun and sees the whole history of life on earth, and especially the appearance of humanity, as "the effect of a mad exuberance."[8]

> It is in the principle of life that the sum of energy produced is always greater than that needed for its production.
> The living organism. . . receives in principle more energy than it needs to maintain its life: the excess energy (wealth) can be used for growth of a system (e.g. an organism). If the system can grow no more or if the excess cannot entirely be absorbed into the growth process then it has to be lost without profit, spent voluntarily or not, gloriously or else catastrophically.

On the level of the individual human being, once the body is fully grown, we get the explosion of sexuality which liberates enormous amounts of energy which are either just wasted or used for procreation, extending the body's potential for growth.

The most general and thorough waste of energy is death. Therefore, on the level of societies, war is the obvious catastrophic spending. For Bataille, the two great wars of this century follow quite logically on a relatively peaceful century devoted to industrial growth. Unemployment he calls a passive spending, or rather passive reduction of the excess. The glorious ways of wasting the excess are great feasts, conspicuous luxury, sacrifices, rituals like potlatch in which wealth is literally destroyed, monuments like pyramids and cathedrals which are far in excess of their practical function as tombs or places of worship, and of course all forms of art.

THESIS 4

Bataille's general economy, his notion of waste and excess explains the persistence of poets and poetry in the face of meager rewards. It makes more sense than putting the poem in a context of useful production, let alone supply and demand, even though it does enter the world of merchandise once it is published and distributed.

EXCURSION

Marx/Engels: "A writer is a productive worker not in as far as he produces ideas, but in as far as he enriches the bookseller who distributes the work."[9]

The IRS shares this view absolutely: When Burning Deck, the small press Keith Waldrop and I run, applied for non-profit status we were told: "If you sell books you're a business. You may be a bad business, but you're a business." In any case it is obvious that the energy that goes into writing a poem is enormous and totally out of proportion to any gain it might bring, even if it should get published by a commercial press and even if we include non-monetary gains like reputation, approbation of a group, etc.

ALARM

Poetry is an extreme case in that not even the most successful poet could live off his or her book sales. So a poet knows from the beginning that he or she will have to make a living in some other way — whereas a successful novelist can hope to live by writing. Although again, the more "difficult" among successful novelists (Hawkes, Coover, Barth, Abish, Angela Carter) all seem to teach at least part time.

As far as publisher or bookseller being enriched, this holds for some books, but I doubt that it ever holds for poetry, and obviously not for the small presses and their distributors which have no hope of even breaking even and must rely on grants or patronage. And I would like to see the bookseller who gets rich by stocking small press poetry. In other words, the whole small press world, rather than getting rich at the poets' expense, is like the poets, engaged in wasting energy, time, money; wasting it beautifully.

Why do they do it?

THESIS 5

There are more crazy people around than you would think.

ALARM

Nobody can be crazy all the time and still be sane. The process of writing, let alone distribution, cannot be *pure* waste. There has to be a balance between the contradictory tendencies toward growth and toward spending.

EXCURSION

Let us for a moment imagine two writers embodying the extreme points of the two orientations. Bataille's distinction between warrior and military societies seems a good analogy [p. 60]. A warrior society, like the Aztecs, engages in wars which do not necessarily enlarge its territory. They are exercises in pure violence, conspicuous combat without calculation. What matters is fighting and waste worthy of the gods. A military society, by contrast, is rather a business enterprise for which war means expansion of territory, power gain, empire building. The latter will be gentler, more rational and civilized, in contrast to the intense ferocity of the Aztecs. Also more apt to survive.

Likewise, for what we might call the reckless writer the essential is the writing, the intensity of the process, of the present moment, the anxiety and glory of making a structure which holds together. The key word here is the *present*, not being constrained by any considerations of the future in which the work might be read, appreciated, sold. It is a moment of being most completely myself, whether we call it unalienated or mad. In contrast, if I am concerned with building a career I write as an investment rather than spending (though I still spend more energy than justified by the material returns). My eye is on the market, maybe just on the approval of a group, in any case on the future. I voluntarily submit to the order of reality, to the laws which ensure the maintenance of life or of career. Whereas the reckless writer would, in these terms, and at least at the moment of writing "rise indifferent to death."

ALARM

As I said, nobody is pure. For all our anarchic intensity, sooner or later we want our mss. published. We want to be both reckless *and* read. It is once again a case of Valéry's famous two dangers that threaten the world: order and disorder.

EXCURSION

Barthes' *Pleasure of the Text* applies this same distinction to reading. Reading as *jouissance*, an orgasmic pleasure, versus reading as an educational activity, an effort of understanding and interpretation. Again, only as an abstraction can we separate the pleasure in the effort of understanding out from the purer orgasmic pleasure. But Barthes has given us an interesting word.

THESIS 6

The social function of poetry is pleasure.

Pound said: ecstasy, the kind of pleasure which is an enormous anarchic and subversive force, which is why societies and religions, including those of Capitalism, Marxism and Freudianism are suspicious of it and try so hard to regulate it.

ALARM

This kind of subversion does not at all fit our initial thesis of a more constructive critical role. But it might well fit with the notion that writing and the writer do not really have a place inside the social structure at all, but are outside it, opposite.

EXCURSION

Edmond Jabès writes throughout his work about the "non-place" of the book and the writer. This non-place (which perhaps rejoins Oppen's "unacknowledged world") goes farther than the distance from the exercise of power which is often thought to qualify the intellectuals to speak on matters of politics. It also goes farther than marginality: it goes into otherness. Roland Barthes, while admitting that he occupies an official pigeonhole ("intellectual") calls his inner sense of his position "a-topian," being outside even the notion of place. He explicitly contrasts it with u-topias which traditionally are a direct reaction to an actual situation and propose an answer or counter-model, whereas an a-topia is strictly negative.[10] Even Adorno joins in seeing the task of art not in function, but non-function.[11]

ALARM

Is this wishful thinking? a desire to deny how deeply we are part of our society, how impossible it is to escape the place that birth, education, profession assign us? Is it not trying to make a virtue out of personal alienation? Maybe partly. But it proceeds from the essence of literature which is a negative, not "real," a mere as if, especially as it is no longer endowed with priestly function. But for this very reason its existence alone constitutes an alternative to what is and hence a criticism of it.

So we have circled around to

THESIS 7

which reaffirms THESIS 2:

By its very nature of being "other" literature *cannot help being critical*, cannot help being "an action against the inadequacy of human beings." This is Brecht, who draws the conclusion that "all great men were literary."[12]

It is high time we get to the question of how a poem could bring this about.

THESIS 8

Not by direct communication with a reader. For one thing, it is impossible to know our readers (beyond maybe five friends). I am in a dialogue when I write a poem, but not with a prospective reader, not even the "ideal reader," but with language itself. Of course I hope that eventually there will be readers who through my poem will in their turn enter into a particular dialogue with language and maybe see certain things as a consequence. We might approximate this in a diagram where the circle represents the language environment shared in varying degrees by author and reader.

Language

W = Writer
P = Poem
R = Reader

I mean this dialogue with language quite literally. When I begin working, I have only a vague nucleus, an energy running to words. As soon as I start *listening* to the words, they reveal their own vectors and affinities, pull the poem into their own field of force, often in unforeseen directions, away from thesemantic charge of the original impulse.

EXCURSION

Jabès: "The pages of the book are doors. Words go through them, driven by their impatience to regroup. . . . Light is in these lovers' strength of desire."

Oppen: "When the man writing is frightened by a word, that's when he's getting started."

Olson: Not the "thing" [and not the "mot juste"] but what "happens between."[13]

THESIS 9

A poem is primarily an exploration of language. This view is shared by linguists like Roman Jakobson and Paul Valéry:

EXCURSION

Valéry:

> When the poets repair to the forest of language it is with the express purpose of getting lost; far gone in bewilderment, they seek cross-roads of meaning, unexpected echoes, strange encounters; they fear neither detours, surprises, nor darkness. But the huntsman who ventures into this forest in hot pursuit of the "truth," who sticks to a single continuous path, from which he cannot deviate for a moment on pain of losing the scent or imperiling the progress he has already made, runs the risk of capturing nothing but his shadow. Sometimes the shadow is enormous, but a shadow it remains.[14]

When I say poetry is an exploration of language, this is not a retreat from the social because language is the structure that is shared by society and this otherness which is poetry. It also does not mean that there is no reference. It only means reference is secondary, not foregrounded. The poem works by indirection, but the poet's obsessions and preoccupations will find their way into the text. Jabès again: "What I believe, hear, feel is in my texts which say it, *without sometimes altogether saying it.*"

EXCURSION

In the early stages of my writing all the poems were about my mother and my relation to her. Rereading them a bit later, I decided I had to get out of this obsession. This is when I started to make collages. I would take a novel and decide to take one or two words from every page. The poems were still about my mother. So I realized that you don't have to worry about contents: your preoccupations will get into the poem no matter what. Tzara ends his recipe for making a chance poem by cutting out words from the newspapers and tossing them in a hat: "The poem will resemble you."[15]

THESIS 10

The poem will not work through its content, through a message which in any case would speak only to the already converted, but through its form.

EXCURSION

Brecht:

> The presentation has to be unusual to get the reader out of the shelter of his habits, so that he pays attention and understands and, we hope, will react less in accordance with norms.[16]

Gertrude Stein, *Composition as Explanation*:

> Everything is the same except composition and as the composition is different and always going to be different everything is not the same.[17]

Adorno:

> [Since] art is by definition an antithesis to what is . . . it is separated from reality by the aesthetic difference. . . . It can only act on it through its *immanente Stimmigkeit*, the intrinsic rightness of the relation of its elements [i.e. through its form]. Only as a totality, through all its mediations, can the work become knowledge, not in its single intuitions.[18]

EXCURSION

I would like to give two examples of poems with explicit social content.

The first is Charles Reznikoff's *Testimony*:

1

Forty feet above the ground on a telegraph pole,
the lineman
forced the spur he wore into the pole and,
throwing his other leg around it,
leaned over

to fasten a line with his nippers
to the end of a crossarm
by a wire around the glass cup on a pin.

The line, hauled tight
hundreds of feet ahead of him
by means of a reel,
broke,
and the crossarm
broke where it was fastened to the pole:
he fell headlong
to the stones below.

2

It was a drizzling night in March,
The street lamps flashed twice:
a break in the connection,
and all hands were looking for it.

When the policeman saw him first,
the colored man was carrying a short ladder
that the hands used
in climbing the electric-light poles.
The policeman next saw him hanging on a pole,
his overcoat flapping in the wind,
and called to him but got no answer.

They put the dead body on the counter of a shop nearby:
the skin was burnt on the inside of both his hands;
his right hand was burnt to the bone.
The insulation was off of part of the "shunt cord" he had carried
and his skin was sticking to the naked wire.

3

There were three on the locomotive:
the flagman, the fireman, and the engineer.
About two hundred yards from the man —
stone-deaf —

the flagman commenced ringing the bell;

within about a hundred yards
the engineer commenced sounding his whistle:
thirty or forty short blows.

The man did not get off the track or look around. . . .[19]

This seems to contradict what I said about indirection. But by operating with distance, without any kind of commentary or explanation or even just fuller details, Reznikoff goes against our expectation of empathy. He lets the flat language of the news note stand as is, but accumulates the instances into a testimony to a society which not only causes such daily disasters in the name of industrial progress, but reports them in this manner.

The German poet Helmut Heissenbüttel very often works with Gertrude Stein's technique of avoiding of nouns and replacing them by words with an implicit reference to context, like pronouns, connectives, auxiliaries and dependent clauses. He often uses the refusal to name for social and political comment. The unstated words assume the aura of the taboo, and all the relative clauses, the its and thats imply hedging. This can be very funny, for instance when the taboo is sexual as in "Shortstory" where by the end everybody has had "it" with everybody else, including himself. In contrast, take an excerpt from the poem "Final Solution":

they just thought this up one day
who just thought this up one day
it just occurred to them one day
whom did it just occur to one day
someone of them it just occurred to someone of them
someone of them just thought it up one day
one day just someone of them just thought it up
or perhaps a number of them thought it up together
maybe it occurred to a number of them together
and how did they do what had occurred to them

if you want to do anything at all you've got to be for something and not just anything you just think up but something you can be for alright or at least something that many like to be for or at least something you think many like to be for

and so they just thought it up one day

they thought it up and they hit on it when they wanted to start something but what they hit on wasn't something you could be for but you could be against or better yet something you could get

most people to be against because when you can get most people
to be against something you don't have to be very specific about
what you can be for and the fact that you don't have to be very spe-
cific about this has its advantages because as long as they can let off
steam most people don't care what they are for

and so they hit on it when they'd started to just think up something
like that

they hit on the idea that what you're against must be something
you can see touch insult humiliate spit on lock up knock down ex-
terminate because what you can't see touch insult humiliate spit on
lock up knock down exterminate you can only say and what you
can only say can change and you never really know which way it
will turn no matter what you say against it.

and so they hit on this and did it

so they hit on this and did it and when they had done it they tried
to get most people to go along and when they'd gotten most people
to go along they hit on the idea that what you're against can still
change as long as it's still around and that only what's gone can't
change and so they forced those they'd gotten to go along to de-
stroy what they'd been gotten to be against to regard it like Malaria
mosquitoes or potato bugs which you've got to exterminate. . . .[20]

It is true that we are given a reference in the title, but what the poem is
"about," the reference it constructs, is not so much the "final solution"
itself, but the postwar German feeling about it: the wish not to talk
about it, the wish it would go away, and yet its inescapable presence in
the mind, in the relentlessness of the poem. Its power lies exactly in the
fact that the text does not state what it was "they" thought of, what it was
they could get people to be against. Nothing but this circling around an
unnamed middle could convey so much ambivalence.

THESIS 11

For the form to be unusual is has to go against expectations by break-
ing some convention, rule, established tradition, law, whether literary or
more general.

EXCURSION

Bataille:

Men differ from animals by observing laws, but the laws are ambiguous. Men observe them, but also need to violate them. The transgression of laws is not from ignorance: it takes resolute courage. The courage necessary for transgression is an accomplishment of man. This is in particular the accomplishment of literature whose privileged moment is challenge. Authentic literature is promethean.[21]

Or, as Tristan Tzara put it more succinctly: "We must destroy the pigeon holes."[14]

The possibilities for breaking laws in writing are of course infinite. I would like briefly to talk of two very fundamental targets of attack, logic and meaning.

EXCURSION

I am certainly not the first person to say poetry is an alternate logic. It is not illogical, but has a different, less linear logic which draws on the more untamed, unpredictable parts of our nature.

This is part of what I think my *Reproduction of Profiles* addresses, from which I read at the beginning [of this session]. It works with a logical syntax, all those "if-then" and "because," but constantly slides between frames of reference. It especially brings in the female body and sets into play the old gender archetypes of logic and mind being "male," whereas "female" designates the illogical: emotion, body, matter. And I hope that the constant sliding challenges these categories.

What I worked on consciously, though, was the *closure* of the propositional sentence. This was a challenge to me because my previous poems had mostly worked toward opening the boundaries of the sentence by either sliding sentences together or by using fragments. So here I accepted complete sentences (most of the time) and tried to open them up from the inside, subvert the correct grammar and logical form by these semantic slidings. Needless to say, the opening of closed structures would also be a thought pattern that could be useful in a social context, but while we write we are, as Cervantes says in Don Quixote, working on the back of a tapestry, working out patterns of colored threads without knowing what the picture is going to look like on the front.

EXCURSION

Steve McCaffery has applied Bataille's economics to an attack against the privileged position that meaning holds in literature.[22] He makes "meaning" the equivalent of wealth, the reward and "destination of the de-materialization of writing" which for him is what makes a text into merchandise. So his idea of a "general economy" of writing is the destruction of an absolute, fixable meaning, and this can range from the "nomadic meaning" of metaphors and any other kind of multivalence to sound poems and texts which refuse or at least delay meaning. As an example of the latter he quotes from Charles Bernstein's *Poetic Justice*, where we recognize the meaning of "inVazoOn uv spAz," but not without having been slowed down by the unusual spelling and capitalization.

This is actually closer to Ezra Pound's economics than to Bataille's. McCaffery introduces an abstract-concrete dichotomy:meaning versus the sound and shape of the words, and then uses the analogy of money which is abstract, symbolic energy, to discredit meaning. This is much like Pound, where anything concrete is good, where gold, the concrete metal, "gathers the light against it," but money and all banking operations are abstract and evil. Whereas Bataille wants the waste of energy in all its forms, not just the symbolic ones like objects or money, but human lives, work, anything.

However, I agree that it is one of the important tasks of poems to short-circuit the transparency that words have for the signified and which is usually considered their advantage for practical uses. Susanne Langer says: "A symbol which interests us *also* as an object is distracting."[23] It distracts from the reference, from what is symbolized. But this is exactly what poems want: to attract attention to the word as object, as a sensuous body, keep them from being mere counters of exchange. For Jakobson, it is the poetic function of language to make words "palpable,"[24] and Sartre's *What is Literature?* accepts as the basic difference between prose and poetry that poetry treats words as things rather than signs, that it is more like painting or music than like prose.[25]

ALARM

I have not kept clear borders between genres in this essay, many of whose statements are about literature in general or even all the arts. But perhaps Sartre has put his finger on a crucial difference and we need to rethink all this in terms of poetry versus prose.

EXCURSION

Let me give you one more example from a book of mine, *The Road Is*

Everywhere or Stop This Body:

> Exaggeration of a curve
> exchanges
> time and again
> beside you in the car
> pieces the road together
> with night moisture
> the force of would-be sleep
> beats through our bodies
> denied their liquid depth
> toward the always dangerous next
> dawn bleeds its sequence
> of ready signs[26]

Here the target is more strictly grammatical. The main device is that the object of one phrase turns into the subject of the next phrase without being repeated. I was interested in extending the boundaries of the sentence, of having a nearly unending flow which would play against the short lines that determine the rhythm. And since the thematic field is cars and other circulation systems I liked the immediate effect of speed.

However, it also comes out of my feminist preoccupation. The woman in our culture has been treated as the object par excellence — to be looked at rather than looking, to be loved and have things done to rather than being the one who does. So I propose a pattern in which subject and object function are not fixed, but temporary, reversible roles, where there is no hierarchy of main and subordinate clauses, but a fluid and constant alternation.

ALARM

There remains the huge doubt, the nagging suspicion of a quantitative threshold. So maybe our poems offer a challenge to the ruling grammar, offer some patterns of thinking and perception which might not be bad possibilities to consider. But how many readers does a small press book reach? Even if all 1000 copies of a typical press run get sold, even if they all reach readers how much effect is this book going to have on society? None, I am afraid. I suspect it takes similar patterns appearing in many disciplines at the same time, even though I have acted in this paper as if there existed nothing but society on the one hand and writing on the other. For instance, many of the characteristics of innovative art which bother people to this day (discontinuity, indeterminacy, acceptance of the unescapable human reference point) were anticipated in science by the turn of the century. In contrast, the fact that they are still an irritant in art would seem to show that it takes art to make people aware of the challenge to their thinking habits or that the challenge has to come in many areas. It also gives us an inkling of how *slowly* mental habits change.

EXCURSION

One last word on the development of the small presses which is a curious and more tangible example of interaction with society. In the early sixties, when Keith Waldrop and I were graduate students wanting to start a magazine, the quotes from printers were completely unaffordable, but we found we could buy a small letterpress for $100. We had stumbled into a moment of technological development when offset printing had proved cheaper than letterpress, so printshops all over the country were dumping their machines. And more and more small presses sprang up, not all using letterpress, but in the early days a good many because this particular technology was accessible (as is now computer typesetting). I remember a bookseller in Ann Arbor whose eyes lit up when we told him about the press: "With a mimeo you can start a party, with a printing press a revolution." It is not quite a revolution, but it very quickly became more than just a few kooks printing little books. Over the past 30 years small press publishing has snowballed into an alternative to commercial houses — to the point that it gives them a good conscience about taking even fewer financial risks! They now say: a small press can do this better than we could. But small press publishing has also had enough impact that a conservative agency like the National Endowment for the Arts admits that our literature would be much poorer without it and offers occasional grant help.

Whether all this will produce or contribute to a revolution in our thinking or amount only to a little putsch remains a question.

DISCUSSION

KABU OKAI-DAVIES: Much of what you said seemed to speak to my own situation. For example, your quotation from Jabès: A writer is responsible for even what he does not write. How about when you adopt a language or vice versa, and this language is not able to express your own native language or peculiar experience, i.e, mother tongue and world view, and [yet] the native language hasn't expanded enough to meet the demands of your global experiences. Worst of all you don't know how to write in your mother tongue; yet this language you have adopted is beginning to think for you and therefore interprets your experiences contrary to what you mean. The language you have adopted is subverting your own psychic self. You grow to distrust the language itself. You are caught in a situation where you cannot communicate anymore. So can you hold the writer responsible for even not writing at all? [laughter]: neither the language that he has adopted nor his native language?

BRUCE ANDREWS: Perhaps you could say something about Celan in responding to that question.

WALDROP: This is curious because, maybe to a slightly lesser degree than yours, this is also my problem. I came to English when I was — well, I had had it in school but I came to this country [from Germany] when I was 21. So I changed languages also. And I know what you mean, this very strange feeling that you have no language at all because your native language has sort of evaporated or seems not relevant and the new language is not really yours, so they fight each other. This is hard to live with, to an extent, but it is also actually an advantage, because it makes you very conscious that you don't ever own the language, that the language is larger than you, that it is not simply a tool that you are the master of that you can use. And I think that this is a useful, a healthy position to have this sort of distance of being caught between the structures. And it also means that you really have different patterns always present so that you in a way are always less susceptible to be gullible to these phrases that do influence our thinking. This "language thinks for us" which can be good and bad. So I think it works both ways, as a problem and also as an advantage.

OKAI-DAVIES: My problem is different than a Singer or a Brodsky who can write in their native languages — Yiddish or Russian. I can't write in Ga or Ashanti (Twi). I was not taught to read and write in my native language since the formal education in Africa is still Eurocentric in language and orientation. And though many of the African languages are written now, each [individual] language does not serve the national communication interest, because of the multi-linguistic — dialect — situation that exists in Africa today [with] many tribes in one nation. For example, Ga is the language of the Gas who inhabit central and east of Accra. Twi is the language of the Ashantis — the majority of the Akan people. Ghana alone, out of the whole of Africa, has ten linguistic regions and over thirty-six complete dialects which in most cases can stand as individual African languages.

So the problem is, you start writing in English and you get to a very peculiar Ghanian or African experience which if you want to do the inner translation and put it in English you destroy the whole thing. And if you want to communicate and use the English language to communicate to your African people, they don't understand you. So some African writers have adopted the method of Africanizing the European languages, especially English, by using African words in sentences where necessary — and that obviously ceases to become English. About half of what you write out as a book is what you call glossary or something else — an Afro-English dialect. You end up writing a dictionary thinking it is a novel [laughter].

WALDROP: But you see, that might really lead to a useful new form, which could be a bridging. Celan is a very interesting case. Since he barely survived the concentration camp and his whole family did not, he had a massive block against German. But he continued to write his poems in German. His solution was partly to subvert the language, to make it more and more wrenched and partly go back to archaic words, but in a way create his own language inside the German. And since it has a wrenched, tortured feel, he makes us constantly aware of the anguish he must feel at having to use a language he must consider instrumental in trying to eradicate his people. So, this might be another point. You can subvert from the inside. I think you should go on working on this. You sound frustrated at this point, but this might lead to something.

LEE ANN BROWN: I was interested in what you were saying about the semantic sliding in *The Road Is Everywhere or Stop This Body* and *The Reproduction of Profiles?*

WALDROP: Well, actually, I was only using it for *The Reproduction of Profiles*. In *The Road* it's [there] a little too because there are various circulation systems which are used interchangeably. So at one moment [you are] with a car and the next moment you are with money and the next moment with the circulation of semen or blood. There is a sliding from one frame of reference to the other. I came to this by trying to get away from small metaphors, to push the metaphor out into the structure, making it large. Nowhere in *The Road* is there a line that says that circulation of cars is *like* the circulation of blood. There is no one image that puts those areas in relation. But the whole book, by moving from one to the other, implies it and thus breaks down boundaries.

BROWN: Could you talk more about the sentence structure in *The Reproduction of Profiles*.

WALDROP: This book mostly uses grammatically correct sentences (modeled on the very closed propositional sentences of logic, specifically Wittgenstein's). But these correct sentences don't make "sense" because of semantic slides, mostly on puns, mostly pitting the body against logic. Take, for instance, this beginning of a poem I read earlier tonight: "You told me if something is not used it is meaningless and took my temperature which I had meant to save for a more difficult day." We have, on the one hand, a position on economics in which use is declared good, and saving, by implication, bad. On the other hand, we have the body and its temperature. The sliding — and the fun — occurs in the punning use of "taking." The two contexts question and subvert each other. The givens of the body make nonsense of the economy of "take and use," but then again confirm it since there is literally no way of saving one's body temperature — except in the sense that we can use illness as an excuse.

Q: I wanted to come back for a second to the political and your feminist position. Because I think that it is rather difficult when you write as a woman poet that you have to resist or subvert two kinds of thing at the same time. Because you are fighting against the stereotypes in society but then there is another thing, the stereotype discourse that you ought to have as a feminist writer. How do you feel, as a woman poet, in relation to the feminist anthologies, presses — to the feminist movement, in general?

WALDROP: That's pretty involved. Let me just stick to writing. I don't want to write "about" any issues, not even feminist ones, I prefer exploring the forest to hewing a road, even if the road is in a good direction. But I think my feminist consciousness inevitably gets in (like my other assumptions). Sometimes as irony, as when I speak of a field "which, lacking male parameters, must be nowhere."

Actually, I have some poems that are explicitly feminist. There is one about the theme of looking and being looked at. I reread at some point the tale of Psyche and Eros. Sure, it's an allegory about love and the soul. But the literal tale hinges on the woman not being allowed to look at her lover: she is only to be looked at, i.e. she is treated like an object. I

use this in my poem "Psyche and Eros." It's one of the most direct po-
ems I've written. I retell the tale with this slant, and I say it's not so terri-
ble really what she does: she "opens more than her legs" — she opens
her eyes, laying claim to being a subject rather than an object. And that
precipitates the crisis in this story.

Here I have worked with a feminist *theme*. In a different way, the con-
stant flip-over of object into subject in *The Road* (e.g. "the dawn" in "to-
ward the always dangerous next / dawn bleeds its sequence / of ready
signs") addresses this same theme, though not *as* theme. On the surface
I talk about our car culture — though also about sexual relations. But
indirectly, on the level of grammar, this technique attacks a rigid sub-
ject-object relation by practicing reversibility. And since the woman as
"love object" is a prevalent archetype in our culture I think this tech-
nique has definite feminist/political implications. Of course, this is
hindsight. Consciously, I was working on a formal problem, on eroding
the boundaries of the sentence, sliding sentences into one another. This
has been my experience: on form you have to work consciously, where-
as your concerns and obsessions surface all by themselves.

These sexist patterns are very persistent, even in people that have the
best intentions. I was talking with a man who is the furthest thing from
macho that you can imagine. He was asking me some questions about
The Reproduction of Profiles and I said that the second part, especially,
brings in very much the female body as a challenge to logic. And he
said, "Oh that's funny, because it didn't strike me as very erotic." —
Look, I said, the female body is not just an object of eroticism; it is
many other things. Of course he said he didn't mean that but these
things go very deep.

Q: But I imagine that you must have some difficulty with the more ex-
plicit, politically engaged writing, don't you? Or with the exclusion of
poets like yourself and Susan Howe, or say Lorinne Neidecker, from,
for example, the Gilbert and Gubar anthology of women's writing?
There's an extra difficulty being a women poet and writing the kind of
poetry you write: you are out of everywhere [laughter].

WALDROP: I take that as a compliment. I've more or less claimed this
is the position of poetry.

I think there is a definite need for the kind of anthology you're talking
about, but I wouldn't expect to find Susan Howe's explorations of lan-
guage in it. But then I wouldn't expect to find them in most non-feminist
thematic anthologies either. It's not what people are looking for. They are
looking for statements of position you can rally to, for experiences you

can feel you can identify with, for things they already know. For comfort-poetry.

Q: I was very struck by the fact that you only quoted men. There must have been some expression or thought on the subject by women.

WALDROP: I know and am not happy about it. For the theoretical part, I'm afraid it's a matter of not having read the right texts by the right time. (By "right" texts I mean that that would fit my context.) I had thought of using Leslie Scalapino, but the Reznikoff and Heissenbüttel seemed the clearest, because most technically opposed, exemplifications of the particular point.

JEFFREY JULLICH: I appreciate your talk a great deal. You referred to the gender dichotomy as a subject often misperceived as a subject-object relation, and you referred to this as "crude dichotomy." I cannot overlook the diagram which has been on the board this whole time, which seems to me might [suggest] the unspoken assumptions that all of your propositions follow out of, which is that the author stands in relation to the reader in a subject-object dichotomy: that through this vehicle the author can produce these changes in the reader.

And yet you used a phrase just now, "that's what they're looking for," which really reverses the axis, and says that the reader is in some way going to do the determining: that the uses to which the literature is put depends on the needs of the reader. *Ulysses* which was an oppositional work, is now a token of a certain kind of intellectual wealth. Artaud and Valéry could be quoted back to back, which is — you couldn't get them anywhere near each other. And I just wondered how it would change your propositions if that axis might not be just another "crude dichotomy." Because the reader may determine the literature.

WALDROP: This is a very good point. It's partly a crude dichotomy, but it is not as crude as it would be if we posited a direct communication. If the author does not directly communicate with the reader, he or she does not tell the reader how to read the work, nor does the reader tell the writer how to write. Readers can do this only in the case of the businessman-writer who writes strictly to the demands of a market or genre. But this person I have bracketed all along as one who is not going to do what I consider real writing.

If I think my little diagram is a little less crude it is because the "vibration" area allows for some openness. It is not a situation of "control," it is not even as symmetrical as I have drawn it, except that both parties are *active*.

JULLICH: Do you think it would change the truth-value of any of your theses, such as that the work needs to surprise, that it must be oppositional? If the reader can take a revolutionary text or a revolutionary song and turn it into a sign of cultural chic or an advertisement, would this possibility change the truth-value of your propositions?

WALDROP: Well, the truth-value of my propositions I am not altogether sure of to *start* with.

ALAN DAVIES: What would be dichotomous — I'm going to build on what you said, I think — about a direct relationship between the so-called reader and the so-called writer? Let's not say "the writer communicates to the reader" because that's like saying "the writer fucks the reader" or something, and might conceivably be problematic [laughter]. But let's say there is a direct understanding between them, what would make that dichotomous? In other words, I think you [Jullich] are absolutely right, that the confusion of the relationship as you [Waldrop] have drawn it is the answer to all the questions you have asked about the failures of poetry. This confusion . . .

WALDROP: What is the confusion?

DAVIES: These so-called vibrations and the fact that the writing is kind of off to the side and out of balance. That it's either miswritten or misperceived, and that those misgivings are elevated and privileged.

WALDROP: Well they can be and they can be turned even into radical chic.

JULLICH: At the beginning you looked at the "legislator of the world" quote. Maybe what is wrong with that quote is that it is definitely not the writer [but] the reader who is legislating.

WALDROP: The legislation part I don't think goes very far, again exception made for the businessman-writer whose criterion of quality is sales figures. Otherwise it only goes to the point that the writer can legislate over his/her structure while making it, and the reader can legislate over the way he or she is using the poem, or *if* he/she is going to use it.

JULLICH: There'll be no control over the outcome.

WALDROP: But there isn't any control over the outcome. That is the point. And it is also why I think the relation is not a simple one.

ANDREWS: Following up on what they were saying and embroidering further on your chart: the boundary condition that you have is language.

So, that seems what makes possible these vibrations. It's not some quality of misstatement or misreading; it's the fact that what is being set up is some vibrational activity in the language that the writer sets up for the reader.

I was struck when you were talking that the value you were placing on countering expectations and creating surprise was strictly at the formal level. You weren't really talking about content-oriented statements that would create surprise or counter expectations; instead, the manner in which things were constructed would counter expectations. It seems that those expectations, and the lack of surprise, the habits that you are challenging, would have to be in the normal language use of some larger community — much larger than the actual people reading the text. There would be some gesturing toward a society or a social body that had certain kinds of norms that were fairly general, that you would be thinking of yourself and seeing how writing would counter normal expectations about form — seeing how writing would create surprise [in terms of these norms].

And yet your small press work brought home how specific and narrow [the readership for such work is]. Now there's an entire tradition of countering formal expectations and [readers of these works] might only be looking for things that were surprising to some normal reader who would never touch these books. So that for those readers, the ones that you would actually be writing for, you wouldn't be countering expectations or creating surprise at all. You would be giving them just what they want: exciting, "challenging" texts — but only challenging for those other guys who would never get *these* texts.

WALDROP: I talk on the level of form because that is what I know most about, that's what I work on consciously, but of course the value of surprise and renewal applies to all levels, including the social context.

But you are right: what's called innovation can very quickly become mannerism and the expected thing rather than the unexpected.

ANDREWS: So to the extent that you have a consciousness of your actual readers, as different from the more abstract notion of challenging normal expectations, would this register as a problem?

WALDROP: I have no sense of who my readers are. Of course, there is Keith Waldrop and a few friends I can count on reading whatever I write. But beyond that, what little feedback I get is not that predictable.

ANDREWS: I guess what I'm trying to [contrast is] a fetishizing of the idea of countering expectations for the reader [as opposed to] seeing

[your project] in broadly social terms. If [countering expectations] be-
came a reference point in and of itself, if you had to do that with any in-
dividual reader, then as soon as you found out that the people who were
reading your work were coming out of an avant garde, experimental tra-
dition of readership, you would able to say, "Well. Ah ha! Now I have to
immediately challenge that mode of reading too and I will give them
Adrienne Rich. That'll show 'em [laughter]. I'll batter them over the
head with blatant ideological formulations that have no formal interest
for their tradition and this will shock them, this will surprise them." But
I don't think you are doing that: so it makes sense for you to say then
that you don't really know who your readers are, that the terms are
more social.

WALDROP: I'd like to go back to the nature of surprise. I think we
were taking it too abstractly. Or I was rash agreeing with you. It's true
that an innovative technique can become a mannerism, the idea of
countering expectation can become a fetish, but if it does then obvious-
ly the life has gone out of it and it is being *used* in a mechanical (i.e.
unsurprising) way. This does not exclude that the same technique can
again be used in a fresh, alive, surprising way. It's not as if once we've
encountered a pun and understood how it works we will never again be
surprised and amused by another.

If I reach for a new poem by, say, Susan Howe I obviously bring to it
the expectation of "avant-garde writing" and, more narrowly, expecta-
tions based on her previous work. Now in order to surprise me Susan
Howe does not have to change her style completely and write like
Adrienne Rich (though that would be a shock alright). If the new poem
does something for me it will be because there are all sorts of *small* sur-
prises, conducting wires thrown between words, references, contexts,
ideas, which I did not expect, even though, once I see it, it all fits into
her previous work, presents no radical departure.

What I'm saying is that surprise is a sign of *life*, which means change
and the unexpected, hence a sign of creativity. It works in all sizes, on all
levels, against all norms. And it will stimulate mental activity in the per-
son experiencing it.

This is the one social function of poetry (and art in general) that I am
certain about: it helps keep the synapses functioning, the mind's arteries
from hardening, in writers and readers alike. So rather than legislators I
would call poets (*and* readers) something like the unacknowledged life
maintenance crew of the mind.

Notes

Unless otherwise noted, all translations are by Rosmarie Waldrop.

1. Edmond Jabès, "Repondre à repondre pour," unpublished, 1988.

2. Paul Valéry, *Aesthetics*, tr. Ralph Manheim, Bollington Series, vol. 13, New York: Pantheon Books, 1964, p. 129.

3. Bertold Brecht, *Schriften zur Literatur und Kunst*, vol. 2, Frankfurt: Suhrkamp, 1967, p. 23.

4. There have been several convincing studies of how the little perverted phrases spread and reinforced antisemitism in Germany, e.g. Victor Klemperer, *Die unbewältigte Sprache*, München: dtv, 1969, or Sternberger/Storz/Suskind, *Aus dem Wörterbuch des Unmenschen*, Hamburg: Claassen, 1968.

5. in Urs Jaeggi, *Literature und Politik*, Frankfurt: Suhrkamp, 1972, p.105.

6. Edmond Jabès, *Le petit livre de la subversion hors de soupcon*, Paris: Gallimard, 1982, p. 7 and cover text.

7. Theodor Adorno, *Noten zur Literatur* II, Frankfurt: Suhrkamp, 1961, p. 168.

8. Georges Bataille, *Oeuvres Completes* VII, Paris: Gallimard, 1976, pp. 40, 9, 29. An English translation of this 1949 volume, *La Part Maudite*, has been published as *The Accursed Share*, Cambridge: Zone Books, 1988.

9. in Jaeggi, p. 21.

10. *Roland Barthes par Roland Barthes*, Paris: Seuil, 1975, p. 53.

11. in Jaeggi, p. 7.

12. Brecht, *Schriften zur Literatur und Kunst*, vol. I, pp. 115, 30.

13. See Jabès, *The Book of Questions*, vol. 1, tr. Waldrop, Middleton, Conn.: Wesleyan University Press, 1976, p. 25; Charles Olson, *The Human Universe*, New York: Grove Press, 1967, p. 18. Oppen, in "A Letter," in *Agenda*, 1973, quoted in *HOW(ever)* 1,#3 (Feb. 1984): "We do not write what we already know before we wrote the poem."

14. Valéry, *Aesthetics*, pp.48-9.

15. Tristan Tzara, "7 Manifestes Dada," *Oeuvres*, vol. I, Paris: Flammarion, 1975, p. 382.

16. in Jaeggi, p. 52.

17. Gertrude Stein, *Selected Writings*, New York: Modern Library, 1946, p. 520.

18. Adorno, *Noten zur Literatur* II, pp. 163-4, 175.

19. Charles Reznikoff, *Testimony I: The United States 1885-1890: Recitative*, Santa Barbara, CA: Black Sparrow, 1978, pp. 30-33.

20. Helmut Heissenbüttel, *Textbuch* V, Olten: Luchterhand, 1965, p. 12.

21. Bataille, *Oeuvres Complètes*, IX, p. 437.

22. Steve McCaffery, *North of Intention*, New York: Roof Books, 1986, pp. 201-22.

23. Susanne Langer, *Philosophy in a New Key*, New York: Mentor Books, 1948, p. 61.

24. "Linguistics and Poetics," in *Style in Language*, ed. Th. A. Sebeok, Cambridge, MIT, 1960, pp. 356.

25. Jean-Paul Sartre, *Situations* II, Paris: Gallimard, 1948, p. 64.

26. Rosmarie Waldrop, *The Road Is Everywhere or Stop This Body*, Columbia, MD: Open Places, 1978, p. 26.

Poetic Politics

Nicole Brossard

I have divided my presentation into two parts. The first part has to do with the body of writing, its motivations, its energies. The second part has to do with the references and values that surround us and the kinds of linguistic reaction they call for when we disagree with them. I say *when we disagree with them* because I don't believe that one becomes a writer to reinforce common values or common perspectives on reality.

I would like, in this talk, to make space for questions regarding different rituals, different approaches, different postures that we take in language in order to exist, fulfill our needs to express, communicate, or to challenge language itself: hoping that by playing with language it will reveal unknown dimensions of reality. I have been writing for more than 20 years. I have written poetry, novels, texts, essays. Today, I am still fascinated by the act of writing, the processes, the trouble, the pain, and the joy that we go through in order to put in words what we feel, what we recall vaguely but which insists on being recalled, what we envision whether it is full-length images or enigmatic flashes running through our brain like a storm of truth.

Those who are familiar with my work will know that one of most recurrent words in my texts is *body (corps)*. This word is usually accompanied by the words *writing (écriture)* and *text (texte)*. The expression *Le Cortex exubérant* summarizes my obsession with body, text, and writing. For me the body is a metaphor of energy, intensity, desire, pleasure, memory, and awareness. The body interests me in its circulation of energy and the way it provides, through our senses, for a network of associations out of which we create our mental environment, out of which we imagine far beyond what we in fact see, feel, hear or taste. It is through this network of associations that we claim new sensations, that we dream backward in accelerated or slow motion, that we zoom in on sexual fantasies, that we discover unexpected angles of thought.

73

I have always said that writing is energy taking shape in language. Sexual, libidinal, mental, and spiritual energies give to us the irresistible need to declare things, to make new propositions, to look for solutions which can unknot social patterns of violence and death, to explore unknown territories of the mind, to search for each of our identities, to fill the gap between real and unreal. In other words, energy motivates us to write but it also needs to find its *motive* to be able to do this. Energy has to go out and has to come in. The body is its channel. But the body claims to be more than a channel: it thinks of strategies to regularize the flow of energy. The body alone cannot process all energy, it needs language to process energy into social meaning. Among the uses that we make of language, there is a privileged one called creative writing. It is in this sense that I say that writing is shaping figures and meanings within the merry-go-round of energy that traverses us. Filtered by language, this energy finds a rhythm, becomes a voice, transforms itself into images and metaphors. Energy that is too low keeps you silent, energy that is too high makes noise instead of meaning — even though silence and noise can eventually by interpreted as an historical momentum.

Sexual, libidinal, mental, and spiritual energies provided with a *motive* or an *object of desire*, or both, engage us in a creative dimension. When these energies synchronize they offer a privileged moment to a writer. Most of the time we call this "inspiration." These energies can also work alone or in combination. Sexual energy produces a multiplicity of images and scenarios. Libidinal energy creates projects and goals. Mental energy provides for sharpness and for abstraction. Spiritual energy links us to a global environment. Yet all these energies can stagnate or make you mad if they don't meet their object of desire, or organize themselves in such a way that they can at least dream of — or figure out — their object of desire.

Now let me make a distinction between the motive and the object of desire. The motive is something that whatever the situation eternally returns in the work of an artist. The motive is roots, flesh and skin. It is *incontrovertible*. It is inscribed in us as a first and ultimate memory. It is carnal knowledge. All good writers have a strong motive. The motive is most of the time hidden in the core of a work, hidden but recurrent as a theme. It seems to me that motive (a good reason and a pattern) is a personal, existential question that makes one endlessly repeat: why or how come? It is a three-dimensional question caused by a synergetic moment, this moment being either traumatic or ecstatic. With the synergetic moment gone, we are left with this three-dimensional question, a question to which we can only respond with a two-dimensional answer —

that is, a partial answer that obliges us to repeat the question and to try other answers. We answer in two dimensions because we think in a chronological way, one word at the time, one word after the other, while the body experiences life synchronously. Writing, we have to make choices, to separate things. Naming is separation, it portions out reality. Dreams are 3-dimensional but we forget about them or cannot understand them.

As for the object of desire, it is probably always the same one mediated by different people we fall in love with, by books we cannot recover from, by situations to which we respond passionately. For me, a good writer or a good painter always repeats the same motive, the same question, the same statement in all her or his works. Think of Kandinsky, Rothko, Betty Goodwin. Great artists are always driven by a motive while fairly good creators have to rely on their objects of desire: if the object isn't there, then nothing happens but sweat.

It is well known that people give and take energy from one another; that blame, insult, humiliation take away energy; that praise, love, and respect multiply energy. The principle is very simple. But it gets complicated when it applies to the way men and women are positioned in regard to language's patriarchal values. We cannot avoid questioning this cultural field of language, which both provides us with energy or deprives us of it. What I call the cultural field of language is made of male sexual and psychic energies transformed through centuries of written fiction into standards for imagination, frames of references, patterns of analysis, networks of meaning, rhetorics of body and soul. Digging in that field can be, for a creative woman, a mental health hazard.

This second part is more personal. What I propose to discuss is a kind of trajectory in my writing. I would like to show how my politics of poetic form — my Poetic Politics — have been shaped within a sociocultural environment as well as through private life. But I would also like to talk in general terms of the behaviors that we encounter in writing while we make space for ourselves as well as for ideas that we value and themes that we privilege.

Since in principle language belongs to everyone, we are entitled to reappropriate it by taking the initiative to intervene when it gives the impression of closing itself off, and when our desire clashes with common usage. Very young, I perceived language as an obstacle, as a mask, narrow-spirited like a repetitive task of boredom and of lies. Only poetic language found mercy in my eyes. It is in this sense that my practice of writing became at once a practice of intervention and of exploration — a ludic experience. Very early I had a relationship to the language of transgression and of subversion. I wanted strong sensations: I wanted to unmask lies, hypocrisy, and banality. I had the feeling that if language was an obstacle, it was also the place where everything happens, where everything is possible. That I still believe.

I have often said that I don't write to express myself but that I write to understand reality, the way we process reality into fiction, the way we process feeling, emotion and sensation into ideas and landscapes of thought. After all, the difference between a writer and a non-writer is that the writer processes life through written language and by doing so has access and gives access to unexpected, unsuspected angles of reality — which we commonly called fiction.

What about expressions like *strong sensations, transgression, subversion,* and *ludic experience?* Let's start with "strong sensations" and "ludic experience." What do these expressions oppose? For me, they oppose boredom and daily routine; in a word: *linearity.* Behind that there is obviously a statement something like: "I am not satisfied with what society offers me as a future or imposes on me in the present because if I was to follow its directives, it would mean that I would have to lead a boring, middlebrow, puritan life." This means that I value research, intelligence, and pleasure. It also means that I cannot function with cliches and standard values that somehow seem to narrow the possibilities of life: life of the mind as well as life of the emotion. Indeed, our emotional and our critical spirits are more and more eroded.

To be more concrete, let's say that I started to write, in the early 60s in a Quebec, which was at a turning point of our history, a period that we have called the "quiet revolution." Yes, everything was being questioned: education as well as social, political, religious, and cultural life. To my generation, the dream of an independent, French, socialist, secular Quebec provided for audacities, transgressions, and a quest for collective identity. But underneath these changes was essentially the question of identity. Who were we? Who are we? We have a Canadian passport but our soul and tradition are not Canadian, we speak French but we are not French, we are North American but we are not American. As a young person and as a young writer there were three kinds of institutions that had a sour taste to me:

First: *The Catholic Church* because it had a strong influence in almost every field of Quebec society and mainly because of its control on education and sexual life (marriage, contraception, abortion, homosexuality).

Second: *The Canadian Confederation* and all its British and Canadian symbols. I resent profoundly how as French Canadian we were despised and discriminated against by Anglo Canadian politics. I have always made the language issue a personal thing. Today I am still vividly hurt when someone who is living or has been living in Montreal for many years addresses me in English.

Third: *The literary establishment.* When you write you write with and against literature. You write out of inspiration from writers and books, but you also write against mediocrity and the cliches the literary establishment promotes. Maybe it has been unfair to some writers of the generation that preceded mine, but I was fed up with poems talking about landscapes, snow, mountains, and the tormented rhetoric of love and solitude. At the same time, I felt deeply for Quebec literature which the generation of *La Barre du Jour* and *Les Herbes rouges* were about to rediscover and to renew at the same time.

So all together those three realities set up for me a social and literary field that I could oppose and later on transgress and subvert. Very early my poetry was abstract, syntactically nonconventional; desire with its erotic drives had a great part in it. Part of what I was writing was consciously political, at least at the level of intention. Let's say that my "basic intention" was to make trouble, to be a troublemaker in regard to language but also with values of my own embodied by a writing practice that was ludic (playing with words), experimental (trying to understand processes of writing), and exploratory (searching). You see, it brings us back to my values: exploration (which provides for renewal of information and knowledge), intelligence (which provides the ability to process things), and pleasure (which provides for energy and desire).

So from 1965 to 1973, I can say that I would see myself as a poet — an avant-garde poet, a formalist poet. Being a woman was not at stake, didn't seem to be a problem. Of course it was not a problem because in some way I was not identifying with femininity nor with other women, with whom I felt I had nothing to share. I could understand and talk about alienation, oppression, domination, exploitation only when applied to me as a Quebecer. I was a Quebecer, an intellectual, a poet, a revolutionary. Those were my identities. They were all positive and somehow they were valued in those years of cultural changes and counterculture. So in some way by transgressing I was still on the good side.

But in 1974, I became a mother and about the same time fell in love with another woman. Suddenly, I was living the most common experience in a woman's life which is motherhood and at the same time I was living the most marginal experience in a woman's life which is lesbianism.

Motherhood made life absolutely concrete (two bodies to wash, to clean, to move, to think of) and lesbianism made my life absolute fiction in a patriarchal heterosexual world. Motherhood shaped my solidarity with women and gave me a feminist consciousness as lesbianism opened new mental space to explore.

All this to say that my body was getting new ideas, new feelings, new emotions. From then on my writing started to change. It became more fluid, though still abstract and still obsessed with language, transgression, and subversion; but this time I had "carnal knowledge" of what I was investing in words. My frame of references started to change and new words (words that I had never used) started to invest my work: vertigo, cliff, amazon, sleep, memory, skin. I started to use new metaphors to understand things: the spiral, the hologram, metaphors which would help me to drift away from a linear and binary approach. Questions started to flow about identity, imagination, history, and more and more questions came about language and the incredible fraud I was discovering in the accumulated layers of lies told about women through centuries of the male version of reality. Which is to say that I also had to deal with contradictions, paradoxes, double binding, tautology in order to understand what I would call "the father knows best" business. Patriarchy being a highly sophisticated machine, it takes time and energy to understand how it works.

Now I would like to try to answer more precisely the questions raised in this series of lectures on "The Politics of Poetic Form." While writing this essay, I found myself saying: "It is not in the writing that a poetic text is political, it is in the reading that it becomes political." I knew something was true and wrong at the same time with this statement and therefore I decided to divide it in two affirmative statements which are:

A. It is in the writing that a text shows its politics.

B. It is in the reading that a text has a political aura.

I believe that a text gives subliminal information on how it wants to be read. Its structure is itself a statement, no matter what the text says. Of course, what the texts says is important but it is like body language. Body language tells more about yourself and how you want to relate with someone than does your words. I would like to point out three aspects in which a text shows politics: its perspective, its themes, its style.

The perspective. What I call the perspective is an angle from which we orient the reading of a text before it is even read. This can be done by *quotations* beginning or inserted in the text, for example from Virginia Woolf, Marx, Martin Luther King, etc. This can also be done by *dedication* of a poem to someone whose name will ring a political bell. For example, dedicating your poem to Che Guevara, to Valerie Solanas, to Paul Rose, or to even to Ben Johnson. The third way is to *title* your poem or your book in such a way that it will suggest some political metaphors. For example: *Chili's Bones Flowers*, *Clitoris at Sunset*, *The Color Purple* (in which we read subliminally "people of color") or *Give Em Enough Rope* (which can be understood "give them enough rope to hang themselves" or "give him enough rope to do want he wants"). Quotations, dedications, and titles provide for immediate references or statement. They tell a state of mind, they point out literary, cultural, or political networks.

Themes. There are themes that are bound to have if not ideological at least a troubling effect: *Sexuality*, eroticism, homosexuality, lesbianism — something is always at stake with eroticism because it deals with limits, moral, and the unavowable. *Language* — writing about language, pointing out how language works or giving feedback on how what is being read has been written can also imply politics of awareness because it takes away the "referential illusion" of the reader.

Postures. *Disqualifying symbols of authority* by uncovering the lies and the contradictions on which they have been constituted — God, Pope, President, Man, or little man (as in husband, lover, or father). *Valuing marginal experiences* — valuing people who are inferiorized, for example valuing women as subjects.

Style. Shaking the syntax, breaking grammatical law, not respecting punctuation, visually designing the text, using the white space, typesetting as you choose, using rhythms to create sounds: All of these have a profound effect on readers, offering a new perspective on reality through a global formal approach as did for example the impressionists, the cubists, and the expressionists, in painting and as did, in literature, the surrealists, *le nouveau roman*, the post-moderns. Among writers we can name Gertrude Stein, James Joyce, and Monique Wittig for *The Lesbian Body*.

So by changing the perspective, the themes, or the style, somehow you deceive the conformist reader in her or his moral or aesthetic expectations and you annoy her or him by breaking the habits of reading. At the same time, you provide for a new space of emotion and you make space for new materials to be taken into account about life and its meaning; you also offer the non-conformist reader a space for a new experience — travelling through meaning while simultaneously producing meaning.

These interventions send a message in which the poet says: I don't agree with prevalent moral or aesthetic values. I am not respecting the status quo. There is more to life than what we are thought to believe, there is more to language than what we are used to expecting.

While the statement "It is in the writing that a text shows its politics" repels or seduces the reader (most of the time belonging to the dominant culture), the second statement "It is in the reading that a text becomes political" calls for **a process of identification** from the reader belonging to a minority or treated as such.

I believe that a lot of writers belonging to minorities whether sexual, racial, or cultural, or writers who belong to groups who live or have lived under colonization, oppression, exploitation, or a dictatorship, are bound to have a highly loaded personal memory out of which they express themselves as individuals. But inevitably their personal story converges with the one of thousands who have felt and lived the same experience. Memory, identity, and solidarity are at stake when *reading* is taken as political; just as transgression, subversion, and exploration are at stake when *writing* is taken as political.

Anyone who encounters insult and hatred because of her or his differences from a powerful group is bound, soon or later, to echo a *we* through the use of *I* and to draw the line between *us and them*, *we* and *they*.

WE triggers emotions based on solidarity, memory, identification, complicity, proudness, or sadness.

THEY triggers emotions based on anger and revolt. Hatred also: THEY cuts the relation.

YOU (in the plural *vous*) triggers accusations, blame, reproach. It maintains the relation because it is a direct address. *You* calls for negotiation just as *they* calls for struggle.

We all have a I/We story and a We/They story. If you belong to a dominant group, **they** is either laughable, insignificant, or used as a scapegoat. If you belong to an oppressed group, **they** is targeted as enemy because they have proven to be a real threat or danger to your collectivity or your group. As an example, I could draw a personal chart which would read like this:

I/we a writer	you non-writers	politically non-pertinent
I/we poets	you prose writers	politically non-pertinent
I/we women	you men	politically pertinent
I/we feminists	you sexists	politically pertinent
I/we lesbians	you heterosexuals	politically pertinent
I/we Quebecers	you Canadians	politically pertinent

People from groups who have been politically, economically, and culturally silenced or censored have expectations that one of them will speak about them and for them. Women have those expectations, feminists, lesbians, Indians, blacks, Chicanos have those expectations. Those readers want so much to hear or see things about themselves that they can even overestimate the political involvement of a writer. That is why writers from those groups are often asked the question: Are you a political writer? *Etes-vous un écrivain engagé?* A question that embarrasses them and which they will be tempted to avoid by saying that they write what they write because they are creative. Which is true, but not as simple as it seems. For example, while writing a feminist article, I questioned myself wondering who is writing my text: the poet, the feminist or the lesbian. I came up with this answer: The feminist is moral, responsible, fair, humanist, has solidarity. The lesbian is audacious, radical, takes risks, strictly focuses on women. The creative person has imagination and is able to process ambivalent emotion and contradictions as well as transforming anger, ecstasy, desire, pain, and so on, into social meaning.

So altogether, I would say that one's Poetic Politics shapes itself within the weaving movement of personal motive with energy, identity, knowledge, and the ability to process emotions, ideas, sensations into a meaningful response to the world. As for myself, my poetic is essentially to make space for the unthought. As a woman, I am left with a language that has either erased or marginalized women as subjects. Therefore in my poetic I perform what is necessary to make space for women's subjectivity and plurally, to make space for a positive image of women. This task engages me to question language — symbolic and imaginary, from all angles and dimensions.

In conclusion, I would like to say that a good part of my life has gone into writing and it probably will continue to be like that. In the desire and the necessity to reinvent language, there is certainly an intention for happiness, a utopian thrust, a serious responsibility. It is because I feel both profoundly in me that I continue my course of writing. Voyage without end, writing is what always comes back to seek me out in order to distance death and stupidity, lies and violence. Writing never lets me forget that if life has a meaning, somewhere it is in what we invent with our lives, with the aura of streams of words that, within us, form sequences of truth. There is a price for consciousness, for transgression. Sooner or later, the body of writing pays for its untamed desire of beauty and knowledge. I have always thought that the word beauty is related to the word desire. There are words, which, like the body, are irreducible: To write I am a woman is full of consequences.

Coda

Poetry: For me poetry is the highest probability of desire and thought synchronized in a meaningful voice. Poetry is a formal and semantic intuition that is brought forth by our desire, this desire not knowing the laws that motivate it.

Text: The text is a thoughtful reflexive approach of the processes of writing and reading. When we play the text against the poem, it is as if we would like to tame the irrational of the poem. A text can be written without "inspiration", without a story. To write a text, you only need a "motive" to trigger the pleasure of writing and to perform or to explore in language.

Now I would like to establish the rapport — the connection — I have with poetry, prose, writing, and language. This I can say now, but even five years ago I would have been unable to identify this rapport.

A) My rapport with **poetry** has to do with the voice finding its way at the very moment of synchronization of thought and emotion. It is the rapport of intelligence in the sense of comprehension (to take with one self).

B) My rapport with **prose** and novels resembles my rapport with reality as it is in daily life. I find prose and daily life so boring that I can only exist in these two realities by making **ruptures** in the sentence or in the discourse, by seeking surprises and discoveries, by expending meaning. Writing prose, I need to explode the narrative, the anecdotal, the linearity of time, the normal mumbling of characters. That is why my novels are anti-novels that challenge traditional novels.

C) My rapport with **writing** has to do with desire and energy. This rapport is essentially ludic and about exploration. The body and the act of the eyes are mainly involved.

D) My rapport with **language** is a matter of perspective on patriarchal knowledge and on its symbolic hierarchal/dualist field. It calls for *vision* rather than for subversion. It calls for awareness, concentration, sharpness. Vision goes beyond transgression because it brings forth new material.

DISCUSSION

NICOLE BROSSARD: In Quebec, there are a lot of women writing with a feminist consciousness. What's interesting in their writing is that they don't take language for granted. They question it while using it. They know perfectly well that it's not just a matter of telling a story or expressing yourself. This won't make it. They want to get across more information, provide for a new emotion. And this can only be done by taking into account the way you approach language and the way you approach narrative. Reading and writing with a feminist consciousness brings forth an awareness of "poetic politics." But, as I said in my talk, women have a very loaded memory. And I believe that when you have a loaded memory you need space to narrate part of what's in your memory. You use that material for poetic expression, but not without the narrative losing importance.

LYNN CRAWFORD: Given your very interesting comments about pronouns, I wondered, in your own writing, do you have specific things in mind when you use a particular pronoun?

BROSSARD: What I have just described is something which the writer is usually unaware of when using a pronoun. What I can say about my use of pronouns I have made comes only after thought, as one understands a strategy after the battle has been won or lost. This is knowledge through experience. For example, I know by now that using the pronoun *tu* (which is an intimate you) is a way to distance myself in order to understand Rimbaud's famous remark "je est un autre." You can also use *I* as an ultimate resource to ground yourself in existence or as an ultimate statement that you are at the origins of meaning.

The *you* that I was talking of was a plural you (*vous*) which I believe implies some reproach or accusation — "You've done that to me" — but it also keeps a relational tension. Personally, I don't use this *you*. As for *we*, yes I have used it often. But I have many *wes*: We poets, we women, we lesbians, we feminists, we Quebecers. We all have a story of I and we and you. This really matters when you are in a situation of repression or alienation, where it becomes necessary to draw the line between us and them, we and they. In writing it is a very privileged moment when an *I* and a *you* and a *we* can be united. For example, in Quebec literature in the early 60s, in the poetry of Gaston Miron, Jacque Brault, Paul Chamberland: what they were saying about themselves could go for the collectivity. Because they were reflecting on their alienation not just as individuals but as a group. So, what I say for my *I* can also apply to a lot

of us women. Very often when a collectivity is fighting to get out of op-
pression, we encounter this relation of the I/we.

CRAWFORD: In creating an oppositional writing, are you setting up a
new group — a new *we* and *they* — that then excludes everyone else?
Not *you* personally [laughter] . . .

BROSSARD: I am not creating an oppositional writing, I am describing
a pattern that follows its course in the expression of one's identity.
When we are born, society has already set up for us a series of we/they.
To write is to sort them out and to assume those in which we recognize
ourselves and to identify the *they* which are a threat to our development
as a culture or as individuals.

Q: I find your exploration of the ways that language creates boundaries,
and the ways we can change that, very exciting, in ways that in the 1960s
I also found exciting the Afro-American exploration of the limitations
of European-American concepts. I think the politics of the body lends a
lot to that discussion — of how we change language, how we break
down the boundaries of language and rearrange it. I find in this country
most of the discussion of these approaches to words gets caught in a rit-
ual of shock rather than coming from a sincere desire for change in the
body politic.

BROSSARD: The body of writing somehow pays for its consciousness,
pays for its transgression. I could perform quite well in language — you
know a few tricks and you can do nice things — but I'm not interested
in just performing. Because there is so much at stake for me as a woman
that I want to explore and to communicate a new posture, a new per-
spective — and this means working with language in a way that shocks
are necessary, but also memory of the body, sliding into meaning.
Breathing your identity is always a shocking experience which often
takes a writer an entire life. I know personally that breathing a woman
subject in a patriarchal language is something which requires a lot of
concentration, energy, and audacity.

It's relatively easy to express yourself. What's more difficult is to deal
with the many layers of semantics in language. To go beyond the con-
tradictions inherent in the ordinary use of words. We all have emotions,
we all have ideas. But the writer processes the information she or he gets
— whether social or sensual or whatever: it's this processing that makes
for the difference between writers and non-writers.

There are two kinds of pleasure that I think you encounter in writing
and in reading. One pleasure involves dealing with what you recognize

in yourself or outside of yourself. The other pleasure is similar to find-
ing the proper solution to a mathematical problem — the solution to a
metaphor! I don't know if that is a physical pleasure or a mental pleas-
ure — but it's definitely a pleasure!

Bodies are not neutral and so in writing you must not forget where
you belong, where you come from. I think reading and writing with a
feminist consciousness in Quebec has allowed for a new perspective on
the body and on the text. A lot of young writers in Quebec have been
influenced by that to take into account, in their writing, their daily life,
their bodies. So in making space for ourselves we made space for male
writers — poets mainly, the novelists are a little . . . it takes longer
[laughter].

KABU OKAI-DAVIES: I'm wondering about situations where a poet
will use *I* to speak about an experience of a *them*, to intrude into the con-
sciousness of the other — of the other side — rather than further develop
the consciousness of her or his own side. For example, a Jewish poet writ-
ing "I have supervised the killing of a million Jews." That is, to try to enter
into the mind of the destroyer, who is destroying me. I'd rather use the *I*
for them, so that I function from their point of view toward myself.

BROSSARD: I know part of the mind of the other. There are codes you
have to learn. If you are a woman, you have to learn the man's code in
society. If you are black, you have to learn the white's code. If you are
coming from the working class, you have to learn the bourgeois code. If
you are a lesbian or a homosexual you have to learn the code of hetero-
sexuality. I say *have to*: you are obliged to learn them. Society trains us to
assimilate values and games of those who are in power. Deprogram-
ming ourselves from values which colonized our mind is essential but
in order to do so we have to know how the other thinks and plays the
game. For example, I don't know what individual men have in mind,
but I can guess a few things that men in general have in mind because as
a feminist I have been able to identify the system of values and meta-
phors that nourish their conceptions about women.

OKAI-DAVIES: I'm coming from a different linguistic background. In
poetry, if I'm using the English language to express purely African ex-
perience, one naturally comes to the situation where I use this same *I* of
English to reflect an African metaphor. What about this double-faced
nature of the *I?*

BROSSARD: It's not just a matter of the *I* but the language it is a part of
and the meaning of that language. For example, when I use the French

language there is a whole memory of that language that comes with it that does not necessarily reflect my experience as a North American. Some of this is useful to me, some not. But you must always be ready to challenge the language you write with.

STEPHEN LOWY: You identified the binary system with patriarchal society? Does this mean that binary computer operations are patriarchal?

BROSSARD: Binarity might be something the human mind cannot escape. But within the patriarchal system, binarity provides for a *hierarchical* logic that privileges men's values and behaviors.

It is hard for us to discriminate what patterns are human and what patterns are male. Nor do we know what women's patterns are, since these have not been able to be made public through art, writing, and so on. But we do know that male psychic energy has fantasized — constituted — a *corpus* of "knowledge" as to what is right and wrong, what is valued and what is not. This is what I am questioning: this corpus based essentially on a collective male subjectivity that gives us a culture or a civilization that has just one perspective on reality. But if we look at it from another angle, then reality is different. Had women, throughout history, been permitted to project their own fantasy, I think we would have, for example, a different architecture; and probably we would have also a different kind of scientific reasoning process. I don't know how the world would be if women had been able to participate in the elaboration of laws, traditions, religion, etc. I just know one thing: patriarchal binarity has provided for systematic violence against women.

Sound and Sentiment, Sound and Symbol

Nathaniel Mackey

1.

Senses of music in a number of texts is what I'd like to address — ways
of regarding and responding to music in a few instances of writings
which bear on the subject. This essay owes its title to two such texts,
Steven Feld's *Sound and Sentiment: Birds, Weeping, Poetics and Song in Kaluli
Expression* and Victor Zuckerkandl's *Sound and Symbol: Music and the Exter-
nal World*. These two contribute to the paradigm I bring to my reading
of the reading of music in the literary works I wish to address.

Steven Feld is a musician as well as an anthropologist and he dedi-
cates *Sound and Sentiment* to the memory of Charlie Parker, John
Coltrane, and Charles Mingus. His book, as the subtitle tells us,
discusses the way in which the Kaluli of Papua New Guinea con-
ceptualize music and poetic language. These the Kaluli associate with
birds and weeping. They arise from a breach in human solidarity, a vio-
lation of kinship, community, connection. *Gisalo*, the quintessential
Kaluli song form (the only one of the five varieties they sing that they
claim to have invented rather than borrowed from a neighboring peo-
ple), provokes and crosses over into weeping — weeping which has to
do with some such breach, usually death. *Gisalo* songs are sung at funer-
als and during spirit-medium seances and have the melodic contour of
the cry of a kind of fruitdove, the *muni* bird.[1] This reflects and is founded
on the myth regarding the origin of music, the myth of the boy who be-
came a *muni* bird. The myth tells of a boy who goes to catch crayfish
with his older sister. He catches none and repeatedly begs for those
caught by his sister, who again and again refuses his request. Finally he
catches a shrimp and puts it over his nose, causing it to turn a bright
purple red, the color of a *muni* bird's beak. His hands turn into wings
and when he opens his mouth to speak the falsetto cry of a *muni* bird
comes out. As he flies away his sister begs him to come back and have

87

some of the crayfish but his cries continue and become a song, semi-wept, semisung: "Your crayfish you didn't give me. I have no sister. I'm hungry . . . ." For the Kaluli, then, the quintessential source of music is the orphan's ordeal — an orphan being anyone denied kinship, social sustenance, anyone who suffers, to use Orlando Patterson's phrase, "social death,"[2] the prototype for which is the boy who becomes a *muni* bird. Song is both a complaint and a consolation dialectically tied to that ordeal, where in back of "orphan" one hears echoes of "orphic," a music which turns on abandonment, absence, loss. Think of the black spiritual "Motherless Child." Music is wounded kinship's last resort.

In *Sound and Symbol*, whose title Feld alludes to and echoes, Victor Zuckerkandl offers "a musical concept of the external world," something he also calls "a critique of our concept of reality from the point of view of music." He goes to great lengths to assert that music bears witness to what's left out of that concept of reality,or, if not exactly what, to the fact that something *is* left out. The world, music reminds us, inhabits while extending beyond what meets the eye, resides in but rises above what's apprehensible to the senses. This coinherence of immanence and transcendence the Kaluli attribute to and symbolize through birds, which for them are both the spirits of the dead and the major source of the everyday sounds they listen to as indicators of time, location and distance in their physical environment. In Zuckerkandl's analysis, immanence and transcendence meet in what he terms "the dynamic quality of tones," the relational valence or vectorial give and take bestowed on tones by their musical context. He takes great pains to show that "no material process can be co-ordinated with it," which allows him to conclude:

> Certainly, music transcends the physical; but it does not therefore transcend tones. Music rather helps the thing "tone" to transcend its own physical constituent, to break through into a nonphysical mode of being, and there to develop in a life of unexpected fullness. Nothing but tones! As if tone were not the point where the world that our senses encounter becomes transparent to the action of nonphysical forces, where we as perceivers find ourselves eye to eye, as it were, with a purely dynamic reality — the point where the external world gives up its secret and manifests itself, immediately, *as symbol*. To be sure, tones say, signify, point to — what? Not to something lying "beyond tones." Nor would it suffice to say that tones point to other tones — as if we had first tones, and then pointing as their attribute. No — in musical tones, being, existence, is indistinguishable from, *is*, pointing-beyond-itself, meaning, saying.[3]

One easily sees the compatibility of this musical concept of the world, this assertion of the intrinsic symbolicity of the world, with poetry. Yeats' view that the artist "belongs to the invisible life" or Rilke's notion of poets as "bees of the invisible" sits agreeably beside Zuckerkandl's assertion that "because music exists, the tangible and visible cannot be the whole of the given world. The intangible and invisible is itself a part of this world, something we encounter, something to which we respond" (71). His analysis lends itself to more recent formulations as well. His explanation of dynamic tonal events in terms of a "field concept," to give an example, isn't far from Charles Olson's "composition by field." And one commentator, to give another, has brought *Sound and Symbol* to bear on Jack Spicer's work.[4]

The analogy between tone-pointing and word-pointing isn't lost on Zuckerkandl, who, having observed that "in musical tones, being, existence, is indistinguishable from, *is*, pointing-beyond-itself, meaning, saying," immediately adds: "Certainly, the being of words could be characterized the same way." He goes on to distinguish tone-pointing from word-pointing on the basis of the conventionally agreed-upon referentiality of the latter, a referentiality writers have repeatedly called into question, frequently doing so by way of "aspiring to the condition of music." "Thus poetry," Louis Zukofsky notes, "may be defined as an order of words that as movement and tone (rhythm and pitch) approaches in varying degrees the wordless art of music as a kind of mathematical limit."[5] Music encourages us to see that the symbolic is the orphic, that the symbolic realm is the realm of the orphan. Music is prod and precedent for a recognition that the linguistic realm is also the realm of the orphan, as in Octavio Paz's characterization of language as an orphan severed from the presence to which it refers and which presumably gave it birth. This recognition troubles, complicates, and contends with the unequivocal referentiality taken for granted in ordinary language:

> Each time we are served by words, we mutilate them. But the poet is not served by words. He is their servant. In serving them, he returns them to the plenitude of their nature, makes them recover their being. Thanks to poetry, language reconquers its original state. First, its plastic and sonorous values, generally disdained by thought; next, the affective values; and, finally, the expressive ones. To purify language, the poet's task, means to give it back its original nature. And here we come to one of the central themes of this reflection. The word, in itself, is a plurality of meanings.[6]

Paz is only one of many who have noted the ascendancy of musicality and multivocal meaning in poetic language. (Julia Kristeva: "The poet . . . wants to turn rhythm into a dominant element . . . wants to make language perceive what it doesn't want to say, provide it with its matter independently of the sign, and free it from denotation."[7])

Poetic language is language owning up to being an orphan, to its tenuous kinship with the things it ostensibly refers to. This is why in the Kaluli myth the origin of music is also the origin of poetic language. The words of the song the boy who becomes a *muni* bird resorts to are different from those of ordinary speech. Song language, "amplifies, multiplies, or intensifies the relationship of the word to its referent," as Feld explains:

> In song, text is not primarily a proxy for a denoted subject but self-consciously multiplies the intent of the word.
>
> . . . Song poetry goes beyond pragmatic referential communication because it is explicitly organized by canons of reflexiveness and self-consciousness that are not found in ordinary talk.
>
> The uniqueness of poetic language is unveiled in the story of "the boy who became a *muni* bird." Once the boy has exhausted the speech codes for begging, he must resort to another communication frame. Conversational talk, what the Kaluli call *to halaido*, "hard words," is useless once the boy has become a bird; now he resorts to talk from a bird's point of view . . . Poetic language is bird language.[8]

It bears emphasizing that this break with conventional language is brought about by a breach of expected behavior. In saying no to her brother's request for food the older sister violates kinship etiquette.

What I wish to do is work *Sound and Sentiment* together with *Sound and Symbol* in such a way that the latter's metaphysical accent aids and is in turn abetted by the former's emphasis on the social meaning of sound. What I'm after is a range of implication which will stretch, to quote Stanley Crouch, "from the cottonfields to the cosmos." You notice again that it's black music I'm talking about, a music whose "critique of our concept of reality" is notoriously a critique of social reality, a critique of social arrangements in which, because of racism, one finds oneself deprived of community and kinship, cut off. The two modes of this critique which I'll be emphasizing Robert Farris Thompson notes among the "ancient African organizing principles of song and dance":

> *suspended accentuation patterning* (offbeat phrasing of melodic and choreographic accents); and, at a slightly different but equally

recurrent level of exposition, *songs and dances of social allusion* (music which, however danceable and "swinging," remorselessly contrasts social imperfections against implied criteria for perfect living).[9]

Still, the social isn't all of it. One needs to hear alongside Amiri Baraka listening to Jay McNeeley, that "the horn spat enraged sociologies,"[10] but not without noting a simultaneous mystic thrust. Immanence and transcendence meet, making the music social as well as cosmic, political and metaphysical as well. The composer of "Fables of Faubus" asks Fats Navarro, "What's *outside* the universe?"[11]

This meeting of transcendence and immanence I evoke, in my own work, through the figure of the phantom limb. In the letter which opens *From a Broken Bottle Traces of Perfume Still Emanate* N. begins:

> You should've heard me in the dream last night. I found myself walking down a sidewalk and came upon an open manhole off to the right out of which came (or strewn around which lay) the disassembled parts of a bass clarinet. Only the funny thing was that, except for the bell of the horn, all the parts looked more like plumbing fixtures than like parts of a bass clarinet. Anyway, I picked up a particularly long piece of "pipe" and proceeded to play. I don't recall seeing anyone around but somehow I knew the "crowd" wanted to hear "Naima." I decided I'd give it a try. In any event, I blew into heaven knows what but instead of "Naima" what came out was Shepp's solo on his version of "Cousin Mary" on the *Four for Trane* album — only infinitely more gruffly resonant and varied and warm. (I even threw in a few licks of my own.) The last thing I remember is coming to the realization that what I was playing already existed on a record. I could hear scratches coming from somewhere in back and to the left of me. This realization turned out, of course, to be what woke me up.
>
> Perhaps Wilson Harris is right. There are musics which haunt us like a phantom limb. Thus the abrupt breaking off. Therefore the "of course." No more than the ache of some such would-be extension.[12]

I'll say more about Wilson Harris later. For now, let me simply say that the phantom limb is a felt recovery, a felt advance beyond severance and limitation which contends with and questions conventional reality, that it's a feeling for what's not there which reaches beyond as it calls into question what is. Music as phantom limb arises from a capacity for feeling which holds itself apart from numb contingency. The phantom limb haunts or critiques a condition in which feeling, consciousness itself, would seem to have been cut off. It's this condition, the non-objective character of reality, to which Michael Taussig applies the expression "phantom objectivity," by which he means the veil by way of which a social order renders its role in the construction of reality invisible: "a commodity-based society produces such phantom objectivity, and in so doing it obscures its roots — the relations between people. This amounts to a socially instituted paradox with bewildering manifestations, the chief of which is the denial by the society's members of the social construction of reality."[13] "Phantom," then, is a relative, relativizing term which cuts both ways, occasioning a shift in perspective between real and unreal, an exchange of attributes between the two. So the narrator in Josef Skvorecky's *The Bass Saxophone* says of the band he's inducted into: "They were no longer a vision, a fantasy, it was rather the sticky-sweet panorama of the town square that was unreal."[14] The phantom limb reveals the illusory rule of the world it haunts.

2.

Turning now to a few pieces of writing which allude to or seek to ally themselves with music, one sense I'm advancing is that they do so as a way of reaching toward an alternate reality, that music is the would-be limb whereby that reaching is done or which alerts us to the need for its being done. The first work I'd like to look at is Jean Toomer's *Cane*. Though *Cane* is not as announcedly about music as John A. Williams's *Night Song*, Thomas Mann's *Doctor Faustus*, or any number of other works one could name, in its "quieter" way it's no less worth looking at in this regard. First of all, of course, there's the lyricism which pervades the writing, an intrinsic music which is not unrelated to a theme of wounded kinship of which we get whispers in the title. Commentators have noted the biblical echo, and Toomer himself, in notebooks and correspondence, referred to the book as *Cain* on occasion. His acknowledged indebtedness to black folk tradition may well have included a knowledge of stories in that tradition which depict Cain as the prototypical white, a mutation among the earlier people, all of whom were up to that point black: "Cain he kill his brudder Abel wid a great big club . . . and he turn white as bleech cambric in de face, and de whole race ob Cain dey bin white ebber since."[15] The backdrop of white assault which comes to the fore in "Portrait in Georgia," "Blood-Burning Moon," and "Kabnis" plays upon the fratricidal note struck by the book's title.

Indebted as it is to black folk tradition, *Cane* can't help but have to do with music. That "Deep River," "Go Down, Moses," and other songs

are alluded to comes as no surprise. Toomer's catalytic stay in Georgia is
well-known. It was there that he first encountered the black "folk-spirit"
he sought to capture in the book. Worth repeating is the emphasis he
put on the music he heard:

> The setting was crude in a way, but strangely rich and beautiful. I
> began feeling its effects despite my state, or, perhaps, just because
> of it. There was a valley, the valley of "Cane," with smoke-wreaths
> during the day and mist at night. A family of back-country Negroes
> had only recently moved into a shack not too far away. They sang.
> And this was the first time I'd ever heard the folk-songs and spiritu-
> als. They were very rich and sad and joyous and beautiful.[16]

He insisted, though, that the spirit of that music was doomed, that "the
folk-spirit was walking in to die on the modern desert" and that *Cane*
was "a swan-song," "a song of an end." The elegiac weariness and
weight which characterize the book come of a lament for the passing of
that spirit. In this it's like the music which inspired it, as Toomer point-
ed out in a letter to Waldo Frank:

> . . . the Negro of the folk-song has all but passed away: the Negro of
> the emotional church is fading. . . . In my own . . . pieces that come
> nearest to the old Negro, to the spirit saturate with folk-song . . . the
> dominant emotion is a sadness derived from a sense of fading . . . .
> The folk-songs themselves are of the same order: the deepest of
> them, "I aint got long to stay here."[17]

So, "Song of the Son":

> Pour O pour that parting soul in song,
> O pour it in the sawdust glow of night,
> Into the velvet pine-smoke air to-night,
> And let the valley carry it along.
> And let the valley carry it along.
>
> O land and soil, red soil and sweet-gum tree,
> So scant of grass, so profligate of pines,
> Now just before an epoch's sun declines
> Thy son, in time, I have returned to thee,
> Thy son, I have in time returned to thee.
>
> In time, for though the sun is setting on
> A song-lit race of slaves, it has not set;
> Though late, O soil, it is not too late yet
> To catch thy plaintive soul, leaving, soon gone,
> Leaving, to catch thy plaintive soul soon gone.

O Negro slaves, dark purple ripened plums,
Squeezed, and bursting in the pine-wood air,
Passing, before they stripped the old tree bare
One plum was saved for me, one seed becomes

An everlasting song, a singing tree,
Caroling softly souls of slavery,
What they were, and what they are to me,
Caroling softly souls of slavery.[18]

Cane is fueled by an oppositional nostalgia. A precarious vessel pos-
sessed of an eloquence coincident with loss, it wants to reach or to keep
in touch with an alternate reality as that reality fades. It was Toomer's
dread of the ascending urban-industrial order which opened his ears to
the corrective — potentially corrective — counterpoint he heard in
Georgia. In the middle section of the book, set in northern cities, houses
epitomize a reign of hard, sharp edges, rectilinear pattern, fixity, regi-
mentation, a staid, white order: "Houses, and dorm sitting-rooms are
places where white faces seclude themselves at night" (73). The house
embodies, again and again, suffocating structure: "Rhobert wears a
house, like a monstrous diver's helmet, on his head. . . . He is sinking.
His house is a dead thing that weights him down" (40). Or: "Dan's eyes
sting. Sinking into a soft couch, he closes them. The house contracts
about him. It is a sharp-edged, massed, metallic house. Bolted" (57).
Compare this with Kabnis's fissured, rickety cabin in the south, through
the cracks in whose walls and ceiling a ventilating music blows:

> The walls, unpainted, are seasoned a rosin yellow. And cracks be-
> tween the boards are black. These cracks are the lips the night
> winds use for whispering. Night winds in Georgia are vagrant po-
> ets, whispering. . . Night winds whisper in the eaves. Sing weirdly in
> the ceiling cracks (81, 104).

Ventilating song is what Dan invokes against the row of houses, the
reign of suffocating structure, at the beginning of "Box Seat":

> Houses are shy girls whose eyes shine reticently upon the dusk
> body of the street. Upon the gleaming limbs and asphalt torso of a
> dreaming nigger. Shake your curled wool-blossoms, nigger. Open
> your liver lips to lean, white spring. Stir the root-life of a withered
> people. Call them from their houses, and teach them to dream.
> Dark swaying forms of Negroes are street songs that woo virginal
> houses. (56)

Thirty years before the more celebrated Beats, Toomer calls out against an airtight domesticity, a reign of "square" houses and the domestication of spirit that goes with it, his call, as theirs would be, fueled and inflected by the countering thrust of black music.

Not that the beauty of the music wasn't bought at a deadly price. Its otherworldly reach was fostered and fed by seeming to have no home in this one ("I aint got long to stay here"). What the night winds whisper is this:

> White-man's land.
> Niggers, sing.
> Burn, bear black children
> Till poor rivers bring
> Rest, and sweet glory
> In Camp Ground. (81)

The singing, preaching and shouting coming from the church near Kabnis's cabin build as Layman tells of a lynching, reaching a peak as a stone crashes in through one of the windows:

> A shriek pierces the room. The bronze pieces on the mantel hum. The sister cries frantically: "Jesus, Jesus, I've found Jesus. O Lord, glory t God, one mo sinner is acomin home." At the height of this, a stone, wrapped round with paper, crashes through the window. Kabnis springs to his feet, terror-stricken. Layman is worried. Halsey picks up the stone. Takes off the wrapper, smooths it out, and reads: "You nothern nigger, its time fer y t leave. Git along now." (90)

Toomer put much of himself into Kabnis, from whom we get an apprehension of music as a carrier of conflicted portent, bearer of both good and bad news. "Dear Jesus," he prays, "do not chain me to myself and set these hills and valleys, heaving with folk-songs, so close to me that I cannot reach them. There is a radiant beauty in the night that touches and . . . tortures me" (83).

Cane's take on music is part and parcel of Toomer's insistence on the tragic fate of beauty, the soul's transit through an unsoulful world. This note gets hit by the first piece in the book, the story of "Karintha carrying beauty," her soul "a growing thing ripened too soon." The writing is haunted throughout by a ghost of aborted splendor, a spectre written into its much-noted lament for the condition of the women it portrays — woman as anima, problematic "parting soul." These women are frequently portrayed, not insignificantly, singing. The mark of blackness and the mark of femininity meet the mark of oppression invested in music. Toomer celebrates and incorporates song but not without looking at the grim conditions which give it birth, not without acknowledging its outcast compensatory character. "Cotton Song," one of the poems in the book, takes the work song as its model: "Come brother, come. Lets lift it; / Come now hewit! roll away!" (9). Like Sterling Brown's "Southern Road," Nat Adderly's "Work Song," and Sam Cooke's "Chain Gang," all of which it anticipates, the poem excavates the music's roots in forced labor. Music here is inseparable from the stigma attached to those who make it.

This goes farther in fact. Music itself is looked at askance and stigmatized in a philistine, prosaic social order: "Bolted to the endless rows of metal houses. . . . No wonder he couldn't sing to them" (57). Toomer's formal innovations in *Cane* boldly ventilate the novel, a traditional support for prosaic order, by acknowledging fissures and allowing them in, bringing in verse and dramatic dialogue, putting poetry before reportage. This will to song, though, is accompanied by an awareness of song's outlaw lot which could have been a forecast of the book's commercial failure. (Only five hundred copies of the first printing were sold.) *Cane* portrays its own predicament. It shows that music or poetry, if not exactly a loser's art, is fed by an intimacy with loss and may in fact feed it. This comes out in two instances of a version of wounded kinship which recurs throughout the book, the thwarted communion of would-be lovers. Paul, Orpheus to Bona's Eurydice, turns back to deliver an exquisitely out-of-place poetic address to the doorman, then returns to find Bona gone. Likewise, the narrator holds forth poetically as he sits beside Avey in the story which takes her name, only to find that she's fallen asleep. A play of parallel estrangements emerges. His alienation from the phantom reign of prosaic power — the Capitol dome is "a gray ghost ship" — meets her detachment from and immunity to prepossessing eloquence:

> I talked, beautifully I thought, about an art that would be born, an art that would open the way for women the likes of her. I asked her to hope, and build up an inner life against the coming of that day. I recited some of my own things to her. I sang, with a strange quiver in my voice, a promise-song. And then I began to wonder why her hand had not once returned a single pressure. . . . I sat beside her through the night. I saw the dawn steal over Washington. The Capitol dome looked like a gray ghost ship drifting in from sea. Avey's face was pale, and her eyes were heavy. She did not have the gray crimson-splashed beauty of the dawn. I hated to wake her. Orphan-woman . . . . (46-47)

3.

Beauty apprised of its abnormality both is and isn't beauty. (Baraka on Coltrane's "Afro-Blue": "Beautiful has nothing to do with it, but it is."[19]) An agitation complicates would-be equanimity, would-be poise. "Th form thats burned int my soul," Kabnis cries, "is some twisted awful thing that crept in from a dream, a godam nightmare, an wont stay still unless I feed it. An it lives on words. Not beautiful words. God Almighty no. Misshapen, split-gut, tortured, twisted words" (110). The tormenting lure of anomalous beauty and the answering dance of deformation — form imitatively "tortured, twisted" — also concern the writer I'd like to move on to, William Carlos Williams. The harassed/harassing irritability which comes into the "Beautiful Thing" section of *Paterson* recalls Kabnis's "Whats beauty anyway but ugliness if it hurts you?" (83). In black music Williams heard the "defiance of authority" he declares beauty to be, a "vulgarity" which "surpasses all perfection."[20]

Williams's engagement with black music was greatly influenced by his sense of himself as cut off from the literary mainstream. At the time the two pieces I'd like to look at were written Williams had not yet been admitted into the canon, as can be seen in the omission of his work from the *Modern Library Anthology of American Poetry* in 1945, at whose editor, Conrad Aiken, he accordingly takes a shot in *Man Orchid*, the second of two pieces I'll discuss. His quarrel with T. S. Eliot's dominance and influence doesn't need pointing out, except that it also comes up in *Man Orchard*. Seeing himself as a victimized poet, Williams celebrated the music of a victimized people. In a gesture which has since been overdone ("the white negro," "the student as nigger," analogies between "women and blacks"), he saw parallels between their lot and his own. This can also be seen, though in a slightly more subtle way, in the first of the two pieces I'd like to turn to, "Ol' Bunk's Band."

Both pieces grew out of Williams's going to hear New Orleans trumpeter Bunk Johnson in New York in 1945. A revival of interest in Johnson's music was then going on and Williams caught him during a 3 1/2 - month gig at the Stuyvesant Casino on the lower east side. He soon after wrote "Ol' Bunk's Band," a poem whose repeated insistence "These are men!" diverges from the dominant culture's denial of human stature to black people. He goes against the grain of accepted grammar in such things as the conscious "vulgarity" of the triple negative "and / not never / need no more," emulating a disregard for convention he heard in the music. The poem in full:

These are the men! the gaunt, unfore-
   sold, the vocal,
blatant, Stand up, stand up! the
   slap of a bass-string.
Pick, ping! The horn, the
   hollow horn
long drawn out, a hound deep
   tone —
Choking, choking! while the
   treble reed
races — alone, ripples, screams
   slow to fast —
to second to first! These are men!

Drum, drum, drum, drum, drum,
   drum, drum! the
ancient cry, escaping crapulence
   eats through
transcendent — torn, tears, term
   town, tense,
turns and back off whole, leaps
   up, stomps down,
rips through! These are men
   beneath
whose force the melody limps —
   to
proclaim, proclaims — Run and
   lie down,
in slow measures, to rest and
   not never
need no more! These are men!
   Men![21]

The "hound deep / tone," reminding us that Johnson played in a band
known as the Yelping Hound Band in 1930, also conjures a sense of un-
derdog status which brings the orphaned or outcast poet into solidarity
with an outcast people. The repeated assertion "These are men!" plays
against an implied but unstated "treated like dogs."

    Threaded into this implicit counterpoint are the lines "These are men
/ beneath / whose force the melody limps," where "limps" reflects criti-
cally on a crippling social order. The musicians do to the melody what's
done to them, the social handicap on which this limping reports having
been translated and, in that sense, transcended, triumphed over. Wil-
liams anticipates Baraka's more explicit reading of black music as

revenge, sublimated murder. Looking at *Paterson*, which hadn't been underway long when "Ol' Bunk's Band" was written, one finds the same complex of figures: dogs, lameness, limping. In the preface to Book 1 the image conveyed is that of a pariah, out of step with the pack:

> Sniffing the trees,
> just another dog
> among a lot of dogs. What
> else is there? And to do?
> The rest have run out —
> after the rabbits.
> Only the lame stands — on
> three legs . . . . (11)

This leads eventually to the quote from John Addington Symonds's *Studies of the Greek Poets* which ends Book 1, a passage in which Symonds comments on Hipponax's choliambi, "lame or limping iambics":

> . . . Hipponax ended his iambics with a spondee or a trochee in-
> stead of an iambus, doing thus the utmost violence to the rhythmi-
> cal structure. . . . The choliambi are in poetry what the dwarf or
> cripple is in human nature. Here again, by their acceptance of this
> halting meter, the Greeks displayed their acute aesthetic sense of
> propriety, recognizing the harmony which subsists between crab-
> bed verses and the distorted subjects with which they dealt — the
> vices and perversions of humanity — as well as their agreement
> with the snarling spirit of the satirist. Deformed verse was suited to
> deformed morality. (53)

That Williams heard a similar gesture in the syncopated rhythms of black music is obvious by Book 5, where, after quoting a passage on Bessie Smith from Mezz Mezzrow's *Really the Blues*, he makes his well-known equation of "satiric" with "satyric":

> a satyric play!
>   All plays
> were satyric when they were most devout.
>   Ribald as a Satyr!
>
> Satyrs dance!
>   all the deformities take wing. (258)

This would also be a way of talking about the "variable foot," less an aid to scansion than a trope — the travestied, fractured foot.

Williams here stumbles upon, without naming and, most likely, with-out knowing, the Fon-Yoruba orisha of the crossroads, the lame dancer

Legba. Legba walks with a limp because his legs are of unequal lengths, one of them anchored in the world of humans and the other in that of the gods. His roles are numerous, the common denominator being that he acts as an intermediary, a mediator, much like Hermes, of whom Hipponax was a follower. (Norman O. Brown: "Hipponax, significantly enough, found Hermes the most congenial god; he is in fact the only personality in Greek literature of whom it may be said that he walked with Hermes all the days of his life."[22]) Like Hermes's winged feet, Legba's limp — "deformities take wing" — bridges high and low. Legba presides over gateways, intersections, thresholds, wherever different realms or regions come into contact. His limp a play of difference, he's the master linguist and has much to do with signification, divination, and translation. His limp the offbeat or eccentric accent, the "suspended accentuation" of which Thompson writes, he's the master musician and dancer, declared first among the orishas because only he could simultaneously play a gong, a bell, a drum, and a flute while dancing. The master of polyrhythmicity and heterogeneity, he suffers not from deformity but multiformity, a "defective" capacity in a homogeneous order given over to uniform rule. Legba's limp is an emblem of heterogeneous wholeness, the image and outcome of a peculiar remediation. "Lame" or "limping," that is, like "phantom," cuts with a relativizing edge to unveil impairment's power, as though the syncopated accent were an unsuspected blessing offering anomalous, unpredictable support. Impairment taken to higher ground, remediated, translates damage and disarray into a dance. Legba's limp, compensating the difference in leg lengths, functions like a phantom limb. Robert Pelton writes that Legba "transforms . . . absence into transparent presence,"[23] deficit leg into invisible supplement.

Legba's authority over mix and transition made him especially relevant to the experience of transplantation brought about by the slave trade. The need to accommodate geographic and cultural difference placed a high premium on his mediatory skills. He's thus the most tenaciously retained of the orishas among New World Africans, the first to be invoked in vodoun ceremonies, be they in Haiti, Cuba, Brazil, or elsewhere. There's little wonder why Williams's work, concerned as it is with the New World as a ground for syncrestistic innovation, would be paid a visit by the African bridge between old and new. What he heard in Bunk Johnson's music was a rhythmic digestion of dislocation, the African genius for enigmatic melding or mending, a mystery of resilient survival no image puts more succinctly than that of Legba's limping dance.

Legba has made more straightforward appearances in certain works written since Williams's time, showing up, for example, as Papa LaBas (the name he goes by in New Orleans) in Ishmael Reed's novels. Or as Lebert Joseph in Paule Marshall's *Praisesong for the Widow*, a novel whose third section is introduced by a line from the Haitian invocation to Legba and in which one comes upon such passages as: "Out of his stooped and winnowed body had come the illusion of height, femininity and power. Even his foreshortened left leg had appeared to straighten itself out and grow longer as he danced."[24] One of his most telling appearances in the literature of this country, though, is one in which, as in Williams's work, he enters unannounced. In Ralph Ellison's *Invisible Man* one finds adumbrations of Legba which, bearing as they do on the concerns addressed here, deserve more than passing mention.

Invisible Man, like *Cane*, is a work which draws on black folk resources. While collecting folklore in Harlem in 1939 for the Federal Writers' Project, Ellison was told a tale which had to do with a black man in South Carolina who because he could make himself invisible at will was able to harass and give white people hell with impunity.[25] This would seem to have contributed to the relativizing thrust of the novel's title and its long meditation on the two-way cut of invisibility. On the other side of invisibility as exclusion, social death, we find it as revenge, millenarian reversal. The prominence of Louis Armstrong in the novel's prologue brings to mind Zuckerkandl's discussion of the case music makes for the invisible, as invisibility is here both social and metaphysical. The ability to "see around corners" defies the reign of strict rectilinear structure lamented in *Cane* by going outside ordinary time and space constraints. Louis's horn, apocalyptic, alters times (and, with it, space):

> Invisibility, let me explain, gives one a slightly different sense of time, you're never quite on the beat. Sometimes you're ahead and sometimes behind. Instead of the swift and imperceptible flowing of time, you are aware of its nodes, those points where time stands still or from which it leaps ahead. And you slip into the breaks and look around. That's what you hear vaguely in Louis' music.[26]

This different sense of time one recognizes as Legba's limp. It leads to and is echoed by a later adumbration of Legba, one in which Ellison hints at a similarly "offbeat" sense of history, one which diverges from the Brotherhood's doctrine of history as monolithic advance. Early on, Jack describes the old evicted couple as "already dead, defunct," people whom "history has passed . . . by," "dead limbs that must be pruned away" (284). Later "dead limbs" plays contrapuntally upon Tarp's

contestatory limp, a limp which, as he explains, has social rather than
physiological roots. It was caused by nineteen years on a chain gang:

> You notice this limp I got? . . . Well, I wasn't always lame, and I'm
> not really now 'cause the doctors can't find anything wrong with
> that leg. They say it's sound as a piece of steel. What I mean is I got
> this limp from dragging a chain. . . . Nobody knows that about me,
> they just think I got rheumatism. But it was that chain and after
> nineteen years I haven't been able to stop dragging my leg. (377-78)

Phantom limb, phantom limp. Tarp goes on, in a gesture recalling
the protective root Sandy gives Frederick Douglas in the latter's *Narra-
tive*, to give Invisible Man the broken link from the leg chain he dragged
for nineteen years. Phantom limb, phantom limp, phantom link: "I
think it's got a heap of signifying wrapped up in it and it might help you
remember what we're really fighting against" (379). This it does, serving
to concentrate a memory of injustice and traumatic survival, a remem-
bered wound resorted to as a weapon of self-defense. During his final
confrontation with the Brotherhood, Invisible Man wears it like a set of
brass knuckles: "My hand was in my pockets now, Brother Tarp's leg
chain around my knuckles" (462).

4.

"The trouble has been," Olson writes, "that a man stays so astonished
he can triumph over his own incoherence, he settles for that, crows over
it, and goes at a day again happy he at least makes a little sense."[27]
Ellison says much the same thing towards the end of *Invisible Man* when
he cautions that "the mind that has conceived a plan of living must nev-
er lose sight of the chaos against which that pattern was conceived"
(567). This goes for both societies and individuals, he points out.
Legba's limp, like Tarp's leg chain, is a reminder of dues paid, damage
done, of the limbs which have been "pruned away." It's a reminder of
the Pyhrric features every triumph over chaos or incoherence turns out
to possess. The spectre of illusory victory and its corollary, the riddle of
deceptive disability or enabling defeat, sit prominently among the
mysteries to which it witnesses. "No defeat is made up entirely of de-
feat," Williams writes in *Paterson* (96).

In *Man Orchid*, the second piece which grew out of Williams's going to
hear Johnson's band, the stutter plays a significant role. What better
qualification of what can only be a partial victory over incoherence?
What limping, staggering, and stumbling are to walking, stuttering and
stammering are to speech. "*To stammer* and *to stumble*, original *stumelen*,

are twin words," Theodore Thass-Thienemann points out. "The use of the one and the same phonemic pattern for denoting these two different meanings is found in other languages too. Stammering and stuttering are perceived as speech *im-pedi-ments*."[28] The stutter enters *Man Orchid* largely because of Bucklin Moon, the author of a novel called *The Darker Brother*. Moon was at the Stuyvesant Casino on the night of 23 November 1945, the second time Williams went to hear Johnson's band. He ended up joining Williams and his friends at their table, among whom was Fred Miller, editor of the thirties proletarian magazine *Blast* and one of the co-authors of *Man Orchid*. Because of his novel and his knowledge of black music, Moon was incorrectly taken by them to be black, though Miller asked Williams two days later: "Would you ever think that Bucklin Moon was a Negro, if you passed him — as a stranger — in the street? He looks whiter than a lot of whites."[29] Moon evidently spoke with a stutter whenever he became nervous and unsure of himself, which was the case that night at the Stuyvesant Casino. Miller goes on to offer this as a further peculiarity: "a stuttering or stammering Negro is a pretty rare bird indeed: your darker brother is articulate enough, when he isn't too frightened to talk." Like Legba's limp, Moon's stutter would come to symbolize a meeting of worlds, a problematic, insecure mix of black and white.

At the Stuyvesant Williams suggested that he and Miller publish an interracial literary magazine. Miller was enthusiastic at the time but soon lost interest. He suggested within a couple of weeks, however, that he and Williams collaborate on an improvisatory novel which was to be written as though they were musicians trading fours: "You write chap. I, send it to me, I do the 2nd Chap., send mess back to you, you do 3 — and so on." Williams liked the idea and *Man Orchid* was launched. They spent the next year working on it, off and on, bringing in a third collaborator, Lydia Carlin, in March. The work was never completed and what there is of it, forty pages, remained unpublished until 1973. It's going too far to call it a novel and outright ludicrous to call it, as Paul Mariani does, "Williams's black novel," but the piece is interesting for a number of reasons, not the least of them being its anticipation of the bop-inspired attempts at collaborative, improvisatory writing which became popular among the Beats a decade later.[30]

Wray Douglas, *Man Orchid*'s black-white protagonist, is based in part on Bucklin Moon and intended to embody America's yet-to-be-resolved identity. As Williams writes: "To resolve such a person would be to create a new world" (77). But other than his presumed black-white mix and his stutter not much of Moon went into the figure. Wray

Douglas is clearly his creators' alter ego, the narrated "he" and the narrator's "I" in most cases the same. Want of resolution and the stubborn problematics of heterogeneity are what *Man Orchid* most effectively expresses, the latter symptomized by the solipsistic quality of the work and the former a would-be flight from the resolute self (false resolution) which the solipsism indulges even as it eschews. Two white writers sit down to create a black protagonist whose model is another white writer. The ironies and contradictions needn't be belabored.

The stutter thus becomes the most appropriate, self-reflexive feature of an articulation which would appear to be blocked in advance. Williams's and Miller's prose in *Man Orchid* both stutters and refers to stuttering. Here, for example, is how Williams begins Chapter 1:

> Is it perchance a crime — a time, a chore, a bore, a job? He wasn't a musician — but he wished he had been born a musician instead of a writer. Musicians do not stutter. But he ate music, music wrinkled in his belly — if you can wrinkle an inflated football. Anyhow it felt like that so that's what he wrote (without changing a word — that was his creed and always after midnight, you couldn't be earlier in the morning than that). All good writing is written in the morning.
>
> Is *what* perchance a crime? (One) (or rather two) He ate and drank beer. That is, he ate, he also drank beer. A crime to be so full, so — so (the thing the philosophers hate) poly. So p-p-poly. Polypoid. Huh? (77)

Thinking, perhaps, of the use of singing in the treatment of stuttering, Williams identifies writing with the latter while looking longingly at music as the embodiment of a heterogeneous wholeness to which his writing will aspire, an unimpeded, unproblematic wholeness beyond its reach. Miller's contribution to *Man Orchid* is likewise touched by a sense of writing's inferiority to music. Early on, referring to Bessie Smith's singing, he asks: "What were the little words chasing each other like black bits of burnt leaves across the pages he held — [compared] to that vast voice?" (79). Two pages later he answers:

> More printed words like black bits of burnt leaves. They had the right keyhole, those guys, but the wrong key. The only words that could blast like Bunk's horn or smash like John Henry's hammer were the poet's, the maker's, personal, ripped out of his guts: And no stuttering allowed. (81)

Throughout *Man Orchid*, however, the writer's emulation of the musician causes rather than cures the stutter. Imitating the spontaneity of

improvisatory music, Williams and Miller approach the typewriter as a
musical keyboard on which they extemporize "without changing a
word." Wrong "notes" are left as they are rather than erased, though
the right ones do eventually get "played" in most cases. This results in a
repetitiveness and a halting, staccato gesture reminiscent of a stutterer's
effort to get out what he wants to say. Thus Williams: "American poetry
was on its way to great distinction — when the blight of Eliot's popular
verse fell pon — upon the — gasping universities — who hadN8t
hadn8T hadn't tasted Thames water for nearly a hundred years" (82).
By disrupting the fluency and coherence available to them Williams and
Miller attempt to get in touch with what that coherence excludes, "the
chaos against which that pattern was conceived." This friendly relation-
ship with incoherence, however, constitutes a gesture towards but not
an attainment of the otherness to which it aspires, an otherness to which
access can only be analogically gotten. *Man Orchid*, to give the obvious
example, is a piece of writing, not a piece of music. Nor, as I've already
noted, is the color line crossed. The stutter is a two-way witness which
on one hand symbolizes a need to go beyond the confines of an exclu-
sionary order while on the other confessing to its at best only limited
success at doing so. The impediments to the passage it seeks are ac-
knowledged if not annulled, attested to by exactly the gesture which
would overcome them if it could.

One measure of *Man Orchid*'s flawed embrace of otherness is the pro-
minence in it of Williams's all too familiar feud with Eliot, a feud into
which he pulls Bunk Johnson. Johnson's music is put forth as an exam-
ple of an authentic American idiom, "the autochthonous strain" (85)
whose dilution or displacement by "sweet music" paralleled and antici-
pated that of a genuine "American poetry [which] was on its way to great
distinction" by *The Waste Land*:

> Eliot would not have been such a success if he hadn't hit a soft spot.
> They were scared and rushed in where he hit like water into the
> side of a ship. It was ready for it a long time. Isn't a weak spot al-
> ways ready to give way? That was the secret of his success. Great
> man Eliot. They were aching for him, Aiken for him. He hit the
> jackpot with his popular shot.
>   But long before that, twenty years earlier ol' Bunk Johnson was
> all washed up. Sweet music was coming in and jazz was through.
> But I mean THROUGH! And when I say through, I mean
> through. Go ahead, quit. See if I care. Take your band and go frig a
> kite. Go on back to the rice swamps. See if I care. Sell your ol'd
> horn. See if I care. Nobody wants that kind of music any more: this

is a waste land for you, Buddy, this IS a waste land! I said Waste
Land and when I sez Waste land I mean waste *land*.
      . . . Thus American poetry, which disappeared about that time
you might say, followed the same course New Orleans music had
taken when sweet music displaced it about in 1906 or so. (83-84)

Fraternity with Johnson is less the issue than sibling rivalry with Eliot, a
literary quarrel in which Johnson has no voice but the one Williams
gives him. What it says is simple: "Black music is on Williams's side."
(The Barbadian poet Edward Kamau Brathwaite provides interesting
counterpoint, picturing Eliot and black music as allies when he notes
the influence of Eliot's recorded readings in the Caribbean: "In that dry
deadpan delivery, the riddims of St. Louis . . . were stark and clear for
those of us who at the same time were listening to the dislocations of
Bird, Dizzy, and Klook. And it is interesting that on the whole, the Es-
tablishment couldn't stand Eliot's voice — far less jazz!"[31])
      The possibility that otherness was being appropriated rather than
engaged was recognized by Miller and for him it became an obstacle to
going on. When he began to voice his misgivings Williams brought in
Lydia Carlin, who not only added sexual otherness to the project but a
new form of ethnic otherness as well, in that, though she herself was
English, one of the two chapters she contributed was about a Polish
couple, the Czajas. Her two chapters are much more conventional,
much less improvisatory than Williams's and Miller's and tend to stand
apart from rather than interact with theirs. Her taking part in the project
did nothing to solve the problem and as late as Chapter 7 Miller is asking:

      Now returning to this novel, Man Orchid. Why the orchid? — to
      begin with. There's the old, tiresome and at bottom snobbish liter-
      ary assumption that the Negro in America is an exotic bloom. Ne-
      gro equals jungle. Despite the fact that he has been here longer
      than the second, third, even ninth generation Eurp European —
      Negro equals jungle. Then why doesn't the ofay bank president of
      German descent equal Black Forest? The Rutherford doctor of
      Welsh descent equal the cromlechs? or Welsh rarebit? (111)

As bad if not worse is the fact that the choice of that particular orchid
because of its phallic appearance plays upon a stereotypic black male
sexuality. The distance from this to Norman Mailer's "Jazz is orgasm"
isn't very great, which is only one of a handful of ways in which *The White
Negro* bears upon this predecessor text.
      Miller, though he could agonize as above, was no more free than Wil-
liams was of stereotypic equations. To him Johnson and his music

represent a black essence which is unselfconscious and nonreflective: "Only the Bunks're satisfied to be Bunks, he told himself enviously. Their brain don't question their art. Nor their left hand their RIGHT. Their right to be Bunk, themself" (79). The vitiation of "black" nonreflective being by "white" intellectuality is largely the point of his evocation of Wray Douglas and the trumpeter Cholly Oldham. The latter he describes as having "too much brain for a musician." Oldham stutters when he plays and wants to be a painter:

> There was between Cholly and Bunk — what? a difference of thirty, thirty-five years in age, no more. But the difference otherwise! Hamlet son of Till Eulenspiegel. Showing you what the dry rot of intellectuality could do to the orchid in one generation. Progress (!Up from Slavery. That night-colored Hamlet, he wants to paint pictures now. (82)

Black is nonreflective, white cerebral. So entrenched are such polarizations as to make the notion of a black intellectual oxymoronic. In May, Miller wrote to Williams that it had been a mistake to model their protagonist on Bucklin Moon: "I don't know enough about him and his special type, the colored intellectual (although I've been acquainted with and've liked lots of ordinary Negro folk, laborers, musicians et al)" (73). Small wonder he questioned the idea of an interracial magazine by writing to Williams:

> Is there sufficient Negro writing talent — of the kind we wd. have no doubts about, AS talent, on hand to balance the white talent? I don't believe any more than you that publishing second-rate work with first-rate intentions would serve any cause but that of bad writing. (68)

To what extent was being looked upon as black — as, even worse, that "rare bird," a black intellectual — the cause of Moon's nervousness that night at the Stuyvesant? Could a sense of distance in Williams's and Miller's manner have caused him to stutter? Miller's wife recalls in a letter to Paul Mariani:

> Moon began with easy speech and there was talk at first of the interracial magazine but Moon soon took to stammering. To me Williams was always a warm congenial person, but he would become the coldly analytical surgeon at times and the effect it had on those around him at such a time was quite devastating. (67)

That "coldly analytical" scrutiny would seem to have been disconcerting, making Williams and Miller the agents of the disarray about

which they would then go on to write — as good an example as any of
"phantom objectivity," the social construction of Moon's "mulatto"
selfconsciousness.

What I find most interesting about *Man Orchid* is that it inadvertently
underscores a feature which was then coming into greater prominence
in black improvised music. With the advent of bebop, with which nei-
ther Williams, Miller, nor Carlin seem to have been much engaged,
black musicians began to assume a more explicit sense of themselves as
artists, conscious creators, thinkers. Dizzy Gillespie would don a beret
and a goatee, as would among others, Yusef Lateef, who would record
an album called *Jazz for the Thinker*. Anthony Braxton's pipe, wire-rim
glasses, cardigan sweater, and diagrammatic titles are among the pres-
ent-day descendants of such gestures. The aural equivalent of this more
explicit reflexivity would come at times to resemble a stutter, conveying
senses of apprehension and self-conscious duress by way of dislocated
phrasings in which virtuosity mimes its opposite. Thelonious Monk's
mock-awkward hesitancies evoke an experience of impediment or im-
pairment, as do Sonny Rollins's even more stutterlike teasings of a tune,
a quality Paul Blackburn imitates in "Listening to Sonny Rollins at the
Five Spot":

> There will be many other nights like
> me standing here with someone, some
> one
> someone
> some-one
> some
> some
> some
> some
> some
> some
> one
> there will be other songs
> a-nother fall, another _____ spring, but
> there will never be a-noth, noth
> anoth
> noth
> anoth-er
> noth-er
> noth-er
>   other lips that I may kiss,
> but they won't thrill me like

                    thrill me like
                        like yours
                used to
                        dream a million dreams
                but how can they come
                when there   never be
                a-noth _____[32]

Though Williams and Miller insist that Bunk Johnson doesn't stammer,
the limp he inflicts on the melody is ancestral to the stutter of Monk,
Rollins, and others.

   As among the Kaluli, for whom music and poetry are "specifically
marked for reflection," the black musician's stutter is an introspective
gesture which arises from and reflects critically upon an experience of
isolation or exclusion, the orphan's or the outsider's ordeal, the "rare
bird"'s ordeal. Like Tarp's leg chain, it symbolizes a refusal to forget
damage done, a critique and a partial rejection of an available but bi-
ased coherence. Part of the genius of black music is the room it allows
for a telling "inarticulacy," a feature consistent with its critique of a
predatory coherence, the cannibalistic "plan of living" and the
articulacy which upholds it. *Man Orchid*, where it comes closest to the
spirit of black music, does so by way of a similar frustration with and
questioning of given articulacies, permissible ways of making sense. In
Chapter 6 Williams attempts to make racial distinctions meaningless,
the result of which is part gibberish, part scat, part wisdom of the idiots
("the most foolish thing you can say . . . has the most meaning"). His in-
ability to make sense implicitly indicts a white-dominated social order
and the discourse of racial difference by which it explains or makes
sense of itself:

> Not that black is white. I do not pretend that. Nor white black.
> That there is not the least difference is apparent to the mind at a
> glance. Thus, to the mind, the eye is forever deceived. And philoso-
> phers imagine they can have opinions about art? God are they
> dumb, meaning stupid, meaning philosophers, meaning schools,
> meaning — learning. The limits of learning are the same as an egg
> to the yolk. The shell. Knowledge to a learned man is precisely the
> sane — that's good: sane for same — the same as the egg to the
> hen. No possibility of interchange. Reason, the shell.
>
>   No matter how I try to rearrange the parts, to show them inter-
> changeable, the result is always the same. White is white and black
> is the United States Senate. No mixing. Even if it was all black it
> would be the same: white. How could it be different? (100-01)

The very effort to talk down the difference underscores the tenacity of the racial polarization *Man Orchid*'s liberal mission seeks, to some degree, to overcome — a tenacity which is attested to, as we've seen, in other ways as well, not the least of them being the authors' preconceptions.

5.

The play of sense and nonsense in Wilson Harris's *The Angel at the Gate* is more immediately one of sensation and nonsensation, a complex mingling of endowments and deprivations, anesthetic and synesthetic intuitions. One reads, for example, late in the novel:

> Mary recalled how deaf she had been to the voice of the blackbird that morning on her way to Angel Inn and yet it returned to her now in the depths of the mirror that stood beside her. Half-reflected voice, shaded sound, silent echo. Was this the source of musical composition? Did music issue from reflections that converted themselves into silent, echoing bodies in a mirror? Did the marriage of *reflection* and *sound* arise from deaf appearance within silent muse (or was it deaf muse in silent appearance) from which a stream of unheard music rippled into consciousness?[33]

In dialogue with and relevant to such a passage is a discussion in Harris's most recent critical book, *The Womb of Space*, a discussion which touches upon Legba as "numinous shadow." Harris writes of "metaphoric imagery that intricately conveys music as the shadow of vanished but visualized presences": "Shadow or shade is alive with voices so real, yet strangely beyond material hearing, that they are peculiarly *visualized* or 'seen' in the intricate passages of a poem. *Visualized presence* acquires therefore a *shadow and a voice* that belongs to the mind's ear and eye."[34] Music described in terms pertaining to sight is consistent with inklings of synesthetic identity which run through *The Angel at the Gate*. It's also part and parcel of Harris's long preoccupation, from work to work, with an uncapturable, ineffable wholeness, a heterogeneous inclusiveness evoked in terms of non-availability ("silent echo," "unheard music") and by polysemous fullness and fluency ("a stream . . . rippled").

The Angel at the Gate's anesthetic-synesthetic evocations recapitulate, in microcosm, the translation between media — aural and visual, music and writing — it claims to be. The intermedia impulse owns up to as it attempts to advance beyond the limits of a particular medium and is a version of what Harris elsewhere calls "a confession of weakness."[35] The novel acknowledges that its particular strength can only be partial and seeks to "echo" if not enlist the also partial strength of another art form.

Wholeness admitted to be beyond reach, the best to be attained is a concomitance of partial weaknesses, partial strengths, a conjunction of partial endowments. This conjunction is facilitated by Legba, upon whom *The Womb of Space* touches as a "numinous frailty" and a "transitional chord." In *Da Silva da Silva's Cultivated Wilderness*, an earlier novel which likewise leans upon an extraliterary medium, the painter da Silva's advertisement for a model is answered by one Legba Cuffey, whose arrival infuses paint with sound: "The front door bell pealed it seemed in the middle of his painting as he brooded on past and future. The sound of a catch grown sharp as a child's cry he thought in a line of stroked paint."[36] In this case painting, like music in *The Angel at the Gate*, is an alternate artistic arm with which the novel extends or attempts to extend its reach. "So the arts," Williams writes in *Man Orchid*, "take part for each other" (85).

Music figures prominently at the end of Harris's first novel, *Palace of the Peacock*, where Legba's limp, the incongruity between heaven and earth, is marked by the refractive obliquity and bend of a passage from one medium to another. The annunciation of paradise takes the form of a music which issues through the lips of Carroll, the black namesake singer whose father is unknown but whose mother "knew and understood . . . [that his] name involved . . . the music of her undying sacrifice to make and save the world."[37] The narrator notes a discrepancy between the sound Carroll's lips appear to be making and the sound he hears: "Carroll was whistling. A solemn and beautiful cry — unlike a whistle I reflected — deeper and mature. Nevertheless his lips were framed to whistle and I could only explain the difference by assuming the sound from his lips was changed when it struck the window and issued into the world" (147). The deflection from apparent sound reveals not only the insufficiency of the visual image but that of any image, visual, acoustic or otherwise. Heaven is wholeness, meaning that any image which takes up the task of evoking it can only fail. Legba's limp is the obliquity of a religious aspiration which admits its failure to measure up to heaven, the bend legs make in prayer. As in the *Paradiso*, where Dante laments the poem's inability to do heaven justice by calling it lame, the narrator's evocation of Carroll's music is marked by a hesitant, faltering gesture which whenever it asserts immediately qualifies itself. It mimes the music's crippling, self-correcting attempts to register as well as redeem defects. The music repeatedly breaks and mends itself — mends itself as a phantom limb mends an amputation:

> It was an organ cry almost and yet quite different I reflected again.
> It seemed to break and mend itself always — tremulous, forlorn,
> distant, triumphant, the echo of sound so pure and outlined in
> space it broke again into a mass of music. It was the cry of the pea-
> cock and yet I reflected far different. I stared at the whistling lips
> and wondered if the change was in me or in them. I had never wit-
> nessed and heard such sad and such glorious music. (147)

This is the ongoingness of an attempt which fails but is repeatedly
undertaken to insist that what it fails to capture nonetheless exists.
Legba's limp is the obliquity of a utopian aspiration, the bend legs pre-
paring to spring.

Inability to capture wholeness notwithstanding, *Palace of the Peacock* in-
itiates Harris's divergence, now into its third decade, from the novel's
realist-mimetic tradition. The accent which falls upon the insufficiency
of the visual image is consistent with the novel's earlier suggestions of an
anesthetic-synesthetic enablement which displaces the privileged eye:[38]
"I dreamt I awoke with one dead seeing eye and one living closed eye"
(13-14). And again: "I had been blinded by the sun, and saw inwardly in
the haze of my blind eye a watching muse and phantom whose breath
was on my lips" (16). That accent encapsulates Harris's quarrel with the
cinematic pretense and the ocular conceit of the realist novel, a docu-
mentary stasis against which he poses an anesthetic-synesthetic obliqui-
ty and rush. This obliquity (seeing and/or hearing around corners, in
Ellison's terms) is called "an angled intercourse with history" in *The An-
gel at the Gate* (113), the medium for which is the Angel Inn mirror, de-
scribed at points as "spiritual" and "supernatural." Mary Stella is said to
perceive the world "from a meaningfully distorted angle in the mirror"
(113), a pointed subversion of the mirror's conventional association
with mimesis. Angularity cuts with a relativizing edge: "How unreal, yet
real, one was when one saw oneself with one's own eyes from angles in a
mirror so curiously unfamiliar that one's eyes became a stranger's eyes.
As at the hairdresser when she invites one to inspect the back of one's
head" (21).

Late in the novel Mary Stella's "automatic codes" are said to have
"propelled her pencil across the page of a mirror" (122) — clear enough
indication that the novel sees itself in the Angel Inn mirror, that reflec-
tion and refraction are there the same. Angled perception is a particular
way of writing — writing bent or inflected by music. *The Angel at the Gate*
is said to be based on Mary Stella's automatic writings and on notes tak-
en by her therapist Joseph Marsden during conversations with her,
some of which were conducted while she was under hypnosis. In the

note which introduces the novel mention is made of "the musical compositions by which Mary it seems was haunted from early childhood," as well as of "a series of underlying rhythms in the automatic narratives" (7). Like the boy who became a *muni* bird, Mary Stella, an orphan from the age of seven, resorts to music in the face of broken familial ties — those with her parents in the past and in the present her troubled marriage with Sebastian, for whom she's "the same woman broken into wife and sister" (13). Louis Armstrong's rendition of "Mack the Knife," the song her mother frequently sang during her early childhood, animates a host of recollections and associations:

> . . . the music returned once again coming this time from an old gramophone her mother possessed. It was "Mack the Knife" sung and played by Louis Armstrong. The absurdity and tall story lyric, oceanic city, were sustained by Armstrong's height of trumpet and by his instrumental voice, hoarse and meditative in contrast to the trumpet he played, ecstatic cradle, ecstatic childhood, ecstatic coffin, ecstatic grieving surf or sea.
>   . . . Stella was shivering. The fascination of the song for her mother was something that she grew up with. Mack was also the name that her father bore. Mack was her mother's god. And her mother's name? *Guess*, Ste"a whispered to Sebastian in the darkened studio. Jenny! It was a random hit, bull's eye. It struck home. Jenny heard. She was weeping. It came with the faintest whisper of the sea, the faintest whisper of a flute, in the studio. Mack's women were the Sukey Tawdreys, the sweet Lucy Browns, of the world. Between the ages of four and seven Stella thought the postman was her father. Until she realized that he was but the middleman between her real father and Jenny her mother. He brought the letters from foreign ports with foreign stamps over which Jenny wept. On her seventh birthday the last letter arrived. Her father was dead, his ship sunk. It was a lie. It drove her mother into an asylum where she contemplated Mack clinging for dear life to sarcophagus-globe even as she vanished into the arms of god, bride of god.
>   Stella was taken into care by a Social Welfare Body and placed in an orphanage in East Anglia. (44-45)

Mary Stella's automatic narratives, prompted by her thirst for connection and by "her longing to change the world" (46), instigate patterns of asymmetric equation into which characters named Sukey Tawdrey, Mother Diver, Lucy Brown, and so forth enter. The song, it seems, populates a world, an alternate world. Her music-prompted hand and its inscription of far-flung relations obey intimations of unacknowledged wholeness against a backdrop of social and psychic division. "To be whole," we're told at the end, "was to endure . . . the traffic of many souls" (126).

The novel's concern with heterogeneous wholeness invokes Legba repeatedly — though, significantly, not by that name. As if to more greatly emphasize Legba's association with multiplicity, Harris merges him with his trickster counterpart among the Ashanti, the spider Anancy, tales of whose exploits are a prominent part of Caribbean folklore. An asymmetric equation which relates deficit leg to surplus legs, lack to multiplicity, brings "a metaphysic of curative doubt" (78) to bear on appearances. Apparent deficiency and apparent endowment are two sides of an insufficient image. When Sebastian discovers Mary Stella's attempt at suicide "his legs multiplied" (14), but later "there was no visible bandage around his ankle but he seemed nevertheless as lame as Anancy" (33). Other such intimations occur: Marsden described as a cane on which "something, some invisible presence, did lean" (29), Sebastian asking of the jockey who exposed himself to Mary Stella, "Did he, for instance, possess a walking stick?" (50), and Jackson, Mary Stella's "authentic messenger" (125), falling from a ladder and breaking his leg. The most sustained appearance occurs when Mary Stella happens upon the black youth Anancy in Marsden's study. The "funny title" of a book has brought him there:

> . . . He turned his eyes to the desk. "The door was open and I saw the funny title of that book." He pointed to the desk.
> "Sir Thomas More's *Utopia*," said Mary, smiling against her fear and finding her tongue at last. "I put it there myself this week." His eyes were upon hers now. "I put it . . ." she began again, then stopped. "I brought you here," she thought silently. "*Utopia was the bait I used*." The thought came of its own volition. It seemed irrational, yet true. There was a ticking silence between them, a deeper pull than she could gauge, a deeper call than she knew, that had sounded long, long ago, even before the time when her father's great-great-grandmother had been hooked by an Englishman to bear him children of mixed blood. (26-27)

Mary Stella's pursuit of heterogeneous relations carries her out as well as in. She discovers an eighteenth-century black ancestor on her father's side. That discovery, along with her perusal, in Marsden's library, of seventeenth- and eighteenth-century parish accounts of money spent to expel children and pregnant women, several of them black, arouses her desire for a utopian inclusiveness, the "longing to change the world" which "baits" Anancy. The world's failure to comply with that desire leads her to distance herself from it, to practice a kind of cosmic displacement. Her schizophrenia involves an aspect of astral projection, as she cultivates the "capacity to burn elsewhere" (85) suggested by her middle name: "Ah yes, said Stella, I am a mask Mary wears, a way of coping with truth. We are each other's little deaths, little births. We cling to sarcophagus-globe and to universal cradle" (44).

Displacement and relativizing distance account for the resonances and agitations at work in the text, an animated incompleteness whose components tend towards as well as recede from one another, support as well as destabilize one another. The pull between Mary Stella and Anancy is said to arise from "a compulsion or infectious Cupid's arrow . . . related to the target of unfinished being" (26). Some such pull, together with its other side, aversion, advances the accent on rationality which pervades the novel and has much to do with Harris's distinctive style. The sought-after sense of dispersed identity makes for staggered equational upsets and elisions in which words, concepts, and images, like the characters, are related through a mix of contrast and contagion. The musicality of Harris's writing resides in its cadences, imaginal concatenations and poetic assurance, but also in something else. *The Angel at the Gate* offers a musical conception of the world whose emphasis on animate incompleteness, "unfinished being," recalls Zuckerkandl's analysis of tonal motion:

> A series of tones is heard as motion not because the successive tones are of different pitches but because they have different dynamic qualities. The dynamic quality of a tone, we said, is a statement of its incompleteness, its will to completion. To hear a tone as dynamic quality, as a direction, a pointing, means hearing at the same time beyond it, beyond it in the direction of its will, and going toward the expected next tone. Listening to music, then, we are not first *in* one tone, then in the next, and so forth. We are, rather, always *between* the tones, *on the way* from tone to tone; our hearing does not remain with the tone, it reaches through it and beyond it . . . .pure betweenness, pure passing over. (136-37)

A mixed, middle ground which privileges betweenness would seem to be the realm in which Harris works. He alludes to himself as a "no-man's land writer" at one point (23) and later has Jackson say, "I must learn to paint or sculpt what lies stranded between earth and heaven" (124). An "attunement to a gulf or divide between sky and earth" (123) probes an estrangement and a stranded play in which limbs have to do with limbo, liminality, lift:

> The women were dressed in white. They carried covered trays of
> food and other materials on their head. There was a statuesque de-
> liberation to each movement they made, a hard-edged beauty akin
> to young Lucy's that seemed to bind their limbs into the soil even
> as it lifted them very subtly an inch or two into space.
>
>   That lift was so nebulous, so uncertain, it may not have occurred
> at all. Yet it was there; it gave a gentle wave or groundswell to the
> static root or the vertical dance of each processional body. (122)

What remains to be said is that to take that lift a bit farther is to view
the outsider's lot as cosmic, stellar. Social estrangement is gnostic es-
trangement and the step from Satchmo's "height of trumpet" to Sun
Ra's "intergalactic music" is neither a long nor an illogical one. In this
respect, the film *Brother from Another Planet* is worth — in what will serve
as a closing note — mentioning briefly. That it shares with *The Angel at
the Gate* a theme of cosmic dislocation is obvious enough. That the
Brother's limp is the limp of a misfit — the shoes he finds and puts on
don't suit his feet — is also easy to see. An intermedia thread is also pre-
sent and bears on this discussion, especially the allusions to Dante (the
Rasta guide named Virgil) and *Invisible Man* (the Brother's detachable
eye), where it would seem the film were admitting a need to reach be-
yond its limits. What stronger suggestion of anesthetic-synesthetic dis-
placement could one want than when the Brother places his eye in the
drug dealer's hand? Or than the fact that the movie ends on a seen but
unsounded musical note as the Brother gets aboard an "A" train?

Notes

1. Examples of *gisalo* and other varieties of Kaluli song can be heard on the al-
bum *The Kaluli of Papua Niugini: Weeping and Song* (Musicaphon BM 30 SL 2702).

2. *Slavery and Social Death: A Comparative Study* (Cambridge: Harvard UP, 1982).

3. *Sound and Symbol: Music and the External World* (Princeton: Bollingen Foundation/
Princeton UP, 1956), 371. Subsequent citations are incorporated into the text.

4. Stephanie A. Judy, "'The Grand Concord of What': Preliminary Thoughts on
Musical Composition and Poetry," *Boundary 2*, VI, 1 (Fall 1977): 267-85.

5. *Prepositions* (Berkeley: U of California P, 1981), 19.

6. *The Bow and the Lyre* (New York: McGraw-Hill, 1973), 37.

7. *Desire in Language: A Semiotic Approach to Literature and Art* (New York: Columbia
UP, 1980), 31.

8. *Sound and Sentiment: Birds, Weeping, Poetics and Song in Kaluli Expression* (Philadel-
phia: U of Pennsylvania P, 1982), 34.

9. *Flash of the Spirit: African and Afro-American Art and Philosophy* (New York: Vintage Books, 1984), xiii.

10. *Tales* (New York: Grove Press, 1967), 77.

11. Charles Mingus, *Beneath the Underdog* (New York: Penguin Books, 1980), 262.

12. *Bedouin Hornbook* (Charlottesville: Callaloo Fiction Series/UP of Virginia, 1986), 1.

13. *The Devil and Commodity Fetishism in South America* (Chapel Hill: U of North Carolina P, 1980), 4.

14. *The Bass Saxophone* (London: Picador, 1980), 109.

15. Quoted by Lawrence W. Levine in *Black Culture and Black Consciousness: Afro-American Folk Thought from Slavery to Freedom* (New York: Oxford UP, 1977), 85.

16. *The Wayward and the Seeking* (Washington, D.C.: Howard UP, 1980), 123.

17. Quoted by Charles W. Scruggs in "The Mark of Cain and the Redemption of Art," *American Literature* 44 (1972): 290-91.

18. *Cane* (New York: Liveright, 1975), 12. Subsequent citations are incorporated into the text.

19. *Black Music* (New York: Morrow, 1967), 66.

20. *Paterson* (New York: New Directions, 1963), 144-45. Subsequent citations are incorporated into the text.

21. *Selected Poems* (New York: New Directions, 1969), 115.

22. *Hermes the Thief: The Evolution of a Myth* (New York: Vintage Books, 1969), 82.

23. *The Trickster in West Africa: A Study of Mythic Irony and Sacred Delight* (Berkeley: U of California P), 80.

24. *Praisesong for the Widow* (New York: Dutton, 1984), 243.

25. Levine, 405-06.

26. *Invisible Man* (New York: Vintage Books, 1972), 8. Subsequent quotations are incorporated into the text.

27. *Human Universe and Other Essays* (New York: Grove Press, 1967), 3.

28. *The Subconscious Language* (New York: Washington Square Press, 1967), 96n.

29. Quoted by Paul L. Mariani in "Williams's Black Novel," *The Massachusetts Review* XIV, 1 (Winter 1973): 68. This article is part of "A Williams Garland: Petals from the Falls, 1945-50," edited by Mariani, which includes *Man Orchid*, 77-117. Subsequent citations of Mariani's article and of *Man Orchid* are incorporated into the text.

30. See, for example, "This is what it's called" by Albert Saijo, Lew Welch, and Jack Kerouac in *The Beat Scene*, ed. Elias Wilentz (New York: Corinth, 1960), 163-70.

31. *History of the Voice: The Development of Nation Language in Anglophone Caribbean Poetry* (London and Port of Spain: New Beacon Books, 1984), 31.

32. *New Jazz Poets* (Broadside Records BR 461).

33. *The Angel at the Gate* (London: Faber and Faber, 1982), 109. Subsequent citations are incorporated into the text.

34. *The Womb of Space: The Cross-Cultural Imagination* (Westport: Greenwood Press, 1983), 130-31.

35. "The Phenomenal Legacy," *The Literary Half-Yearly* 11 (1970): 1-6.

36. *Da Siva da Silva's Cultivated Wilderness and Genesis of the Clowns* (London: Faber and Faber, 1977), 8-9.

37. *Palace of the Peacock* (London: Faber and Faber, 1960), 83. Subsequent citations are incorporated into the text.

38. "The eye and its 'gaze' . . . has had a lockhold on Western thought," notes, as have others, Paul Stoller in "Sound in Songhay Cultural Experience," *American Ethnologist* II, 3 (1984): 559-70.

Private Poetry, Public Deception

Jerome McGann

When readers today, especially academic readers, think of "the politics of poetic form" in connection with Romanticism, the names that usually come to mind are Blake and Shelley (for the opposition), or Words-worth and Southey (for the establishment). In the context of 1790-1830, however, and throughout the Euro-American world of the nineteenth and much of the twentieth-century, the name that would have been first on everyone's lips was Byron. A political activist in England where he spoke in parliament against capital punishment, later a social pariah who left England for Italy and Greece where he was deeply involved in revolutionary political groups, he finally — famously — died on the west coast of Greece, in the guerilla encampment of Greek Suliotes whom he had joined and personally financed to fight against the Turks for the liberation of Greece.

English public opinion, after worshipping at his shrine for almost five years (1812-1816), finally decided he was the single greatest threat to the country's public morals and social order. This judgment of Byron is written for anyone to see in the English public press of the years 1816-1824. It seems astonishing to us today, and yet it is the simplest fact. We are surprised partly because we do not easily imagine any single person having the kind of political significance which Byron evidently did have. We are astonished as well, however, because Byron's political life seems to have been so ineffectual — in contrast, for example, to a person like Lenin. But most of all we are surprised because we have come to think of Byron's romanticism not as a political force but as a purely personal one: Byron the great lover, the man not of political but of erotic

119

affairs, the broken dandy of the fast and luxurious world of Regency England.

I will be asking you to rethink the terms of this framework in which Byron and his work have descended to us. And I believe it is important to do so, at this point in time especially, because the contradictions implicit in Byron's personal and political investments have great relevance to our own immediate circumstances.

We begin to glimpse that relevance when we remember perhaps the single most important fact about him and his work: that he was the first writer in English to become a brand name, even a commodity fetish. He was himself well aware of this phenomenon, and was actively — consciously — involved in generating what Benjamin was later to see as an auratic field of poetical relations. Benjamin saw Baudelaire as the poet who defined the character of writing in an age of mechanical reproduction. But to Baudelaire, Byron was the true model and point of origin; and Baudelaire was right.

To understand this better we shall have to go over the ground of romanticism, and the critique of romanticism which Byron's work generated. Byron's departure from England in 1816, heaped with obloquy, would be the emblem of his subsequent cultural and ideological fate. Romantic ideologies came to dominate writing in English for the next hundred years and more, but those ideologies would carefully circumscribe the antithesis embodied in Byron's own romanticism. This would be done by refusing to take seriously Baudelaire's and Nietzsche's readings of Byron's work, by marginalizing him into various inconsequential territories — poet of Regency high life, poet of sentimental love, Satanic poseur, king of light verse and depthless adventure narratives set in exotic places. In his own day, and throughout Europe in the nineteenth-century, Byron was felt to be mad, bad, and dangerous to know. He was generally not read so in the English-speaking world for one simple yet profound reason: his work called into question the most basic premises of writing as they had been recast in the English romantic movement. Byron's work argued that poetry is a discourse not of truth but of illusions and deceits — what Blake earlier called "bodies of falsehood"; and he went on to show the social structure, the rhetoric, by which such illusions are maintained. Briefly, he revealed the secrets of the imagination, made those secrets public information — much as Brecht in the twentieth-century would say that the theatre should do. For trying to leak the files of the pentagon of the poets, Byron would be silenced.

I

Sincerity: this is one of the touchstones by which Romantic poetry origi-
nally measured itself.[1] In a poem's sincerity one observed a deeply felt
relation binding the poetic Subject to the poetic subject, the speaking
voice to the matter being addressed. Romantic truth is inner vision, and
Romantic knowledge is the unfolding of the truths of that inner vision.

Hypocrisy is the antithesis of sincerity. One can be sincere and yet
speak incompletely, inadequately, or even falsely, but it appears a patent
contradiction to think or imagine that one could be sincere and at the
same time speak deliberate falsehoods or develop subtle equivocations.
To do so is to declare that one is "two-faced", and hence lacking that
fundamental quality of the sincere person: integrity.

In this context, rhetorical and premeditated verse may be imagined
prima facie incapable with respect to truth and knowledge. The poetry of
sincerity — Romantic poetry, in its paradigm mode — therefore typical-
ly avoids the procedures of those public forms of poetry, satirical and
polemical verse. When Romantic poetry opens itself to those genres, it
opens itself to the horizon of its antithesis, to the horizon of hypocrisy.[2]

This last move is, of course, exactly what Byron did. We should not be
surprised, then, that he is the one English Romantic who has been com-
monly charged with — who has had his work charged with — hypocri-
sy.[3] This consequence reflects an important and (if I may so phrase it)
two-faced fact about Byron as a writer: that he cultivated rhetorical
modes of verse, and that *he was a Romantic poet who cultivated those modes*.
The distinction is crucial. *Don Juan* is a machine for exposing many
kinds of hypocrisy — cant political, cant poetical, cant moral, Byron
called them — and there is no one, I suppose, who would gainsay the
extraordinary scale of Byron's achievement. Nevertheless, what we have
still to see more clearly is how this satire of hypocrisy is grounded in By-
ron's Romanticism, and how the latter is the very seat and primal scene
of what it means to be hypocritical. In the end we will discover a poetic
truth-function which Byron, alone of the English Romantics, elaborated
and deployed. An essential feature of this work is the understanding that
hypocrisy and the true voice of feeling cannot be separated (even if they
can be distinguished). Paradoxical though it may seem, this is a discov-
ery which may be imagined with peculiar — perhaps unexampled —
clarity through the styles of Romanticism.

At the heart of the Romantic ideal of sincerity are two related prob-
lems, the one a contradiction, the other an illusion. The contradiction is

concealed in the Romantic idea(l) of self-integrity. Byron summed up this problem with great wit and trenchancy:

> Also observe, that like the great Lord Coke,
>   (See Littleton) when'er I have expressed
> Opinions two, which at first sight may look
>   Twin opposites, the second is the best.
> Perhaps I have a third too in a nook,
>   Or none at all — which seems a sorry jest;
> But if a writer would be quite consistent,
> How could he possibly show things existent? (XV st. 87)[4]

This anticipates exactly the critique of the Romantic idea(l) of subjectivity that would be raised so powerfully by Kierkegaard in his analysis of Hegel's paradigmatic representation of the truth-content of that ideal. Kierkegaard's *Concluding Unscientific Postscript* ridicules the "German philosopher" — "Herr Professor" — for the abstraction of Hegel's concept of subjective and phenomenological truth, which cannot be "realized for any existing spirit, who is himself existentially in process of becoming".[5]

I will summarize briefly Kierkegaard's argument on this matter because it helps to clarify the import and structure of Byron's work. According to Hegel, the idea(l) of identity is a dialectical synthesis of "Twin opposites". It is achieved when Otherness, that which is not the subject, is "negated" in the process of knowledge we call consciousness. The objective knowledge that is gained is not positive but phenomenological: not particular subjective or empirical truths, but the metaphysical truth of the process itself.

To this position Kierkegaard raised a simple but difficult problem — his famous "aut. . .aut", the "either/or". Assuming (with Hegel and the entire metaphysical tradition) the principle of identity, Kierkegaard argued as follows: either the truth that is achieved is identical with consciousness, or it is not truth. If the process is the truth, the process is solipsistic (it involves mere tautologies); if it is not solipsistic, contradiction — untruth — remains part of the process. The "negation" that is part of the Hegelian process is either the phantom of a negation or it is a true negation; in the first instance it may be transcended, in the second it may not, but in either case knowledge and truth remain unachieved.

A writer, therefore, cannot "possibly show things existent" and at the same time "be consistent". This contradiction operates because the "process" of subjectivity is an existential and not a logical (or dialectical) process. Kierkegaard's lively prose style is itself an "existential" critique of German philosophical discourse, a revelation of what it actually means to "show things existent". But in this respect Byron's verse far surpasses the Danish philosopher's arguments:

> If people contradict themselves, can I
>   Help contradicting them, and every body,
> Even my veracious self? — But that's a lie;
>   I never did so, never will — how should I?
> He who doubts all things, nothing can deny. . . (XV st. 88)

The lines enact the contradictions they confront. In this passage Byron at once asserts and denies his self-integrity. His contradiction of himself is a lie, the lines declare, but they also declare that his "veracious self" is a lie, and hence they equally give the lie to his denial of his self-contradiction.

The passage, in short, turns itself into an illustration, or an instance, of the problem it is proposing to deal with. It is Byron's poetic, "existential" equivalent of the logical paradox of the lying Cretan. Byron's verse here proposes such a paradox, but it includes its own activity of making the proposal within the paradox, as yet another face of the contradiction.

Later I shall look further into *Don Juan*'s contradictions, but in order to do that we need to understand better the illusions which correspond to those contradictions. If a contradiction exposes itself at the core of Romantic self-integrity, we confront an illusion in the Romantic idea(l) of spontaneity and artlessness. Romantic sincerity only *presents itself* as unpremeditated verse; in fact it involves a rhetoric, and contractual bonds with its audiences, which are just as determinate and artful as the verse of Donne, or Rochester, or Pope. The rhetoric of sincerity in Romanticism is a rhetoric of displacement; the audience is not addressed directly, it is set apart, like the reflective poet, in a position where the discourse of the poem has to be overheard. Among the important consequences of this basic maneuver is the illusion of freedom which it fosters — as if the reader were not being placed under the power of the writer's rhetoric, as if the writer were relatively indifferent to the reader's presence and intent only on communing with his own soul.

Byron's work and his audiences, by contrast, always tend to preserve a clarity of presence toward each other. This remains true even when Byron is working in lyrical forms. In general, it is as if Byron in his work were not simply meditating in public, but were declaring or even declaiming his inmost thoughts and feelings out loud, and directly to others. (The procedure has been aptly described as "trailing his bleeding

heart across Europe.") The difference from the usual romantic practise
is crucial.

II

We observe that difference very early in Byron's work. The first impor-
tant publication in his career as a poet was in fact a text which he did not
write himself, though he had provoked it. I mean Henry Brougham's
shrewd notice of Byron's juvenile *Hours of Idleness* (1807). Brougham reg-
isters and then ridicules Byron's efforts to control and manipulate his
audience:

> the noble author is peculiarly forward in pleading his minority. We
> have it in the title-page, and on the very back of the volume; it fol-
> lows his name like a favourite part of his *style*. Much stress is laid
> upon it in the preface, and the poems are connected with this gen-
> eral statement of his case, by particular dates. . . .
>
> (Rutherford, p. 28)

Brougham understands how the texts of Byron's poems are integrated
into the format of the book in general so that the reading of individual
texts will be framed and controlled by various intratextual markers.
When Brougham pillories Byron, therefore, it is not so much because
the poetry is maudlin or sentimental, but because he detects calculation
and insincerity in the work.

In *English Bards and Scotch Reviewers* Byron strikes back. Though the
work is formally a critical review of the current state of poetry and Brit-
ish culture, the poem is in fact a riposte to the *Edinburgh Review* notice,
an act of self-justification.

> Still must I hear? — shall hoarse FITZGERALD bawl
> His creaking couplets in a tavern hall
> And I not sing, lest, haply, Scotch Reviews
> Should dub me scribbler, and denounce my Muse?
> Prepare for rhyme — I'll publish, right or wrong:
> Fools are my theme, let Satire be my song. (11.1-6)

This is an unusual opening move because Byron does not entirely sepa-
rate himself from the "Fools" who are his poem's theme. The touch of
recklessness in the determination to "publish, right or wrong" is fairly
paraded in these lines. What Byron gains by that move is an effect of
honesty, as if he were — despite his faults as a writer and a person —
more candid and morally courageous than those who will be the objects
of his satire (that is, bad poets like W. J. Fitzgerald and proud reviewers
like Brougham).

One notes as well the imperative address to the reader in the fourth line ("Prepare for rhyme"). This maneuver reminds us of the general literary situation which prevails in Byron's writing even at this first stage of his career. The work, that is to say, operates through a textual interplay which is carried out in the public sphere.

The special strength of *English Bards* is a function of the Brougham review. Charged by Brougham with insincerity in his earlier book, Byron responds in *English Bards* with a new and more powerful style of sincerity. His polemic is grounded in a significant and daring initial decision: not to deny the charges brought against *Hours of Idleness*. Byron does not even deny Brougham's ad hominem critical implications — that Lord Byron, the author of the book, reveals himself in it as a somewhat foolish, calculating, and untrustworthy person.

Byron, in other words, accepts "sincerity" as the critical issue. Launching an ad hominem rejoinder to his Scotch reviewer (whom Byron at the time mistakenly thought was Francis Jeffrey) and his critical cohorts at the *Edinburgh Review*, Byron admits his weaknesses as a writer and his faults of character. This admission is a new sign of his sincerity, and it is the foundation on which Byron reconstitutes his character in this new poem.

Being, as he says, the "least thinking of a thoughtless throng, / Just skilled to know the right and chuse the wrong" (689-90), Byron is a model neither as a poet nor as a "Moralist" (700). Nonetheless, he refuses to disqualify himself from satire. He has "learned to think, and sternly speak the truth" (1058), and the truth is that cultural rectitude in Britain has become random and ineffectual — a praiseworthy poet here, a judicious critic there, but none of them — and least of all Lord Byron — installed (or installable) in a position of authority. Byron's poem exposes the lack of a cultural consensus. More than that, it shows how, in the absence of such a consensus, the merely "righteous" will move to seize authority.

> Thus much I've dared; if my incondite lay
> Hath wronged these righteous times let others say; (1067-68)

Lines like these solicit and even glory in their contrariness. At once aggressive and indifferent, the couplet — which concludes the poem — summarizes the tonal character of the satire as a whole, just as it anticipates the tonal perspective of the celebrated writings soon to follow: *Childe Harold* in particular, but all the Baudelairean Oriental tales as well, and of course *Manfred*.

The challenge reminds us, however, of the equally important matter I touched on earlier: that the structure of the work is communicative

exchange. Throughout his career Byron's books cultivate direct com-
munication with the people who are reading them — addressing such
people (often by name) and responding to what they are themselves
saying (as it were) *to* Byron's poems. His work assumes the presence of
an audience that talks and listens — an audience that may hear as well
as overhear, and that may have something to say in its turn.

We recognize this procedure in numerous passages from *Don Juan*.
The exchange structure is especially interesting when Byron reflects
upon or responds to criticisms directed at his work by contemporary
readers.

> They accuse me — *Me* — the present writer of
>   The present poem — of — I know not what, —
> A tendency to under-rate and scoff
>   At human power and virtue and all that;
> And this they say in language rather rough. (VII st. 3)

In such cases — they are numerous — the act of writing makes itself one
of the principal subjects of the writing. This is not to say that we are sim-
ply witnessing a poem that is written about poetry. That is what we
should say, correctly, about much of *The Prelude* or "The Fall of Hyperi-
on" or a host of other excellent Romantic poems. The situation is slight-
ly but significantly different in Byron's case. Here the act of writing has
thoroughly materialized and socialized the field of the imagination's
activity. In such circumstances we observe how poetry is like most hu-
man events — a dynamic interchange between various parties each of
whom plays some part in the total transaction.[6] Those parties are never
completely visible or present to consciousness — in Byron's poem or
anywhere else; but a poem like *Don Juan*, by calling attention to certain
of its communicative actions, allows one to glimpse the radical hetero-
nomy of the exchanges that are taking place.

Byron is quite sensitive to the presence of his many readers — in-
deed, his acts of writing are equally acts of imagining them into exist-
ence, and then talking with them. Stanzas 27-32 of *Don Juan*, Canto I
narrate the marital troubles of Donna Inez and her husband Don Jose,
but the subtext — the domestic circumstances of Lord and Lady Byron
— exposes the actual structure of Byron's writing here:

> For Inez call'd some druggists and physicians,
>   And tried to prove her loving lord was *mad*,
> But as he had some lucid intermissions,
>   She next decided he was only *bad*. . . . (st. 27)

And so on. One may read these lines, and the entire passage, without any knowledge whatever of the autobiographical allusions; or one may read them with no detailed and particular knowledge, though with some general sense that personal allusions are being made; or one may read them from the inside, as it were, as a person learned in the various references. *Don Juan* has imagined and written to all three of these audiences.

But it has also done more. Besides all those later readers (like ourselves) who are learned in such texts by study and application, the passage has imagined various contemporary readers. Their presences are called to our attention through the surviving proofs of Byron's poem, which were read and annotated by Byron's friend John Cam Hobhouse. In these annotations Hobhouse's principal object was to persuade Byron to moderate various aspects of the satire — for example, the personal swipes at Lady Byron.[7] Alongside the passage just cited Hobhouse wrote, disapprovingly: "This is so very pointed."

The proofs with Hobhouse's annotations were sent to Byron, who entered a dialogue with his friend by adding his own marginalia in response to Hobhouse's strictures. Against that comment by Hobhouse, for example, Byron wrote: "If people make application it is their own fault." The remark is entirely disingenuous, of course, but it emphasizes his awareness of "the people" who might "make application" in texts like these. Hobhouse is one of those people — but then so is Lady Byron; and these two readers, equally imagined through this text, will read in very different ways.

This proof material raises two points which I want to emphasize and pursue. First, the "application" which Hobhouse makes in his reading underscores the variety of *possible* applications: even if we limit the reading group to "the knowing ones", we can see how differently the passage will be read by Hobhouse, Lady Byron, Augusta Leigh, and so forth. Second, those different readings do not stand outside the text; on the contrary, they are part of the work's imagination of itself. Byron is a r eader of his own text here, as his marginal note to Hobhouse indicates. And when we consult the reviews of the first two cantos we find a series of other readers who have been imagined by the writing and who turn u pon Byron's texts in various states of outrage, annoyance, disgust. Our l ater varieties of amusement are to be reckoned up here as well.

Byron's poem thus incorporates a large and diverse group of people i nto itself. The group includes specific persons, like Hobhouse, Lady Byr on, and a host of named or otherwise targeted individuals — literary pe ople (friends, acquaintances, enemies, or simply people he knew or had heard of), politicians, public figures, lovers, and so forth; but it also includes various social, ideological, religious, and political groups (like the bluestockings, the landed aristocracy, the London literary world, the government, the opposition, and a variety of Christian readers). These people are "in" Byron's poem not simply because they are named or alluded to — not simply at the narratological level — but because Byron's text has called them out — has imagined them as presences at the rhetorical and dialogical levels. Because Byron has pulled them into the world of his poem, the poem is forced to overstep its own aesthetic limits, and to move among *them*, in *their* world.

The various public's responses to the poem are therefore included in the writing's imagination of itself. Byron's readers seem most present in those passages where the text appears most shocking or tasteless. The parody of the decalogue in Canto I; the scenes of cannibalism in Canto II; the aftermath of the siege of Ismael when the "Widows of forty" are made to wonder "Wherefore the ravishing did not begin!" (VIII. st. 132): these passages horrified early readers, and many of them still retain their offensiveness. The effects are wholly calculated, however, though for certain readers this fact only increases the offense which they represent.

Byron's calculations are meant to draw readers into the orbit of the poem, to insist upon their presence. The stanzas in Canto I (209-210) where Byron declares that he "bribed my grandmother's review — the British" to write an approving article on *Don Juan* are a good instance of what is happening in Byron's text. The allegation is patently outrageous — an amusing poetical flight which calls attention to Byron's general awareness that his poem might cause "some prudish readers [to] grow skittish". The editor of *The British Review*, however, William Roberts, took it all in high seriousness, and was moved to issue a public denial of Byron's imaginary declaration.[8]

William Roberts thus becomes an accomplice in Byron's writing. *Don Juan* seeks that kind of complicity, imagines its presence at every point. We laugh at Roberts' foolishness for having risen to Byron's bait here, but the more important matter to grasp is that Roberts' reaction *has to be included in our understanding of Byron's poem*, has to be seen as "part of" the work.

Roberts' reaction calls attention to some of the poem's most important discursive procedures. We confront the same kind of situation, for example, when Hobhouse annotates the texts that allude to Lady Byron. Where the poem reads (in reference to Donna Inez and Don Jose):

> She kept a journal, where his faults were noted,
>   And open'd certain trunks of books and letters. . . .
>
>   (I. st. 28)

The text is glancing at one of Byron's most cherished beliefs about his wife and her deviousness ("You know," Byron wrote to his sister, "that Lady B[yro]n *secretly opened my letter trunks before she left Town*").[9] Hobhouse annotates the *Don Juan* text "There is some doubt about this", meaning that he is not sure that Lady Byron actually ransacked Byron's belongings in January 1816. What is remarkable here is the *way* Hobhouse is reading, the way he, like Roberts, refuses to distinguish between the fictive and the factive dimensions of the text. Hobhouse reads the poem as if it were literal statement at the level of the subtext.

Byron's response to Hobhouse's annotation is even more interesting. Against his friend's expression of doubt about the factual truth of Byron's poetic allusion, Byron writes this in the margin:

> What has the '*doubt*' to do with the poem? It is at least poetically true — why apply everything to that absurd woman. I have no reference to living characters.

Here disingenuousness unmasks itself as hypocrisy. Byron's argument that his work should not be read outside its purely aesthetic space is belied by his own continual practise. What Byron's remark indicates, however, is his reluctance to accept fully the consequences of the writing procedures he has set in motion. The writing has collapsed the distinction between factual and fictional space, and it calls various actual readers into its presence. Byron's annotation shows that he still imagines he can control those readers, that he still imagines it is his poetic privilege to keep them in control and to require them to read "in the same spirit that the author writ". But a larger "spirit" than Lady Byron's husband supervenes the act of writing here. The poetry, written "in" that larger spirit, exposes that man as another partisan reader of the poem, and hence as a reader who can claim no authoritative privilege. Hobhouse's critical reading of Byron's text is written in, is part of, that larger satirical spirit. The generosity of Byron's satirical project is that it has licensed his work to bite the hand that feeds it.

III

To the degree that *Don Juan* is committed to telling the truth, the undermining of the narrator's authority has important implications. In laying "Byron" open to criticism, the writing takes away a fundamental

Romantic truth-function. Sincerity, the integrity of the "veracious self",
will not survive the poem's own processes. The poem responds to this
situation by developing a new theory of truth, the idea of "truth in mas-
querade":

> And after all, what is a lie? 'Tis but
>   The truth in masquerade; and I defy
> Historians, heroes, lawyers, priests to put
>   A fact without some leaven of a lie.
> The very shadow of true Truth would shut
>   Up annals, revelations, poesy,
> And prophecy. . . .

This being the case, Byron concludes:

> Praised be all liars and all lies! (XI sts. 37-38)

The project of Don Juan is itself an instance of the truth in masquerade:
for while six volumes of the work were published under Byron's author-
ity, they were all issued anonymously. Note or text, the name Byron
never passes the lips of the poem. That Byron was its author everyone
knew, nor did he try to conceal the fact; but he did equivocate, as we see
from the "Reply" he wrote (but never published) to the attack made on
Don Juan in Blackwood's Edinburgh Magazine of August, 1819.

> With regard to Don Juan, I neither deny nor admit it to be mine
> — everybody may form their own opinion; but, if there be any who
> now, or in the progress of that poem, if it is to be continued, feel, or
> should feel themselves so aggrieved as to require a more explicit
> answer, privately and personally, they shall have it.
> I have never shrunk from the responsibility of what I have written.[10]

Byron here insists on maintaining the fiction of the author's anonymity
even as he all but acknowledges the poem as his production. Not to
come forward explicitly as the author of Don Juan meant that the work
could operate as a masquerade performance whose many roles and atti-
tudes would all have to be understood to have been assumed by one
person. Furthermore, the work is properly to be designated a masquer-
ade rather than a theatrical perfomance because the encounters with the
poem's audiences do not take place across the distance marked by a
proscenium. The poem engages its interlocutors — even when those
people are a group or a class — in much more intimate and personal
ways. The style is, as the work says, "conversational".

Still, the truth that lies in masquerade remains contradictory. In his
enthusiasm for his new theory of truth the narrator exclaims "Praised
be all liars and all lies!" But the propositions concealed in that sentence
— that all liars and lies are worthy of praise, and that the speaker of the
sentence assents to this idea — are both belied by *Don Juan*. The text is
happy to praise many lies and liars, even the lies of lying women which
the younger Byron, drowning in his sentimental sexism, once had so
much trouble with; and the narrator stands behind the text in all those
instances. But one liar stands outside the pale: "shuffling Southey, that
incarnate lie" (X st. 13).

The exception is extremely important so far as *Don Juan* is concerned.
I pass without comment the obvious fact that Southey's exceptional po-
sition gives the lie to — contradicts — the universal praise of liars. This
is important, but not so important as another contradiction. To the de-
gree that Byron can perceive untruth incarnate in Robert Southey, to
that extent Byron comes forward in his masquerade as one possessed,
however unselfconsciously, of truth. A kind of negative ground of truth,
Southey becomes one of the still points in the turning world of *Don Juan*.
The veracity of the Byronic self is defined through its differences from
and with Robert Southey.

But even here we encounter a problem, as one may see very easily
from that passage in Canto III which centers in "The Isle of Greece"
ballad. At the plot level, the ballad is sung by the Romaic poet kept by
Lambro on his island fastness. The song becomes the occasion for a ser-
ies of reflections on poets like Southey who sell themselves to authority,
or fashion their work to catch the main chance. The textual difficulty
arises because, in developing the attack on Southey's crassness and lack
of integrity, the poem uses details and illustrations which are drawn
from Byron's own work and career. As I have given the details of this sit-
uation elsewhere,[11] I will simply here underscore the general point: that
in drawing the portrait of the "sad trimmer" poet (III st. 82) in the like-
ness of Robert Southey, Byron's poem creates an unusual palimpsest in
which the faces of Southey and Byron, those arch antagonists, are super-
imposed on each other. The two men are, in the full meaning of that
paradoxical phrase, "Twin opposites".

When truth operates in masquerade, then, even negative grounds of
truth fail to keep their identity. If bad "moralists like Southey" (III st.
93) are not the reeds on which the poem can lean, perhaps — as numer-
ous readers have suggested — we are to count on the play of *Don Juan*'s
ironies. Integrity and stability lie in the work's flaunting of its own
contradictions, in the Romantic irony we observed playing through the

passage about Byron's "veracious self" in Canto XV. There Romantic
irony is invoked, as so often in the poem, to expose and transcend its
own contradictions.

But Romantic irony is not the work's ground of truth either. We
glimpse this even through the example of Southey, who is not known in
Don Juan through plays of Romantic irony. He is known rather through
hatred — the same way that Brougham and Castlereagh are known. The
poem's equation of Byron and Southey, therefore, cannot be assimi-
lated into *Don Juan*'s ironical self-understanding, for it is an equation
which, though real, stands outside — in true contradiction to — the ho-
rizon of the work's self-consciousness. Byron can be witty at his own ex-
pense, or at Southey's expense, but his wit is not engaged in face of the
Byron/Southey parallel. His wit cannot be engaged here because
Southey is not in the end a figure of fun for Byron, he is a figure of all
that is hateful and despicable.

The issue of Southey and the presence of anger and hatred in *Don
Juan* are the touchstones by which we can measure the poem's contra-
dictions. The argument in the margins between Byron and Hobhouse,
noted earlier, eventually spills, like so much else, into the public text:

> And recollect [this] work is only fiction,
> And that I sing of neither mine nor me,
>   Though every scribe, in some slight turn of diction,
> Will hint allusions never *meant*. Ne'er doubt
> *This* — when I speak, I *don't hint*, but *speak out*.
>
>   (XI st. 88)

Which is all very well except that the poem not only practises such an art
of allusions, in Canto XIV it explicitly declares itself committed to the
mode. *Don Juan* is written in a secret code, the text declares, because the
work contains so "much which could not be appreciated / In any man-
ner by the uninitiated". (XIV sts. 21-22) It is important to see that these
two passages — these two positions — do not cancel each other out in
the poem. *Don Juan* is constructed to show that there is a sense in which
— or perhaps one should say that there are times when — both asser-
tions apply; just as there are occasions when each of these attitudes
would have itself belied by the text.

Thus *Don Juan* does something more than set in motion Byron's ver-
sion of Kierkegaard's either/or problematic. The poem's contradictions
deconstruct all truth-functions which are founded either in (metaphy-
sical) Identity or (psychological) Integrity, as we have seen. In their place
is set a truth-function founded (negatively) in contradiction itself, and

(positively) in metonomy: to the negative either/or dialectic *Don Juan* adds the procedural rule of "both/and". That procedural rule is Byron's version of what Hegel called "the negation of the negation".

The latter, in its Byronic form, means that the terms of all contradictions are neither idealistically transcended nor nihilistically cancelled out. They simply remain in contradiction. The both/and rule means that the writing of the poem must "invariably" produce not simply the dialectic of "Opinions two", but somewhere "a third too in a nook", that third being, minimally, the awareness of the unresolved character of the original opposition.

It is through its many forms of contradiction that the poem declares its truth-function to consist in the setting of problems and not the presentation of solutions. The point of the work is to test the limits of what it itself is able to imagine, and to carry out those tests by setting imagination against imagination.

The poem, we should therefore say, learns from itself, even though the knowledge it acquires must remain provisional, subject to change, and even sometimes unassimilated at the authoritative level of its consciousness. Byron's private argument with Hobhouse in the margins of the proofs of Cantos I-II would eventually find itself publically displayed in the contradictory passages set down in Cantos XI and XIV respectively, where those two imaginations expose their respective limits. This kind of thing happens repeatedly in the work. The writing seems bound to imagine the truths in its own lies as well as the falsehoods in its own truths. In *Don Juan*, Byron's imagination of Southey has a fatal appointment to keep with his imagination of himself.

This structure of provocations does not arise, however, from the ideology of Byron's own "creative imagination". It is rather the consequence of *Don Juan*'s rhetoric, which insists upon the presence of an objective world of various readers. One of these readers is the person we call Lord Byron, the writer of *Don Juan*, though even in *his* case, as we have seen, the person subsists in a multiplied — perhaps we should say, a fractured — identity. But it is the many other readers — Hobhouse, Lady Byron, the reviewers, the public in general — who stand as the work's most plain figures of otherness and objectivity. "Prepare for rhyme", *Don Juan* in effect says to them all — and in so saying the work lays itself open to the preparedness — the selfconsciousness — it insists upon in those it has summoned.

Don Juan is seriously interested in what they all have to say — the foolish things of William Roberts, the more thoughtful things of his friend Hobhouse, the critical and antagonistic things of everyone. In Canto

VII, for example, when Byron protests against those who attacked him for underrating and scoffing "At human power and virtue, and all that", Byron defends the morality of the work "as a *Satire* on the abuses of the present states of society" (BLJ 10.68), and on the illusions of those who were unable to see those abuses.

But the reviewers and pamphleteers insisted that *Don Juan* was something far different. Jeffrey's notice in the *Edinburgh Review* (Feb. 1822), while respectful of the work in certain ways, summarizes the negative line of attack. *Don Juan* is "in the highest degree pernicious" to society because it, like all Byron's writings, has "a tendency to destroy all belief in the reality of virtue".

Though *Don Juan* vigorously dissents from such a judgment, it also assimilates the judgment to itself, adds its own assent to that judgment even as it maintains, at the same time, its dissenting line.

That both/and maneuver is unmistakeable, for example, at the beginning of Canto XIII. In Canto XII Byron had reiterated his position that *Don Juan*'s goal is the "improvement" (st. 40) of society: "My Muse by exhortation means to mend / All people (st. 39). But at the opening of Canto XIII this passion for virtuous improvement, it appears, has waned somewhat:

> I should be very willing to redress
>   Men's wrongs, and rather check than punish crimes,
> Had not Cervantes in that too true tale
>   Of Quixote, shown how all such efforts fail.
>
> Cervantes smiled Spain's Chivalry away;
>   A single laugh demolished the right arm
> Of his own country; — seldom since that day
>   Has Spain had heroes. While Romance could charm,
> The world gave ground before her bright array;
>   And therefore have his volumes done such harm,
> That all their glory, as a composition,
> Was dearly purchased by his land's perdition. (sts. 8, 11)

The argument repeats the most commonplace line of attack taken towards *Don Juan* by contemporary readers. Its force here as a self-critical move is only emphasized by the explicit parallels which *Don Juan* draws at various points between itself and *Don Quixote*. Furthermore, since Byron has been deliberately pursuing this quixotic line at least since the first two cantos of *Childe Harold*[12], the repetition of it here underscores the "truth" of the idea which Jeffrey had formulated for so many: that all of Byron's writings, and not just *Don Juan*, tend to undermine "the reality of virtue".

Byron's work is so replete with turnabouts of this kind that we tend to read its basic structure as dialectical, and hence to approach its truth-functions in an epistemological frame of reference. This is to see the work as fundamentally critical — the great pronunciamento of what Carlyle would call the "Everlasting Nay". But the critical spirit that drives Byron's work is inadequately represented as a dialectical form. True, the work itself frequently encourages such a representation:

> And if I laugh at any mortal thing,
>   'Tis that I may not weep; and if I weep,
> 'Tis that our nature cannot always bring
>   Itself to apathy, for we must steep
> Our hearts first in the depths of Lethe's spring
>   Ere what we least wish to behold will sleep: (IV st. 4)

This passage begins with a dialectical gesture as the first two lines put us on the brink of a neatly turned antithesis. With the third line, however, we veer off unexpectedly — not in the direction of the laughter initially imagined but toward "apathy" and forgetfulness. These, it turns out, are neither wanted nor attainable here, though they are raised up as imaginable goals. In the end the passage does not tell us what would follow if the text were to "weep" instead of laugh. Forgetfulness, indifference, and laughter would, by the logic of this argument, all be equally possible.

This famous passage displays in miniature an important point: that in Byron's writing, contradiction is not dialectic, it is asymmetry. Metaphoric transfers yield to the transactions of metonymy which themselves branch out along rhizomatic lines. The order of things in the work therefore turns out to be wholly incommensurate:

> Ah! — What should follow slips from my reflection:
>   Whatever follows ne'ertheless may be
> As apropos of hope or retrospection,
>   As though the lurking thought had followed free.
>   (XV st. 1)

Writing "what's uppermost, without delay" (XIV st. 7) may equally mean description, narration, direct address; it may mean to write spontaneously or reflectively; it may mean gathering similes in a heap, developing an argument, opening a digression. It might mean copying out something (a quotation, a pharmaceutical prescription) or it might mean not writing anything at all, but simply editing.

The "ever varying rhyme" (VII st. 2) of *Don Juan* seems to me a direct function of its choice of a rhetorical rather than a lyrical procedure. The

decision has pitched the work outside the bounds of its subjectivity and
forced it to take up many matters which it may have imagined but which it
could not comprehend. As a result, the writing will not — indeed, cannot
— achieve anything but provisory and limited control over its own materi-
als. It continually enters into contradictions, but the contradictions do not
typically emerge out of a structure of their own internal logic. Rather, con-
tradictions come to the work at odd angles — for instance, through struc-
tures of the unforeseen and the haphazard:

> For ever and anon comes Indigestion,
>   (Not the most "dainty Ariel") and perplexes
> Our soarings with another sort of question: (XI st. 3)

What undermines authority in *Don Juan* is the presence of many com-
peting authorities, all of whom have been called to judgment. Some of
these authorities are not human beings at all but circumstantial powers:
Indigestion, for example, or puberty (or age), boredom, or different kinds
of chance events (like the assassination of the military commandant of
Ravenna, Luigi dal Pinto).[13] If all are summoned to judgment, all are
equally capable of introducing unauthorized topics and problems — sur-
prises for or threats to the text which have to be taken into account. The
poem may then consciously engage with these materials or not, and when
it does (or when it does not) its engagements (and refusals of engagement)
will themselves be highly idiosyncratic.

Don Juan develops its masquerade by pretending to be equal to itself
and to all its heterodox elements. This pretense to understanding and
truth is carried out, however, in the contradictory understanding that it *is* a
pretense; and the ground of that contradictory understanding is the pres-
ence of others who are to observe and respond to the pretenses being
made.

That differential of a real otherness is most clearly to be seen in the
texts that resist incorporation by Romantic irony. Because Byron's mas-
querade is not all in fun, for example — because many persons have
been invited who are each other's mortal enemies — *Don Juan*'s pre-
tenses are not all embraceable in a comic generosity. Benevolence may
be universal, but it is not everything. Savagery and tastelessness are
therefore *Don Juan*'s surest signs of a collapse of its integrity, a rupture in
its pretensions to the truth. Did Byron's text imagine or anticipate the
public outcry that would be raised at the passage which sneered at
Southey's and Coleridge's wives as "milliners of Bath" (III st. 93)? Was
it equal to that outrage and to the meaning which the outrage repre-
sented? We would have to say that it *was* only if we also said that, in this

passage, meaning deploys itself as an unreconciled differential.

At the end of Canto XIV, when the narrator teases us about the possible outcome of Adeline's and Juan's relationship, he forecasts the actual event which will prove crucial to their lives in the plot of the poem.

> But great things spring from little: — Would you think,
>   That in our youth as dangerous a passion
> As e'er brought man and woman to the brink
>   Of ruin, rose from such a slight occasion,
> As few would ever dream could form the link
>   Of such a sentimental situation?
> You'll never guess, I'll bet you millions, milliards —
> It all sprung from a harmless game of billiards. (st. 100)

A superb masquerade of truth, the passage is not at all what it may appear: for concealed in its reference to a "harmless game of billiards" involving Juan and Lady Adeline is a private recollection of just such a game once played in 1813 by Lady Francis Wedderburn Webster and Byron.[14] But of course it was not a game of billiards at all, it was a game of hearts. In his wonderful description of the scene at the time to Lady Melbourne Byron observed that

> we went on with our game (of billiards) without *counting* the *hazards*
> — & supposed that — as mine certainly were not — the thoughts
> of the other party also were not exactly by what was our ostensible
> pursuit. (BLJ 3.134)

Lady Frances and Lord Byron played out the truth of what was happening in a masquerade. They were making love, not playing billiards, but the larger truth — as Byron's letters at the time show — was that the lovemaking was itself masked in a series of sentimental moves and gestures.

Don Juan pretends it is forecasting the lives of its fictional characters, but while its mind is on that game of billiards, it is on something else as well, a different game of billiards which was, like the other game, not simply (or "harmlessly") a game of billiards at all. The text here, in other words, executes a complex set of pretenses as a figure for the kind of truth which poetry involves.

That truth is best seen, perhaps, in the interpretive stanza which follows the one I just quoted.

> 'Tis strange — but true; for Truth is always strange,
>   Stranger than Fiction; if it could be told,
> How much would novels gain by the exchange!

> How differently the world would men behold!
> How oft would vice and virtue places change!
>   The new world would be nothing to the old,
> If some Columbus of the moral seas
> Would show mankind their souls' Antipodes. (XIV st. 101)

Once the mask of truth is exposed in the first stanza, we understand how the thematized discussion in this stanza is equally a mask of truth. This happens because the text has revealed itself as a dialogical event in which various parties may be imagined to be participating. We may imagine, for instance, Lady Frances reading this interpretation, or Lady Melbourne, or any number of Byron's "knowing" friends — or, for that matter, other readers, people who are unaware of the subtext. Each would have a different way of interpreting the interpretation. Furthermore, in each of those cases the authoritative interlocutor, let us call him "Byron", would undergo an identity shift, for the masque of truth would have to play itself out differently in each of the exchanges.

When truth comes in masquerade, propositions and states of affairs are called into question, are called to an accounting; and this includes the propositions and states of affairs which the poetical work itself appears to aver or define. Thus we might say of the poem, after Sidney, that it affirms and denies nothing — that it is, in our contemporary terms, a "virtual" reality. That idea is often represented in *Don Juan*, as when the text insists that it denies, admits, rejects, and contemns "nothing". But "in fact" the work denies, admits, rejects, and contemns various things, though sometimes — as in the text I am alluding to — it "in fact" denies, admits, rejects, and contemns "nothing". *Don Juan* is not a virtual reality, it is a particular deed in language. It is — to adapt a phrase from Bruno Latour's work — poetry in action.

What is "true" in the poem therefore always depends on context and circumstances. The concept of truth itself is revealed as open to change. What does not change, I think, is the structure in which knowledge and truth are pursued and (however provisionally or idiosyncratically) defined. This structure is rhetorical and dialogical — not an internal colloquy but a communicative exchange.

Finally, that structure is to be seen as a masquerade for two important reasons: that the parties to the exchange may be concretely defined, and that they may share each other's consciousness. The both/and form of the masquerade establishes the possibility of identity precisely by putting identity in question. In the same way, the pretense involved in the masquerade, being kept in the foreground, sets in motion an exchange of awarenesses from both sides of the encounter.

This is perhaps to put it all far too abstractly, so I close by asking you to imagine the billiard passage being read by different parties, and to measure the differentials of truth which would emerge through those readings. After you imagine it being read (say in 1823, the year the text was published) by Lady Frances, then imagine Lady Frances's husband, Byron's friend Wedderburn Webster, coming to the passage ten years after that billiard game at Aston Hall which, at the time, Webster knew nothing about. If you make the latter imagining you might recall as well — would Webster have recalled it? — that on the very evening of the perilous billiard game Webster, in company with his wife and his other guests, loudly proposed a bet to Byron "'that *he* [Webster] for a certain sum wins any given *woman* — against any given *homme* including *all friends* present[']'" (BLJ 3.136); and recall as well (would Webster have had the moral strength to make such a recollection?) that Byron "declined" the challenge with, as Byron put it, "becoming deference to him & the rest of the company". What *truth* Webster's reading would have involved — *however* he read the passage!

The point is that Webster's reading, though we do not have it or even know if it were made, is part of this text's imaginings — and *that* is an important truth about *Don Juan*, and about Byron's writing in general.

DISCUSSION

JEROME McGANN: . . . I feel a little odd, because there's no reason for most of you to be as invested in Byron's work as I am, and I'm not sure how familiar you are with the sort of thing he does, especially since Byron, although tremendously famous to the nineteenth century and even to the beginning of the twentieth century, in the English-American world of cultural studies, [has] come to seem an odd, if not distinctly marginal writer — as opposed to, for example, the centrality, especially in the Romantic frame of reference, of, say, Keats or Wordsworth.

DEBORAH THOMAS: Why do you think that is?

McGANN: Well, because of the dominance — the acceptance of the rules of the poetry of sincerity. Byron's poetry never is sincere in that sense. Even his most sincere poetry is always masked in some way, it always has a hidden secret. It's always looking at itself and *aware* that it is doing something according to a convention. Sometimes, he is the prisoner of the convention, even when he is aware that he is the prisoner of the convention; at other times he is not — he plays with the convention.

JAMES SHERRY: Where does this poetry of sincerity come from?

McGANN: If you read Keats's "On First Looking Into Chapman's Homer," or probably any Wordsworth poem, you know you are reading a poetry which takes itself seriously. John Stuart Mill said that this kind of poem had the structure of "overheard" musings. That was a very powerful structure, because it gave a kind of sacredness to the musings of the poet. The poetic space was not to be invaded by persons from Porlock. You were to stand back and sort of watch the poet in a vatic posture. The sign of the poem's sincerity was the fact that it was in communion with these higher things: you weren't paying attention to the world, you weren't talking, it wasn't a rhetoric.

Wordsworth just denounced Byron's work as factitious, as doggerel, as poetry that, — well remember Keats's famous comment on Byron: "Lord Byron cuts a figure but he is not figurative." It's a shrewd comment. What he means is that Byron is like the Elvis Presley of his day, or James Dean or something like that [laughter]. He's very conscious of the transactions that are going on between himself and his audience. Keats sees that, doesn't like it, and satirizes it. Byron has his own way of denouncing Keats, equally witty, perhaps, and to the point. He calls it the onanism of poetry, he says [Keats] is frigging his imagination, which is true.

SHERRY: Is Byron consciously going after the other Romantic poets? Is he trying to undercut them? And if so, where does he go wrong, how does he lose out in this duel?

McGANN: Yes he is. It seems to me it's a sociological problem. Byron very definitely is aware of his class situation [in the] special sense that he knows his class is doomed. It's like he's alive and already dead. So it's a kind of dialogue where he can look at a scene from outside. He has that special privilege of a person who no longer has any stake in what's happening. He knows it's a middle class world. The middle class and its power structures, its ideologies, are winning. That means that he will lose. He's resentful of that, [but] it gives him a peculiar kind of privilege.

At the beginning of his life, Byron imagined that he would in fact be an aristocrat to join this middle class revolution. He saw himself as a liberal reformer. He went into Parliament on those terms, and he quickly became completely disillusioned with this procedure. It took him about two weeks to realize that he was not cut out for this role [laughter]. So, he became cynical, nihilistic, with all the stylistic and poetic privileges that come with that.

Now, Keats, Wordsworth, and especially Coleridge, who is the main ideologue and cultural guru of Romantic theory, promulgate a series of aesthetic positions that Byron eventually will come to just vomit on [laughter]. But they are the positions that will dominate the theory of poetry for 150, 175 years, more, even to our own day. It seems to me only in the theater of postmodernism are these ideas actually beginning to crumble. Up until the Vietnam War, it seems to me they held perfect and total sway. They do not hold sway anymore.

SHERRY: I get the impression that Byron was a victim of who he was.

McGANN: It's hard to see him as a victim, though. I mean, he was so successful.

He's a byword, as everyone in this room must know, of the person who is beautiful, rich, successful. He couldn't be more famous or successful in all of his outward circumstances, and yet through all that he is unhappy. That's the meaning of Byronism: to be completely successful and beautiful and happy and so forth, and to have everything you want, and to be desperately unhappy [laughter].

NICK LAWRENCE: Was his fame due to the middle class?

McGANN: Yes. But it's a very complicated situation, because it's the Regency. When you think of Romanticism — if you have any reason to think about Romanticism [laughter] — [you're not likely to] think about the Regency, [about] Holland House and certain fast, upper class worlds. The Regency period was fast and immoral — as the movie says, "Live fast, die young, and have a good-looking corpse." That might have been its motto. [The Regency] was not at all the middle class world [with the] bourgeois set of parameters [that usually come to mind with] Romanticism. [But] Romanticism and the Regency were one, historically. And to that extent Byron is more truly of his age, whatever you want to call it, than probably any other writer at that time (except perhaps George Crabbe, whom nobody ever reads anymore) because he ran in both these worlds: the aristocratic and the middle class. . . .

[With the ascent of the middle class], the aristocracy either gets out, the way Byron sort of dropped out, or agrees to become middle class. But it is allowed to keep its trappings. You can stay rich, you can keep your houses, you can keep all the emblems, but you have to perform emblematic ideological functions within a middle class society. To me that is a definition of Victorianism. But Byron was nihilistic; he said no. It was a suicide.

LAWRENCE: I'm interested because he often championed early eighteenth century satire when none of the other Romantics did. If the Romantic ideology has dominated academia's reception of poetry, it has also managed to exclude a serious satirical tradition.

McGANN: Among the Romantic writers, Blake, Shelley, and Byron write satire. The others do not. Wordsworth specifically said he hated satire. Later on, Tennyson, famously, denounced satire as an immoral mode.

Part of what I was trying to talk about here was that style or that way with language: because satire has to be a public discourse, there have to be transactions across. In the poetry of sincerity, that's precisely what you forbid. You have an overheard situation. The poet looks in his heart, or her heart, and writes. And then you as a reader sort of look over the shoulder and participate: but you don't have an exchange going on between the writer and the reader, [which] is the nature of a satiric discourse.

LAWRENCE: Do you think it is class-related, as a genre? Because the early eighteenth century satirists were often middle class, too.

McGANN: I don't know whether I'd say it is class-related, but it is related to a desire to manage social dysfunctions. It's like system-management: You don't want satire as part of the system because Romantic satire says that the system is dysfunctional. It's not unlike the sort of thing we see in the Bush campaign now, or [with] Reagan, where it is imperative that you speak positively; if you want to speak negatively [it must] be within the limits of negativity.

One of the reasons why Byron is a kind of impossible writer through this whole period is that he really is a nihilist. Baudelaire knew it, and Nietzsche knew it. He was not assimilable. There are things that he will do that are simply not to be done. You write a poem about a siege and then the people who take the town come in and they start looking around and they are *not* raping [laughter]. The text is very careful to say: Now of course in all these kinds of situations there is always a lot of raping going on, but in *this* one no raping occurs. And then the "Widows of forty," who are in their houses, open their shutters and say, "When is the raping going to happen!" People read this in *Don Juan* and they were horrified. It's a kind of joke that you're not supposed to tell.

Because of this, because of this aspect of Byron's writing, it's difficult for the culture, seen in an Arnoldean sense, to take him to its bosom. You don't teach your children this kind of thing.

There is a lot of tastelessness in *Don Juan*, or what has been called tastelessness. I think that those passages are important to pay attention to. They are at the limit [which] the culture will not accept. Mostly, a culture wants to absorb its archive. It wants to take it and say: We love it, it's wonderful, here is another example of why our civilization is great. "The best that has been known and thought in the world." But Byron writes: "Wherefore the ravishing did not begin!" Arnold could not have said that [laughter]. But Benjamin would say that.

That kind of writing is not allowable in a framework that is defined by works like the *Biographia Literaria* or "The Preface" to *Lyrical Ballads* or any of Arnold's — the usual run of texts that stand behind curricular delivery systems of English-American poetry.

BRUCE ANDREWS: Speaking of cultural delivery systems, I wondered if you could talk about the consequences of the modernists' appropriation of Romantic ideology and specifically what happens as they repress this self-acknowledgement of conventionality, this self-acknowledgement of dialogue that you are talking about in Byron.

McGANN: Here I think there is a difference between early modernism and late modernism. I really think that there was a distinct break with the conventions of the nineteenth century, say in 1912 with *Tender Buttons* and all the early efforts of modernism. It seems to me that what you're describing doesn't happen until later. A good example of it would be — which I think is a great poem — "The Four Quartets." It's quite a late poem, but it illustrates what you're saying. As I read, say, *The Waste Land* — leaving aside the problem of its plot, which is kind of despicable — its local procedures, section-by-section, its Poundian procedures, seem to me tremendous.

ANDREWS: I was talking about the canon as you end up confronting it in the academy, in which a work like *Tender Buttons* obviously doesn't exist. I know very little about the reception of Byron among those figures in the early period of the century. That's what I was curious about, because if that acknowledgment of this communicational transaction, this economy of dialogue, was present, it seemed that it would have given all its practitioners a great resource to break through this self-enclosure that you get with the other Romantics.

McGANN: Byron was a tremendous lost resource.

It is in fact true that Pound began *The Cantos* with Byron and Browning in mind. Now Browning didn't have anything to do with Byron. They're very different, but stylistically they have a lot in common, at least from

Pound's point of view. The ur-*Cantos* are consciously aware of Byron's model. He then becomes more interested in Browning and the whole sort of Byron thing drops away. Remember the ur-*Cantos*, how consciously satiric they are. That drops away.

Pound was really interested in the problem of voice: how to get many voices operating within a poetical text. And he saw *Don Juan* as an obvious [model]. The problem is that when Byron manages voices, he is a [fantastic, seductive] mimic. And so, if you read the text through a Browning filter, you won't see the rhetoric that I've been trying to describe to you here.

STEPHEN LOWEY: In his era, do you think he was misread?

McGANN: The thing that most strikes me about the reception history of Byron is that the best readers I think were the readers who were reading him at the time. The reviewers, friends, enemies: they know what's happening. Many of them hate it, but then they should. Byron call out that hatred, deliberately.

DON BYRD: There are different kinds of time involved here. You probably wouldn't say that Wordsworth or Coleridge were best read by their contemporaries.

McGANN: No. Wordsworth said he had to create the audience for his poetry.

BYRD: To a certain extent they're writing in "eternity." I wonder if underlying the Romantic ideology isn't, in some sense, a kind of academic ideology, and I don't mean that in any narrow sense, but the remembering function — the way a culture remembers itself. The one thing that an academy can't do is confront the circularity of the issue of its sincerity about sincerity or its insincerity. This is the one place that that self-referential moment that Byron makes so much use of comes alive for an academic tradition: how sincere are we going to be about sincerity, and can we actually transmit the idea of insincerity in some way without involving ourselves in a logically impossible situation. So it seems to me that the kind of writing-in-time that Byron represents, that some of the fine poets in this room represent, perhaps isn't by its very nature the kind of poetry that is not going to be remembered, in that high sense.

McGANN: You raise an impossible question [laughter]. My way of trying to come to grips with that ultimate paradox is: I think of Arnold when he says that great writing, or whatever writing, is the best that has been known and thought in the world. And then, sixty years later, Benjamin says: "Every document of civilization is at the same time a document of barbarism." And it seems to me that if you are going to carry out academic writing, you have to carry it out under those two epigraphs. I don't know how you can do it. You somehow have to manage it, though. But you cannot give up either one. If you give up the Arnold, from a critical perspective what you do is you hand the archive over to people who really oughtn't to have it. So you cannot. There is some sense in which the best that has been known and thought in the world are these terrible things that Byron does, and yet if you assimilate them and pull them in and they lose their edge, then . . .

BYRD: . . . then they're not that anymore. And so exactly the self-referential paradox that Byron exploits so beautifully in a way makes it impossible for that to be done with a historical canon.

McGANN: I suppose in the end what happens is that contemporary writing rewrites the past.

One personal object I have in view at this point — I don't think I'll every write again about Romanticism, maybe here and there but not in any major way — [is] to be able to find a way — it's a pedagogical problem — to help people in a classroom situation to read the archive out of the frames of reference of contemporary writing.

CHARLES BERNSTEIN: It seems to me that a lot of what you are saying about the complexity of the issue of sincerity also applies to left and oppositional poetry: that much of this writing has not taken to heart, or to non-heart, the limits of the Romantic ideology of sincerity. Even in rejecting the vatic role of the poet, some of this writing nonetheless relies on unambiguously positive images and values of, say, a community, or various programmatic goals or aims. The Byronic mode that you propose here is as antithetical to that as it is to the Arnoldian values you discuss.

McGANN: No question. The writers that you are talking about are not interested in [the sort of considerations I'm suggesting here]. And they're right not to [be], I think, given that they believe about how writing ought to be carried out. [But] I believe they have miscalculated the social-historical situation. They have adopted an avant-garde position in a kind of traditional sense: that you can adopt an unproblematic negative position, and that by it you can actually have some political leverage. I think that's wrong.

Notes

1. For two good generic discussions of sincerity in Romanticism see David Perkins, *Wordsworth and the Poetry of Sincerity* (Cambridge, Mass., 1964); Lionel Trilling, *Sincerity and Authenticity* (Cambridge, Mass., 1972).

2. Romantic drama — for example, the drama of Coleridge, Shelley, or Byron — presents a special case of Romantic absorption. No literary mode is more socialized than the drama: this is an historical and an institutional fact which declares itself in the relation which persists between theatre and drama. The development of "closet drama" — which is what happened in Romanticism — clearly breaks down that relationship, or at least throws it into a crisis. The separation of the drama from the theatre is an index of Romanticism itself.

3. The charge was first raised in the controversy over Byron's "Poems on his Domestic Circumstances", and particularly in relation to "Fare Thee Well!". John Gibson Lockhart's comment on *Don Juan* — "Stick to *Don Juan*: it is the only sincere thing you have ever written" (quoted in Andrew Rutherford, ed., *Byron: The Critical Heritage* (New York, 1970), p. 183; hereafter cited as "Rutherford") — nicely captures the problem of Byron's sincerity, for that view exactly flew in the face of the dominant line of contemporary criticism. The latter would have been able to say much the same thing that Lockhart said, only for *Don Juan* it would have substituted *Childe Harold*.

4. *Lord Byron. The Complete Poetical Works*, ed. Jerome J. McGann (Oxford, 1980) V.614. All quotations from the poetry will be from this edition.

5. Soren Kierkegaard, *Concluding Unscientific Postscript*, trans. Walter Lowrie (Princeton, 1941), p. 171.

6. This is not to suggest that (say) *The Prelude* or "The Fall of Hyperion" are not themselves just as involved in communicative exchanges as Byron's work; on the contrary, in fact. Byron's work simply foregrounds these exchanges in a clearer way.

7. The annotations discussed here and below are to be found in the editorial notes for the relevant passages from *Don Juan*, in *Lord Byron. The Complete Poetical Works*, op. cit.

8. Byron extended the absurd textual situation by writing a (prose) response to Roberts which he signed "Wortley Clutterbuck" and published in *The Liberal*. For further details see William H. Marshall, *Byron, Shelley, Hunt and the Liberal* (Philadelphia, 1960), 86-88, 113-14.

9. *Byron's Letters and Journals*, ed. Leslie A. Marchand (London, 1973-82) V.93. Hereafter cited as "BLJ".

10. The text here is from *Lord Byron. Letters and Journals*, ed. Rowland E. Prothero (London, 1898-1901) IV.475.

11. See "The Book of Byron and the Book of the World," in my *The Beauty of Inflections. Literary Investigations in Historical Method and Theory* (Oxford, 1985), pp. 255-93.

12. See especially Byron's Preface to Cantos I-II where he ridicules the romanticism of the chivalric order.

13. See Canto V sts. 33-39.

14. For details see Leslie A. Marchand, *Byron. A Biography* (New York, 1957), I, pp. 413-18.

Canons and Institutions:
New Hope for the Disappeared

Ron Silliman

The diagnosis begins with symptoms: when Joseph Ceravolo died late last summer, I passed word of this to Joyce Jenkins, the editor of *Poetry Flash*, only to learn that, by her own account, she had never heard of this New York School poet. Lest this be thought of as merely an index of her own conservative aesthetics, or of her work habits as a reader, I had precisely the same response from Andrew Schelling, co-editor of the late lamented *Jimmy & Lucy's House of "K"*, a critical journal that was, among other things, seriously committed to exploring the legacy of the New American poetry. Both the *Flash* and *Jimmy & Lucy's* are publications with a visible impulse to comprehensiveness. Further, Schelling is a buyer for Moe's, the Berkeley used book emporium whose poetry collection is the largest and most comprehensive in the San Francisco region, and whose smaller new poetry book sampling is significantly broader in its representation of titles and authors of non-academic poetry than such stores as City Lights, Cody's or Black Oak Books. Now, while Ceravolo was something of a recluse as far as the poetry scene was concerned, and may never have given a reading on the west coast, he did publish at least four books, one of which, *Spring in This World of Poor Mutts*, was the first Frank O'Hara Award volume in 1968 and, as such, was published by Columbia University Press. Ceravolo's anthologizations include fourteen poems in the Padgett/Shapiro collection, *An Anthology of New York Poets*, a 1970 trade paperback from the Vintage division of Random House that was widely distributed and influential. When he died, this fine lyric poet was only 54. How is it that a writer with this public a career could have escaped the notice of two editors committed to knowing what is going on in contemporary poetry?

Ceravolo here is only a symptom and just one of far too many from which I could choose. To cite another, at the time of his apparent suicide in 1971, Lew Welch was a highly visible west coast poet who had signed a contract to bring out a large selection of work from his small press books with a New York publisher. He'd been teaching at the University of California extension in San Francisco for years, had been a poet in residence at colleges elsewhere, and was invariably included in any discussion of west coast poetry alongside his two old Reed College buddies, Gary Snyder and Philip Whalen. I recall Clifford Burke, a poet, printer and publisher active around San Francisco in the 1960s saying, only half-facetiously, that you couldn't trust a poet who kept Lew Welch's poems any further than arm's length from their bed. Today, the erasure of his influence on American verse appears almost complete. Only one of his books is still in print, and the place where we are most apt to come across the name Lew Welch now is in music magazines, a footnote in background pieces about the stepson whom he helped to raise, rock star Huey Lewis.

I am haunted by such disappearances as these from the public discourse and conciousness of poetry not only because of the manifest unfairness that results when the hard-earned labors of fine artists goes unnoticed and unrewarded, but because poetry itself is impoverished whenever and wherever its rich and diverse roots atrophy. A poetry without history strikes me as bordering on the unintelligible, its social value, its very use to us in our daily lives, seems to me questionable, and its fate a mere choice between oblivion and the still worse doom of perpetually repeating itself. Yet instances of literary forgetfulness such as these — and I could speak for days simply listing others — indicate that poetry, particularly in the United States, is a profoundly amnesiac discourse. The stereotypic figure of the artist unrecognized in her or his own time who emerges decades or centuries later to become one of the building blocks of western civilization is really the reverse side of a more ominous token: our society discards enormous quantities of that which it could benefit from, and this includes poetry. The shelf life of a good poet may be something less than the half-life of a styrofoam cup.

So I discover that in this sense I'm a conservative: I want to preserve the heritage that I believe American poetry can offer to writers and readers today. A heritage that I find to be both troubled and fragile in much the same way that America's wilderness is troubled and fragile, for the public disappearance of the work of a decent poet is not so terribly different from the extinction of a species in the wild. As a poet in the wild myself, each new absence alters my ecosphere and diminishes my existence.

Thus it is obviously not enough if what remains is merely a trace or record, some last remnant housed in a zoo, a museum or a library.

Ceravolo and Welch were both associated with that broad phenomenon known as the New American poetry, an ensemble of literary tendencies so populous and diverse that there is no evidence (and, indeed, no reason to believe) that the two ever met one another. Among the principle surface characteristics shared by most, though not all, of the New Americans, were a distaste for what they identified as academic poetry and a commitment to the the relationship between poetry and speech. A poem of Ceravolo's:

Drunken Winter

Oak oak! like like
it then
   cold some wild paddle
so sky then;
flea you say
"geese geese" the boy
June of winter
of again
Oak sky[1]

A poem by Welch:

Olema Satori

                            for Peter Coyote

Walking from the gate to the farmhouse,
Buzzards wheeling close as 20 feet,
to the West a ridge of
redwoods, fir, that
goofy Pt. Reyes pine,

walking on a dirt farm road,

small birds darting from the grass,
cows, burnt hills,
tongue of the Pacific,
ridge and the Last Ocean,
my boots,
walking,

"This is all you get,"
Olema said.

And I said, "That's
twice as much as I could ever hope for."

And Peter said,

"You can have the whole thing,
with fur covered pillows,

at the same price."[2]

Even from these two short poems, it is evident that such basic character-
istics as anti-academicism and a bias towards speech could mean radi-
cally different things to different poets. For many New Americans, to be
"nonacademic" meant not just an avoidance of the bureaucratization
that is an escapable feature of life in any large institution, nor even pri-
marily that — Welch, after all, taught, while Ceravolo had a book pub-
lished by a university press — but opposition to a received tradition of
Eurocentric closed verse forms. Even this last phrase is subject to multi-
ple interpretations: Welch's poem reflects influences from William
Carlos Williams to the descriptive emphasis of Japanese poetics to the
invocation of the Miwok figure Olema. His use of variable spacing be-
tween stanzas places Welch firmly in the Olson generation of the
Pound/Williams tradition. By contrast, Ceravolo's poem employs de-
vices right out of dada and surrealism, received Eurocentric culture but
with a twist, and Ceravolo's definition of speech is parataxis (the poem
is almost a list) rather than the discursive. Both works here seek and at-
tain closure, although hardly that of a rhymed sonnet whose regimented
iambics march stiffly to a predictable halt.

I could go on at length about why I think these poems and others like
them are valuable and worth our continuing attention. But what I want
to consider here instead is the broader issue of the erasure of these poets
(and so many others like them) from public consciousness even within
the cozy, almost claustrophobic confines of the poetry world. If the ab-
sence of disappeared poets such as Welch and Ceravolo are our symp-
toms, my diagnosis will hardly come as a surprise: the process of public
canonization, that which socially converts the broad horizon of writing
into the simplified and hierarchic topography of Literature, capital L, is
a disease. We could extend this metaphor further, and I will: the mecha-
nisms of public canonization are pathological and its proponents are
malignant. The question before us this evening is treatment.

I do not want this argument to be confused with a leveling of value, a
literary pluralism in which all poems would be equal for all readers. Val-
ue in writing is a definable relationship. What it is not, however, is a con-
junction between tradition and the individual talent. For in and of itself,
tradition is nothing: it does not exist. Tradition is a bibliography with im-
plications. It is what one has read and how one links these together.

And not just any One, but each and every specific person, that poten-
tially infinite regress of subject positions. Thus one cannot define value
without specifying the reader at stake: valuable for whom? to what end?
What does it mean that we valorize the Shakespeare of Caliban and Cor-
iolanus, of Othello and Shylock? How are we to judge the poetry of an
Ezra Pound, whose anti-semitism in a time of death camps was at least a
matter of conviction, compared to the mere murderous opportunism of
a Paul de Man? These are hardly idle questions. I *do* value the fact that
Pound dramatically extended the technical vocabulary and potential of
poets. I also value quite seriously his recognition that the social organi-
zation of writing, the simple act of putting poets and writers in touch
with one another, was an integral and necessary part of the literary proj-
ect. But I value *more* the poetry of Williams and Zukofsky, whose rather
different contributions to technique strike me as being as profound as
Pound's, even though both start with him as a point of departure, and
whose poems are not filled with the loathing, hatred and fear that is the
ultimate content of *The Cantos*.

The critique of public canonization is not therefore a denial of value
and a surreptitious defense of the status quo. Argued and read properly,
it should be an insistence on value's rootedness in the real life of the in-
dividual reader, not out of some abstract valorization of pure difference,
but because differentials are profoundly social. The process of public
canonization actually reverses this relation of value: in generalizing
(and, typically, dehistoricizing) aesthetic principles, public canonization
subjects the reader to them and obliterates social difference. The dis-
tinction between the individual subjective canon of a specific reader and
the social organization of public canons, such as we find in the Norton
anthologies and college curricula, lies precisely in the factor of power.
Public canons disempower readers and disappear poets. They are con-
scious acts of violence.

One of these acts of violence has been that which has incorporated a
few, and only a few, of the New American poets into a broader canoni-
cal history of the poetry of the 1950s and '60s. Interestingly — and it
would be a topic for an evening's discussion in itself — , one sector of
the New American poetry that has been excluded very nearly in its en-
tirety from the public canon is the genre of the lyric, the principle
domain of both Joseph Ceravolo and Lew Welch. Alan C. Golding, in his
excellent history of American poetry anthologies, offers this analysis of
the academic winnowing of the New American poets, following Robert
Lowell's distinction between the "cooked" poetry of the academy as rep-
resented by the Donald Hall, Robert Pack and Louis Simpson anthology,

New Poets of England and America versus the "raw" of Donald Allen's
New American Poetry:

> Two main kinds of anthology have emerged both as part of and
> in response to this pluralism. One is the teaching anthology. . . .
> The other continues the tradition of the revisionist anthology de-
> signed to increase awareness of particular noncanonical poetry. . . .
> It is not primarily intended for the classroom, even though it may
> be used there. The editors . . . are rarely scholars, more often poets
> — poets aiming not at the aesthetic and social orthodoxy that
> Bryant, Emerson, and Whittier promoted, however, but at hetero-
> doxy. From their inception, American poetry anthologies have
> usually pushed a political or literary program, so the contemporary
> revisionist anthology is not a new *kind* of anthology. Only recently,
> however, have the revisionist programs that reached a wide public
> discourse become so many and so vocal, and their number reflects
> the nonacademic anthologists' increased power to shift the canon.
> Many of these polemics from editors outside the academy have
> succeeded. Anthologists like [Donald] Allen have gained their
> favored poets admission into the canon. Allen's "raw" poets are
> represented almost equally with Hall, Pack, and Simpson's
> "cooked" poets in the major academic anthologies today.[3] Yet in
> one sense these poets enter the canon as the victims of a catch-22.
> Much of the interest and vigor of a book like *The New American Poetry*
> lay in its extracanonical status. The book's tone and contents as-
> sailed the walls of the academically established canon, eventually
> broke them down, and Charles Olson, Robert Duncan, and such
> were admitted. But when these poets became tentatively canon-
> ized, their combative rhetoric was assimilated by the cultural
> institution it assailed and lost much of its point. As numerous
> studies of the avant-garde show, this is the likely fate of any
> extracanonical group or individual seeking the acknowledgment of
> canonization.[4]

While Golding's analysis is perhaps the most thoughtful and balanced
consideration of the canonical fate of the New American poetry we have
yet had, it is problematic for several reasons. The public canon itself, at
least in this passage, is treated as though it were an entity, Pound's old
five-foot bookshelf, some thing or place to which one might aspire to be
admitted, rather than the ensemble of socially competing discourses it
more accurately is. There is an assumption that an insurgent editor such
as Donald Allen possessed the power *from without* to determine which

of the New Americans would get in through the gate. Yet when we note that the week Ceravolo passed away Helen Vendler published an article in the *New York Review of Books* on the work of Jimmy Schuyler, when we consider how Harold Bloom appropriated and conceptually tamed the poetry of John Ashbery for the academy, or how M. L. Rosenthal constructed his Rube Goldberg theory of confessional poetry so as to yolk the bubbling exuberance of an Allen Ginsberg to the ennui of Robert Lowell, or whenever we read that Michael Palmer, Charles Bernstein, Ron Silliman, Susan Howe, Bob Perelman, Clark Coolidge or Lyn Hejinian is the "best" (or maybe merely the least repellant) of the language poets, what we observe instead is a process by which those who seek to control access cynically pick and choose in the hope that their selection will prove the least disruptive to the current hegemonic balance. Certainly the longterm public success of the poetry of Denise Levertov had little to do with the significance of her poetry to her peers among the New Americans.

Most crucially, Golding asserts that the New American poets were "seeking the acknowledgment of canonization." While it is difficult to know what exactly is intended by that statement, it is worth considering the motivations underlying the New American project and other so-called avant-gardes. The explicit argument is that these poets sought (and ultimately settled for) access to an elite, rather than its displacement or something more re- or de-constructive in nature. If by "the acknowledgment of canonization" Golding means the continuation of one's work in print and the consciousness of a small (and identifiably specific) fraction of the reading public, and if the sole alternative to such acknowledgment is the total oblivion of literary amnesia, to become one of the disappeared, then of course the answer must certainly be Yes, that is at least among what was being sought, but this is such a weak definition of public canonization as to basically trivialize the question. Golding's own test of canonic success is the number of contributors from the Allen collection who appear in three teaching anthologies from Oxford and Norton, ranging from a low of eight to a high of fourteen. Yet *The New American Poetry* included Helen Adam, Brother Antoninus, John Ashbery, Paul Blackburn, Robin Blaser, James Broughton, Paul Carroll, Gregory Corso, Robert Creeley, Edward Dorn, Robert Duncan, Larry Eigner, Lawrence Ferlinghetti, Allen Ginsberg, Barbara Guest, LeRoi Jones, Jack Kerouac, Kenneth Koch, Philip Lamantia, Denise Levertov, Ron Loewinsohn, Michael McClure, David Meltzer, Frank O'Hara,

Charles Olson, Joel Oppenheimer, Peter Orlovsky, James Schuyler, Gary Snyder, Gilbert Sorrentino, Jack Spicer, Lew Welch, Philip Whalen, John Weiners, and Jonathan Williams — and this listing fails to name nine of the contributors. Of the 35 I've mentioned, at least 60 percent are absent from each of the three "major" anthologies Golding surveys. Thus Golding's own criteria serve rather to reinforce the rather different argument that what really took place was more a hegemonic academic strategy of divide and conquer via token incorporation against which the New Americans found themselves relatively powerless. A case by case examination of these poets would demonstrate that actual motivations differed substantially with each person. The most ambitious, Olson and Duncan, both perceived their own poetry as part of a larger project of constructing a new public canon, not necessarily more heterodox than that which they confronted, but rather utterly different and extending well beyond the borders of poetry, the ultimate purpose of which was to have served as the foundation for a new paradigm of knowledge and agency in social life itself. Some, such as Levertov, may in fact eagerly have sought access to the public canon as Golding suggests; but far more common appears to have been the desire of creating an entirely new poetic canon, an alternative tradition, the establishment of which was perceived as an end in itself, something to be shared rather than imposed on others. Still other New Americans cared not a fig one way or the other and just wanted to write their poems. Jack Spicer distrusted the entire process of public canonization and was perpetually satirizing and subverting it.

The fate of these writers suggests that the problem needs to be rethought. The epistemological ambitions of Olson and Duncan (whose projected master paradigms, incidentally, were not identical) have largely been reduced to signifiers of eccentricity. The construction of an alternative canon has been only partially successful: it is unable to keep poets such as Welch and Ceravolo, Steve Jonas and Harold Dull, Gail Dusenbery and d alexander, Frank Stanford and Carole Korzeniowski, John Gorham and David Gitin, Ronnie Primack and Sotere Torregian, Ebbe Borregaard and Lindy Hough from joining the ranks of the disappeared; it is doubtful that there are more than a dozen literature programs in the nation where the New American poetry is treated as more than a subaltern variant, an anticipation of the hippie anti-institutionalism of the 1960s; in the forty-one years since Olson published *Call Me Ishmael* and Duncan *Heavenly City, Earthly City*, the record of the New American poetry with regards to public awards such as the Pulitzer

Prize or the Yale Younger Poets has been just short of a complete shutout;
the history of grantsmaking bodies like the NEA and the Guggenheim
Foundation is nearly as bad. Like Duncan and Olson's counter-para-
digms, Spicer's subversions are discounted as marks of an eccentric.

Seen from the perspective of a relatively fixed and stable public can-
on, even if an imaginary public canon, the problem confronting any
outsider poetry is unsolvable, a double bind. Thus, poets and readers
committed to any alternative or marginalized poetics need to jettison
the question of canonization altogether as a frame for thinking through
strategies for the social survival of their work. My prescription for the
treatment of this disease of canonization is that poets must substitute an
institutional strategy for the canonic one. There is an absolute and es-
sential difference between contesting canons and contesting institutions.
The first strategy inescapably is forced to posit a legitimacy to the con-
cept of a public canon itself, something we have already demonstrated
to be false, whereas the latter is predicated on the reality that institutions
themselves are inescapable facts of a pre-existing social landscape. As
importantly, and as the historic fate of the New American poetry more
than luridly demonstrates, questions of canonicity, of the survival of po-
ets and poetry, are determined institutionally, rather than between texts
or aesthetic principles.

The questions which flow from this perception are reasonably obvi-
ous: *which* institutions? and what might the components be of an institu-
tional strategy? The answers are in fact problematic. The primary insti-
tution of American poetry is the university. In addition to its own prac-
tices, it provides important mediation and legitimation functions for vir-
tually every other social apparatus that relates publically to the poem.
The university provides the context in which many, and perhaps most,
poetry readers are first introduced to the writing of our time; it may
even be, as has sometimes been argued, the context in which the major-
ity of all poems in the U.S. are both written and read. Regardless of what
we think of the situation, the university is the 500 pound gorilla at the
party of poets.

It has not always been this way, and one could in fact trace the short
history of the poem's relationship to the university, dating back just 160
years to the 1828 appointment of Thomas Dale to the Chair of English
Language and Literature at London University, the very first professor of
English literature. (Ironically, his employment was part of an effort by his
superiors to legitimate and democratize writing by spurring on reading
societies and book clubs.)[5] Such a history would trace the growth of the
English Department and, within it, the first American literature specialists

at the end of the 19th century, the first conscious major project of canon construction in the U.S., *The Cambridge History of American Literature* in 1917, the increased presence of poets on campus as professors of academic disciplines, and the sequence of paradigm shifts that would occur in English departments starting with the hegemony of the New Critics during World War II. After all, many of the New Critics were themselves poets, although a significant element of their critique of their predecessors was that earlier philological, historical, biographical and sociological approaches had been insufficiently professional; close reading as the New Critics proposed it was a pseudoempirical advance toward a literary science. This strategy by the New Critics, however, combined with their conservative aesthetic commitments to leave them especially vulnerable to criticism later in the 1940s and early '50s by Romantic Revivalists, such as Northrup Frye and Geoffrey Hartmann, who argued that the New Critics not only had downgraded romantic poetry but were themselves not so terribly professional as critics, citing as evidence precisely the fact that many New Critics wrote poetry. I take it as no accident that this debate occurred exactly when the post-Second World War expansion of the educational system gave many English departments sufficient critical mass to set up the first generation of creative writing programs, nor was it an accident that the most influential of these programs, the Iowa Writers Workshop, was situated at one of the primary centers of New Criticism, the University of Iowa. One consequence of this debate was to cleave critical thinking about the poem, particularly among academics, from the writing of the poem itself. Thus academic poets of the 1950s, if they were serious intellectuals, moved away from criticism and theory toward translation as a socially acceptable means of thinking about the poem (for example, Richard Howard, W. S. Merwin, Richard Wilbur and Robert Bly). Creative writing programs in turn became entrenched sites not only for the orthodoxy of the conventional academic poem, that received Eurocentric tradition, but in order to establish their own marginal autonomy within the framework of English departments and literature programs skeptical of the professional claims of mere versifiers, developed into sites of hostility to theory and critique per se that have never been matched by the self-professed anti-intellectuals of the anti-academic tradition. Thus, in that brief moment during the late '60s when the Iowa Writers Workshop felt compelled to incorporate some tokens of the New American tradition, it made very calculated choices in temporarily employing Ted Berrigan and Anselm Hollo.

As we have seen, to be anti-academic meant different things to different New American poets. However, with the exceptions of Olson, Duncan, Spicer and possibly Ginsberg, it seems evident that the category was largely a canonical, rather than an institutional one. Black Mountain College, precisely because it had been designed (and marginalized) as an alternative university some 15 years before Charles Olson became rector there, never was in a position to serve as more than an exemplary Other to a rapidly growing educational establishment after World War II — that it collapsed economically and closed during a period of enormous expansion for the American academy is an index of its impact on education (although not on the arts). The original Poetics Program at New College of California — not to be confused with the current program there — was a similar example of a counter-curriculum too little, designed too narrowly, and situated too far from academic sites of power to have much impact, although (as I will return to later) it offers us with the best strategic example to date. The program at the Naropa Institute is likewise marginalized. But for the vast majority of New American poets, anti-academicism, because it was grounded in opposition (and some horror) to the conservative aesthetics that had become identified with the New Critics, meant no organized counter-strategy whatsoever, beyond avoiding committee work whenever possible if one had a teaching job.

There's an analogy here between 20th century political life in this country and the quandary faced by oppositional poetic tendencies in the United States with regards to the academy. For decades, the American left has been bedeviled by the problem of how to institutionalize its victories, and thus how to sustain victory of any sort whatsoever. Civil rights, a woman's political control over her own body, preventing America from intervening militarily in the life of other nations — these are all instances where the left can be said to have had some success on a national scale over the past thirty years, and yet it is evident just how tentative, sporadic and ultimately reversible these successes are. They prevail only so far and so long as they are institutionalized. To deal with the institutional *political* process in this society is to be faced with sobering alternatives: either one works in and through the Democratic party, an entirely corrupt institution — and one, incidentally, that is noticeably weaker than the academy — either directly or indirectly (for example, through single issue organizations) or one works through marginalized third party formations that are structurally prohibited from achieving any substantial lasting power whatsoever; if one pays attention to history, it is painfully obvious that there is no such thing as a third party alternative in the United States, and indeed that a third party politics is not a politics at all, but rather a substitute in the place of a politics that may appear to be entirely corrupt and inevitably corrupting. If one chooses to avoid electoral politics, however, which may appear to be a personally "cleaner" alternative perhaps, one must then select from one of three alternatives: (1) to abandon politics altogether (and, in a strict sense, *polis* as well) and thus any hope of enacting change in society at any level; (2) to wait and work for a revolution that may never come, given that revolutions have only occurred in the transition from pre-bourgeois to bourgeois states and thus may be specific to one historical moment, a narrow window through which the U.S. and Western Europe have long since passed; or (3) to attempt change at cultural, rather than political (by which I mean institutional) levels, where accomplishments, while real, are infinitely more fragile because they can be easily negated by a reaction at the institutional level.

Thus the left turns to the Democratic Party much the way outsider poets face the academy, with all the emotional conflicts one might expect of a starving person trying to pick edible scraps of nourishment out of a pile of vomit. It makes people crazy, leaves the articulate stammering with frustration, and has caused numerous explosions of seemingly inexplicable fury directed at almost random targets. Nobody began to write poetry, this loveliest of addictions, in order to wade through puke, but, as Jack Spicer phrased it in the last line of his final poem, people *are* starving. I would suggest that this double-bind is at the very least one contributing factor in the self-destructiveness we find so prevalent in the world of poetry, whether that manifests itself with a gun, the way it did in the cases of Lew Welch, d.a. levy and Richard Brautigan, or more slowly with a bottle, the way Spicer and Darrell Gray died. If the broadest outlines of my argument are couched in the medical metaphor of symptom, diagnosis and treatment, it is because real people are dying horrible, alienated deaths partly as a result of the conditions of poetry in our society. Outsider poetics has been stuck for decades at the moment of diagnosis. It is time to begin treatment.

Because the impact of the academy as an institution on poetry is so conflicting for so many writers, and because the academy is also pervasive and inescapable, most outsider poets respond to it privately. They may work in it or consciously avoid doing so, and, if the former, they can operate all the way from aggressive and successful careerists to perpetually bungling part-timers who sabotage their every attempt to gain a foothold of vocational security, but they do so *as individuals*, silently and without anything approximating a collective response to this central institution of their lives as writers.

It is just the incoherence of this collective response in the face of an omnipresent mediating institution that calls to mind the left's equally pained relation to the Democratic Party. The diverse tendencies of the left can even be categorized with some precision just by their stance toward the Democrats. Consider, for example, the difference between the Democratic Socialists of America (DSA), perhaps the largest group on the American left, and democratic socialists who situate themselves more in the Trotskyist tradition, such as the American organization that calls itself Solidarity. DSA, which has strong ties to labor at the leadership level, refused to endorse any candidate in the 1984 primaries, because many key members were working for Walter Mondale, while others supported Jesse Jackson. Virtually all of the tendencies and grouplets that were to form Solidarity supported Jackson in '84 precisely because they saw his campaign as an alternative to traditional Democratic Party politics. Solidarity theoreticians such as Mike Davis castigated DSA for its failure to support Jackson. In 1988, however, with no other candidate even remotely in the progressive tradition, DSA endorsed Jackson early and provided his campaign with a significant number of workers. DSA, in short, saw and used Jackson in 1988 as a road *into* the Democratic party. Solidarity also supported Jackson, but saw the Dukakis nomination and Atlanta compromise as predictable sell-outs of the working class, the poor, women, gays and ethnic minorities. Misreading Jackson's own motivations completely, they conceived of his campaign as an opportunity to fragment the progressive wing off of the Democratic Party toward some unnamed new formation, and their slogan at the time was "Bolt, Jesse, Bolt!" The ultraist puritans on the Trotskyist spectrum, the Sparticist League, saw Jackson as little more than a front man for a racist and corporatist Democratic Party. Yet John Judis, columnist for the independent socialist weekly *In These Times*, blasted DSA for its endorsement of Jackson; in Judis' view, Jackson was the ultraleftist and DSA's work in his behalf was a means of playing at participation in the Democratic Party, while actually isolating itself off from any serious hope of influence. The range of positions here is telling. The left, because it isn't a unified subject and so doesn't have a single, clearly agreed upon sense of its motivation or goals, relates to this ambiguous institution of the Democratic Party in such a fashion as to minimize whatever potential impact it could have. The difference between the left's relationship to the problem of an inescapable mediating institution and that of outsider poets, however, is that the former has at least thought and argued long and hard about the issue.

To follow this analogy a little further, the functional relationship between the mediating institution and a community of oppositional poetry is profoundly *not* the same as that of the Democratic Party to any socialist tendency. The problem facing poets is not how to either "take

over" or even necessarily alter the institution as a whole (although I
wouldn't want to preclude that), but rather more one of that institu-
tion's relationship to it as a specific, identifiable community. In this
sense, the question confronting outsider poetry much more closely ap-
proximates the Democratic Party's relationship to any single issue or-
ganization or cause, what the Habermasians and Foucaultians like to
characterize as New Social Movements and the Reaganauts long ago de-
graded as special interests.

While the range of stances toward mediating institutions taken by so-
cial movements is no less various than those of self-conceived political
tendencies such as socialists, the record with regard to the institutionali-
zation of their positions is not. Each of the left victories I mentioned a
moment ago were predominantly the work of social movements.[6] The
history of movements like these is virtually unanimous on the point that
all tend to gravitate over time toward mediating institutions, regardless of
what their original stance toward them may have been, or else they suffer
defeats and dissolve outright. One incidental result of this process is that
a small but significant number of professional politicians are themselves
veterans of social movements; a larger group of professional politicians,
while not veterans of these movements, articulate (and may even perceive
themselves as the institutional conduits for) their causes. This, I should
note, also means that the anti-electoral left conceives of new social move-
ments as filled with opportunists, easily bought off, with little conscious-
ness of the deeper issues underlying even their own causes.

I have suggested throughout this talk that a feature of mediating institu-
tions is in fact that they are inescapable. All forms of organizing that at-
tempt to bypass, deny or avoid them are, I believe, social forms of psycho-
logical denial built out of an inner need to reject internal conflict and
complexity. That sounds harsh, but denial of this sort, we should remem-
ber, is a basic and healthy defense mechanism for anyone confronted with
oppressive circumstances. What is not healthy is to perpetuate this state
indefinitely. The situation with regards to writing is essentially identical.

So the question here is treatment: what is to be done?

Obviously, continued forms of denial are not to be recommended.
This would include not only pure avoidance, either on an individual or
a group level, but also the more complicated, passive-aggressive modes,
such as Andrei Codrescu's trashing of the academy and academic poe-
try in the introduction to his anthology *Up Late: American Poetry Since
1970*, while working as a professor himself and including poets in his
book such as William Hathaway whose sole discernible relationship to
the writing otherwise contained in that volume is the fact that he was a

colleague of Codrescu's on the LSU faculty in Baton Rouge.

It is even time to say out loud that there is nothing inherently wrong with being an academic poet. Descriptively, that term is an even worse generationalization than the misnomer language poet. It identifies the site of their practice, perhaps — although not always — and possibly tells us a little, although not much, about the writer's subjective canon, but it is ultimately silent with regards to many more critical issues, such as the role of the reader, the function of history, or the potential and responsibilities of the poem. The term academic poetry inhibits those who use it from developing a fully nuanced reading of the very writing it seeks to identify. How are we to distinguish a Bill Knott or a James Tate from a Timothy Steele or a Frank Bidart? How is James Merrill different from Alan Dugan? Where does one situate a Wendell Berry, a Denise Levertov or a Bill Merwin? In what ways might Jorie Graham and John Hollander conceivably be the same? In practice, the category "academic poetry" has been a mechanism for evading the very topic it names, and in this it has served as an inverse parallel to the term language poetry. Both rubrics deserve to be relegated to the dustbin of history.

In place of the homogenizing category of academic poetry, what we need now is a far more critical and specific taxonomy of the divergent writings subsumed by that term. We need to be able to distinguish a Henry Taylor from a Dave Smith from a Brad Leithauser from an Amy Clampitt. We need to understand how poets like Peter Wild, James Scully, Michael Harper, Howard McCord and Robert Peters fit into a possible reading of the broad terrain of American verse, and for some of the very same reasons that the work of Joseph Ceravolo and Lew Welch must not be allowed to disappear. We need to be able to read a poem like Vikram Seth's *Golden Gate* in a way that will enable us to understand how its use of narrative techniques derived from mass culture models such as the sitcom differs, if in fact it does, from a style predicated on the cartoon or underground comic, such as Edward Dorn's *'Slinger*.

So abandoning the term "academic poetry" is a move not in the direction of disengagement, but towards a fuller, more deeply critical investigation. (Some "academic" poets *should* be threatened by this loss of their name.) This is one step towards addressing the problem of dualisms in poetry. But it is only that, one step, and by itself not nearly enough. Abandonment of the category of the academic is simply the first moment in the articulation of a strategy aimed at the institutions of poetry, beginning with the academy. By definition, such a strategy must be institutional, rather than canonic, aesthetic or theoretical.

Also by definition, an institutional strategy requires a position from

which the institution itself can be addressed. Here, of all the oppo-
sitional tendencies in poetry, language poetry, so called, finds itself in an
interesting situation. Although historically self-defined within an "anti-
academic" tradition, its long-term engagement with social, aesthetic and
linguistic theory provides language poetry with both a vocabulary and
potential mechanisms for posing the institutional question that, for ex-
ample, the anti-theoretical college workshop tradition lacks. This theo-
retical involvement has for good reason attracted the attention of main-
stream academic critics as diverse as Andrew Ross and Jerome McGann,
a point that the anti-theoretical detractors of language poetry compul-
sively reiterate.

Yet, also because language writing, so called, has been situated within
the anti-academic tradition, its practitioners operate, with a few note-
worthy exceptions, almost entirely at the professional margins of the
academy, present perhaps but in the capacity of part-timers, visiting fac-
ulty, editors, secretaries, grants writers, librarians or as members of de-
partments other than literature or English. If anything, language poetry
to date has had a far deeper penetration of the computer industry than
it has of the academy. The exceptions to this marginalization, who can
be counted on the fingers of one hand after an industrial accident, are
people who in every instance but one were hired *prior to and/or in spite of*
their identification with this literary tendency.

The ambiguity created by this double-edged relationship to the acad-
emy is itself an opening, an opportunity for intervention. At one level,
and I mean this both literally and non-perjoratively, language poetry is
already integrated into the institutional discourses of the academy, even
if this penetration is thus far marginal. In part, this is because the larger
renaissance of theory (of which language poetry itself can be viewed as
one expression) is a profoundly institutional phenomenon, one that
(like language poetry) can be traced directly to the political culture of the
1960s, and especially to the collapse of that culture after 1968. On
another and far more pertinent level, however, language poetry is one
of the very few contemporary literary-theoretical tendencies whose fo-
cus and commitment are explicitly centered *outside* of the academy.[7]
While it would be a false dualism to suggest that the poetry commu-
nities of the major coastal urban areas, the predominant sites for the
practice of language writing, are any more "real" than the audiences of
undergraduates and MFA students elsewhere, the fact is that the literary
scenes of New York, San Francisco, San Diego and Washington are less
transient than the constantly recycled population of college students,
and this contrast serves as much to foreground the distinction as it does

to suggest explanations as to both why and how the broader anti-academic tradition has managed thus far to survive.

The double-edged relationship of language poetry to the academy foregrounds one of the primary features of that institution: the university is not a monolith, but rather an ensemble of competing and historically specific discourses and practices. This is something that at least some leftists have understood since Fred Block's "The Ruling Class Does Not Rule" first appeared in 1977.[8] Rather than being reducible to any reified identity, for example that of "the enemy," the academy is a ground, a field for contestation. This being the case, the question of treatment, of intervention, of an institutional strategy opens up into a set of further questions:

> one, for which this talk is an attempt to begin to sketch
> out an answer, is What is the positionality of language po-
> etry and other oppositional poetic tendencies *within* this
> ensemble of practices;
> a second, even more important issue is that of goals, What
> would such an institutional strategy seek to accomplish,
> both within the institution and more broadly;
> lastly, What strategies are most appropriate to achieve
> these ends?

Many of the goals of an institutional strategy are implicit in the diagnosis itself. The delegitimation of the public canon is the most obvious. This in turn will require the legitimation of the social specificity of readers and the institutionalization of difference, a project for which there are many potential allies. One historical adjunct of this increased pluralism is that the strategy by which most English departments and literature programs represent the late 20th century, by hiring specialists in pre-Second World War modernism who then "cover" the next forty-five years with only marginal sympathy or understanding, must be called into question. Every literature program should have one and preferably several specialists in the period 1945-70, the time of the New American poetry.

In addressing the canonization process per se, the question of the status of the teaching anthology itself needs to be posed, from the Norton collection on down. Even the most well-intended teaching anthology, simply by virtue of containing its subject between two covers, insinuates a public canon. In turning an ensemble of practices into a unified table of contents, always with an implicit narrative through which somebody wins, teaching anthologies are means of "dumbing down" the complexity of a subject. By contrast, any period would be better represented by a series of what Alan Golding terms polemic anthologies just because

their distinctness conveys the reality of contestation and partiality inher-
ent within a reading — it's a positioned presentation. The raw and the
cooked should be different books, so to speak, so that students might
learn more about themselves by discovering which they prefer. One
need only look to the loss of focus that occurred when the Donald Allen
anthology, *The New American Poetry*, was revised by the late George
Butterick into a teaching version called *The Postmoderns* to see that the po-
lemic function of *any* anthology, its argument, is a primary dimension;
teaching anthologies do not lose this aspect, they conceal it so as to ma-
nipulate readers. Thus the teaching anthology is an ideological — not
an educational — device.[9]

Beyond the question of canonization lies the problematic tension be-
tween theory and practice in poetry. Typically, its expression has been
couched in the terms of poetry versus critique, and, as we have seen, a
substantial portion of the evolution of both workshop anti-intellectua-
lism within the academy and the anti-academic counter-tradition out-
side of the university can be traced to stances adopted in response to the
history of this distinction. We must remember, however, that dualisms
exist at the site of a gap, and that gaps occur at the point where continui-
ty is felt as contradiction. Difference may be all, as some versions of
post-structuralism seek to argue, but difference is always also a social
construct. Here, oppositional poetics clearly have a vested interest in
challenging the chasm set up between theory and practice in poetry, not
only because it is an artificial and inaccurate boundary — every poem,
each trope, each linebreak has its epistemological, ontological and
socio-political implications (although it is important to keep in mind
that these are not transhistorically inherent within the device, but rather
specified by a contextuality that shifts with every reader and each ap-
pearance of a given text) — but also because oppositional poetics have a
vested interest in challenging this gap since it is the precise distinction
upon which the English department itself has been founded. The gap
between theory and practice, that apparent but unreal contradiction, is
ultimately what Jack Spicer intended by the term English Department
itself, a phrase he uttered solely as a curse.

Many poets have understood for some time that no such gap exists.
Williams' dictum of "no ideas but in things," after all, can be read as an
endorsement of ideas embodied in practice, and *Spring & All* is a powerful
argument for this position. The portraiture of Stein's *Tender Buttons* is ulti-
mately no less theoretical than Pound's *Cantos*. Olson's use of spatial nota-
tion, a verse technique Robert Duncan called composition by field, is no-
where more visible than in his theoretical masterwork, "Proprioception."

Like the teaching anthology, the poem without theory exists solely as a concealment, the hiding of a primary dimension for the purpose of causing its effects to seem "natural" or "self-evident."[10] As I said earlier, my argument for pluralism is not to be misconstrued as a leveling of values, and I would gladly judge any poem or poetics by how it both constitutes and relates to its readers in terms of such a manipulative dissociation. That is why some "academic" poets deserve to feel threatened by an institutional strategy that takes them more seriously, rather than simply rejecting them out of hand. Some "anti-academic" poets, like Tom Clark and Andrei Codrescu, have every reason to feel likewise.

If the distinction between theory and practice is identified as illusory, the institutional role within the academy of the creative writing program is called into question. If the original rationale behind these programs was to keep one side of that equation, theory, from organizationally overwhelming the other, practice, it has achieved this only by lobotomizing one sphere of poetic activity, isolating it from the other. In actuality, many if not most workshop teachers now include reading as an integral component of their classes, although the supplementary nature of this inclusion at least partially reinforces the hierarchy of values inherent in the distinction itself. Here I would propose, as a partial strategy for the institutional erasure of this gap, a curricular strategy quite close to the original Poetics Program at New College of California. This master's degree program was an alternative to the normative creative writing MFA in that there were no classes that could be called writing workshops. Poets instead were taught to read and think about poetics. There were classes focusing on specific aspects of form, such as number, as well as others that looked at various traditions, periods, and the literatures of other nations and cultures. While the program had its own quirks, such as a bent toward theosophy and sufiism, its mission of creating poets (not critics) through the study of poetics was an embryonic model of what a serious institutional writing program might aspire to. One step within a broader institutional strategy thus should be to establish similar programs elsewhere, and/or to move existing MFA "tanks" further in this direction. As a tactical move, this intervention may be the key to treatment in that it addresses the larger issue at the most institutional level.

Beyond this, however, lies the question of the relations of oppositional poets to the broader institution, whether or not these poets are vocationally positioned within it. It is worth noting that our two primary goals, deconstructing public canonicity and rejoining theory to practice (and practice to theory), are themselves identifiable components of the

programs of other tendencies within the academy. Nor should it be sur-
prising to discover that each could be traced to at least some version of
post-structuralism, broadly conceived.[11] Within the competing practices
we find contesting within the academy, there are many possible allies.
Obviously there are the critics and theoreticians of other literary tradi-
tions and tendencies which have been excluded from the public canon,
often for reasons of race, gender, class or region.

There are also critics who conceive their own writing as having, as
Barrett Watten would phrase it, linguistic values, critics, that is, who seek
to insert practice into their own theory. These academicians who per-
ceive their own theoretical work as possessing an inherent value are only
one segment of a larger contingent quite visible within the university
that takes theory itself to be a primary, if not *the* primary, function of the
English department. There is, however, a distinction to be drawn here
between those who would argue this because they are, in their own ways
and from their own historical and institutional positions, working their
way back toward an integration of theory and practice, from those oth-
ers (probably more numerous) who argue the primacy of theory merely
as a mechanism for personal institutional dominance.

The issue recalls a debate between leftists with regards to their role in
the Democratic Party. Is the function of an intervention for the purpose of
"taking over" the institution, the hegemonic acquisition of power as such,
or is it instead a mechanism for reorganizing and even strengthening
the institution in question? Mainstream Democrats are deservedly wary
of working with ultraleftists whose participation is simply a moment
within a larger program, the goal of which might be the fragmentation
or dissolution of the Democratic Party itself. Because the treatment I am
suggesting here is both poetry and reader centered, and because it is
predicated upon a recognition of the structural organization of Ameri-
can verse via the mediating institution of the academy, a program of
pure negativity would be self-contradictory and perhaps self-destructive.
Strengthening the position within the university of those academics who
are concerned with the integration of theory and practice within their
own writing, for example, would bolster the institution, even if (or, per-
haps I should say, even as) this divides them from the opportunists and
power addicts who've found theory a convenient vehicle for self-promo-
tion. Here the potential divisiveness of any strategy of intervention has
positive implications for the academy.

Divisiveness is not just an issue in the case of an intervention, but an
integral aspect of it as a strategy for those outsiders who would participate
in the institution at whatever level, not in the search for some sinecure,

but to reorganize the ensemble of academic practices. Redirecting crea-
tive writing programs toward poetics, for example, will require a break-
down of massive amounts of hardened institutional inertia. Unfor-
tunately, but unsurprisingly, a program like that at San Francisco State,
where all but one of the tenured faculty are white males, and where only
one or two even sporadically publish in any genre whatsoever, is not
that exceptional. A pluralization of the poetry publishing progams of
university presses — a level of the academy that is even more arthritic
and senile than MFA programs — will have to begin with the de-
legitimation of what is presently being done. That the preservation of
the work of poets such as Lew Welch, Jack Spicer and Paul Blackburn
has fallen entirely into the hands of independent small publishers con-
stitutes a fundamental refusal of responsibility on the part of the state.
This is not to suggest that the conservative-to-reactionary poetry prog-
rams of such schools as Pittsburgh, Wesleyan, Princeton and Yale
should not exist, but that they must be contextualized in terms of the
failure of these schools and others to present the full range of what has
been written in recent American history.

   For the progression of this disease, which I will now christen as ca-
nonic amnesia or Vendler's Syndrome, is not to be checked, let alone
treated, without such contextualization as is possible only through the
concerted *and collective* effort on the part of not just a half dozen commit-
ted individuals, but virtually an entire generation of outsider poets and
their allies, an institutional intervention that has virtually no precedent
in American literary history. But without this intervention, aesthetic
practice raised to an institutional strategy, the contributions of writers
such as Lew Welch, Joseph Ceravolo and literally hundreds of others,
ourselves included, can only fade into oblivion.

DISCUSSION

ROGER HORROCKS: It seems to me that it's not only a matter of
getting the poets into the canon, not only a matter of getting poets onto
the staff. The most common phenomenon is the way in which almost
anybody can be read within the hegemony of readings. After a few
years, Olson is accepted into the canon and is simply read like Pound
[or Eliot]. And the same with theory. Roland Barthes is now just another
great French writer.

   So it seems to me that my experience [in New Zealand], trying to work
on the edges of the academy, is that you can't control the big structures
which actually control the range of readings. You [can] start to get

utopian and think maybe we can take over the whole institution, which maybe is going to happen twenty years down the line. Or you tend to get reduced to talking just about those little institutional problems, which are important, but you end up just discussing structures. But the big issue, which I've never solved, is the issue of reading, and the way in which reading is a reflection of a hegemony of the political power struggle.

RON SILLIMAN: I don't think anyone should propose, should imagine, should hallucinate, the idea that there is such a thing as either socialism or literacy in a single classroom, let alone in a single curricular strategy. What I do think there is is the possibility of linkage between the individuals within a faculty, between the individuals within different programs, between individuals across campuses.

I think it is quite interesting that this phenomenon that I've become linked with, called "language poetry," actually has this bicoastal presence, quite unlike any of the tendencies within the New American poetry. It has managed to involve people who interact over broad ranges of distance geographically. I take that as a sign that people are more conscious about the need to work with each other today than people were thirty years ago. How far that can be carried and what can be accomplished within that [shrugs] . . . — I'm essentially a skeptic: the problem of hegemonic institutions and the state is an omnipresent shadow with which one has to struggle in order to find what light can be discovered at all.

NICK PIOMBINO: I would like to underline one or two things that I thought were most useful in terms of the dilemma you were talking about: which is really the relevance of poetry; or how are we as poets and readers to claim its relevance, its application, and its use to us? How are we to express that? How are we to manifest it in some way?

You pick a very clear symptom of the presence of something that's not too well about the current state of our poetry when you remark that someone like Ceravolo or Lew Welch is forgotten so quickly. Your use of psychological defenses as a way of analyzing the current situation was really very acute. For example, you speak about denial, and you give very good examples; but you could have also mentioned splitting, which I think would really specify the problem.[12] I couldn't agree with you more that to solve a problem means to diagnose it correctly. In other words, if we don't really detect where the problem is we don't have any hope in the world of getting things better. When you start talking about something like splitting I think you are really putting your finger on where the problem might be. You could apply the splitting notion to the term "academic poet" because when we say "an academic poet" what we are really saying is "a bad poet." (The poet, for example, doesn't have to be in the academy.) Using terms to split the bad from the good is really the clearest way to know that the phenomenon of splitting, which is an *unconscious* defense, is actually happening.

SILLIMAN: I got laughter in this room at three or four points where the humor was predicated on an assumption of exactly that split. I think there are "bad" poets in both traditions, I think there are "good" poets in both traditions. I have a bias, obviously, as to which of those I think have more "good poets per capita."

PIOMBINO: I hate to say this, it pains me to say this, but I believe that if we are going to have poetry be healthier, we really have to give up the idea of bad poetry completely. In other words, if we believe that poetry has a use, an overall use, we have to find its use to a person who writes it even badly.

SILLIMAN: I think you're right. I think the question then becomes one of efficacy: this is an effective poem because it works for the poet; this is a more effective poem because it works for the poet and a group of others. In those terms, I have certainly written poems that were not effective for me, so I know that occurs.

There is this really weird schizophrenia in "writing about writing" in our time between the level of discourse which is theoretical and which is therefore elegant and interesting to look at, and that is which is infrastructural, which shows up in publications from COSMEP or Poets & Writers, or from the fifty state arts councils around this country, the sort of article that tells you which margin to put the staples on in small press things, and so on. It's very difficult for anybody, myself included, to recognize that the division between those two meta-genres is in fact a serious problem: one needs to be able to talk theoretically about staple placement in a fashion that is not simply sarcastic.

The shifting from the canonical to the institutional strategy represents an attempt to try and rub these two very disparate things together, which is why I brought what I thought of as being the least pleasant example of this problem in the world, the Democratic Party, into the talk — I thought its sheer repulsiveness would force the issue.

ALAN DAVIES: I wonder, Ron, whether you can solve institutional problems by looking at institutions. Or even whether you can solve problems by looking at the problem. And I wonder whether you can answer these questions by taking sides.

SILLIMAN: I don't think that the sole answer to this whole problem of institutions is institutional. [But] there is a large part of [the answer] which is unavoidably institutional.

I don't mean to fall into crude empiricism here [laughter]. In any analytical process which is a stage in a larger process, you have to begin somewhere. I began not in a random place exactly, but not necessarily a central place.

You cannot address problems without in fact asking questions, without converting them into questions. To take a "real world" situation, someone with a drinking problem has to recognize that one doesn't have control, in order to develop a critical distance on the problem and to begin to create a sequence of, literally, steps by which one then answers that problem. But the only way one can address that problem is to remove it from oneself by turning it into that kind of question. So in fact I think you always go through that step.

DAVIES: What about just stopping? In other words, why do you want to predicate the need for this kind of . . .

SILLIMAN: I guess because I don't think the mind and body are separate.

DAVIES: . . . process, instead of saying, you know, kind of, fuck that and doing the next best thing. Why think about it so much? In other words I see you — I like following your thought, but I see you institutionalizing yourself as you think and as you communicate in the way that you do, as you generate ideas in the way you do, and as you present them in this place to this body of people. And I don't like to see that happen.

ANDREW LEVY: What is the value or efficacy of the kind of exposition that you are using tonight? So much of the theortical writing that is being published in different public forums such as your collaborative piece in *Social Text* is basically very traditional discursive essays. It's the same style that you can read almost anywhere: it's just that the subject is different. So, what is the value of that, rather than going ahead and displaying what you are talking about, even within a theoretical or critical forum. There seem to be fewer places now that welcome that kind of alternative prose or critical thinking.

SILLIMAN: It is question of the direction of the writer's intention toward a specific audience and that audience is in fact socially different from place to place, magazine to magazine, even with regards to a single text. Different texts for different audiences. If you don't take the audience into account, writing becomes a solipsistic gesture. I have to stop to ask what the writer thinks they are doing in those terms.

The readership for $L=A=N=G=U=A=G=E$ was no less specific than that for *The Tenderloin Times*[13]. And each very specifically factored in the reader.

NOTES

1. *An Anthology of New York Poets*, ed. by Ron Padgett and David Shapiro (New York: Vintage, 1970), p. 284.

2. *Ring of Bone: Collected Poems 1950-1971* (Bolinas: Grey Fox, 1979), p. 123.

3. In a footnote to this sentence, Golding cites the numbers included from each book in three such "major academic anthologies": the New Americans are represented 31 times, the academics 37. In an election, this 45 to 55 percent differential would be considered a landslide, not "almost equally."

4. "A History of American Poetry Anthologies," in *Canons*, edited by Robert von Hallberg (Chicago: University of Chicago, 1984), p. 300.

5. "The Social and Historical Significance of the First English Literature Professorship in England," by Franklin E. Court, *PMLA*, vol. 103, no. 5, October, 1988, pp. 796-807.

6. This is not to suggest, for example, that the Communist Party did not play a significant and quite noble role in the civil rights movement, but only that the articulation and legitimation of a new right, or of a substantive limitation on the state has been successful only when it has been presented in a "de-politicized" (i.e., non-party) form, such as via a social movement. A closer examination of these victories spells out the fundamental place occupied by institutions, as against by abstractions such as "the political will of the people." The right of a woman to make the decision over whether or not any pregnancy should be brought to term, with abortion as an available option, depends far less on the fact that two-thirds of all Americans agree women should possess self-determination with regards to their own bodies than it does on the composition of the Supreme Court. Two-thirds of all Americans also agree that the U.S. should *not* be conducting surrogate warfare in Central America via the contras, a position that has only sporadically and incompletely been institutionalized. And the success of a minority of Americans in making the so-called Pro-Life position a defining issue within the Republican Party has the potential to directly constrain women's self-determination of the fate of their own bodies. Agency over one's own physical person is entirely dependent on the institutionalization processes of the state.

7. Language poetry shares this institutional ex-centricity — and I mean that term in its most literal sense — with the poetics of identity that have emerged around some, although not all, feminist, lesbian and gay, and ethnic minority communities.

8. *Revising State Theory: Essays in Politics and Postindustrialism* (Philadelphia: Temple University Press, 1987), pp. 51-68. The article first appeared in *Socialist Review*.

9. One immediate goal of an institutional strategy might thus be to have *The New American Poetry* brought back into print to replace *The Postmoderns* (a book which itself has been consigned to the limbo of "out of stock" for some years now).

10. Hank Lazer's analysis of Louis Simpson's willful misreading of William Carlos Williams' poetics is a brilliant demonstration of how this intent functions in practice. See "Language Writing, or Literary History and the Strange Case of the Two Dr. Williamses," draft ms. of a talk given February, 1989, unpublished.

11. This is quite different from suggesting that language poetry, for example, is either a post-structuralism proper and/or derivative thereof. It is, however, an historical tendency that grew up reacting to and conditioned by many of the same social phenomena as did post-structuralism. There are of course nearly as many types of post-structuralisms as there are post-structuralists, and while it seems safe to say that we are certainly no longer within whatever brief epoch might have been structuralism, one possible version of post-structuralism would be that which continues to place emphasis on the root of its term: *structure*.

12. Piombino explains that splitting is an unconscious mental defensive maneuver which wishes to cause a divisive split between two aspects of reality, usually accomplished by labelling one all good and one all bad.

13. *The Tenderloin Times* is the community newspaper I edited between 1978 and 1981.

Encloser

Susan Howe

ENVELOP   FENCE   PEN   COOP   CORRAL   CAGE   WALL

PRESENT

Patricia Caldwell's *The Puritan Conversion Narrative: The Beginnings of American Expression*, explores a body of materials not figured in our literary canon. The texts she examines are testimonies delivered by individual Puritans in the gathered churches of England and New England between the 1630's and the Restoration. Few of these religious narratives have survived. On the American side there are fifty-one. They were recorded in a small private notebook by Thomas Shepard, the minister of the First Church in Cambridge, Massachusetts, between 1637 and 1645 as they were being delivered, or shortly afterward. The first complete edition of these narratives, edited by George Selement and Bruce Wooley, wasn't published until 1980. Some of the testimonies had previously appeared in various anthologies but none given by women. Apart from the court records of Anne Hutchinson's trial, and a few brief "relations" in John Fiske's notebooks, these narratives represent the first voices of English women speaking in New England. As in Hutchinson's case, their words have been transcribed by male mediators who were also community leaders.

The voice of a form in absence Itself. In new worlds — with lesser claim — the way origins envelop us. To what end and in what manner do I use her voice?

Caldwell's book studies the verbal accounts of both sexes. Her work is an example of revisionist scholarship that is helping to form a fuller reading of American cultural history. *The Puritan Conversion Narrative* movingly demonstrates how careful examination and interpretation of individual physical artifacts from a time and place can change our basic assumptions about the New England pattern and its influence on American literary expression.

PLATO'S PHARMACY: *The Heritage of the Pharmakon: Family Scene* (D 142)

Jacques Derrida:

> This scene has never been read for what it is, for what is at once sheltered and exposed in its metaphors: its *family* metaphors. It is all about fathers and sons, about bastards unaided by public assistance, about glorious legitimate sons, about inheritance, sperm, sterility. Nothing is said of the mother, but this will not be held against us. And if one looks hard enough as in those pictures in which a second picture faintly can be made out, one might be able to discern her unstable form, drawn upside-down in the foliage at the back of the garden. (D 143)

What if the faintly drawn second picture at the back of the garden suddenly tells the scene for what it is?

What if she incarnates the scene?

What if her unstable upside-down form was never separable from the pivotal sheltered exposed Fatherson, and his glorious clothes, and that patch which echoes the skull itself, and parts of books in foreground corners supporting the weight of the skull, and that zigzag area from architectonic to rhythmic structure?

The past is present. We are all part of the background.

THE OXFORD ENGLISH DICTIONARY

> Encloser [f. Enclose *v.* + -ER.] 1. One who encloses; *esp.* one who appropriates common land.

WEBSTER'S THIRD NEW INTERNATIONAL DICTIONARY

> Enclosure: [ME *enclosure*, fr. MF, fr. OF, fr. enclos + ure] 1: the act or action of enclosing: as a: the separation of land from common ground by a fence or barrier b: separation (as for fire protection) of one part of a building from others. 2: the quality or state of being encompassed or shut up (books musty and damp from long~) 3: something that encloses (as a barrier) 4a: something enclosed in a package or letter (each envelope contained miscellaneous~s) b: an

enclosed or fenced in area (a ranch and its outlying~s) 4: the part of
a monastery or convent strictly reserved for the religious of the com-
munity to the exclusion of outsiders (as those of the opposite sex) 5:
the regulation that establishes and is designed to preserve the enclo-
sure of a monastery or convent (an order with a very strict~)

Turned back from turning back

as if a loved country

faced away from the traveler

No pledged premeditated daughter

no cold cold sorrow no barrier

E N C L O S E R

Thomas Shepard: *Anagram* — O, a map's thresh'd (W III.513)

My writing has been haunted and inspired by a series of texts, woven in shrouds and cordage of Classic American 19th century works, they are the buried ones, they body them forth.

The selection of particular examples from a large group is always a social act. By choosing to install certain narratives somewhere between history, mystic speech, and poetry, I have enclosed them in an organization although I know there are places no classificatory procedure can reach where connections between words and things we thought existed break off. For me, paradoxes and ironies of fragmentation are particularly compelling.

Every statement is a product of collective desires and divisibilities. Knowledge, no matter how I get it, involves exclusion and repression. National histories hold ruptures and hierarchies. On the scales of global power what gets crossed over? Foreign accents mark dialogues that delete them. Ambulant vagrant bastardy comes looming through assurance and sanctification.

Thomas Shepard:
> A long story of conversion, and a hundred to one if one lie or another slip not out with it. Why the secret meaning is, I pray admire me. (W II.284-5)

When we move through the positivism of literary canons and master narratives, we consign our lives to the legitimation of power, chains of inertia, an apparatus of capture.

Brother Crackbone's Wife:
> So I gave up and I was afraid to sing because to sing a lie, Lord teach me and I'll follow thee and Lord will break the will of his last work. (C 140)

A printed book enters social and economic networks of distribution. Does the printing modify an author's intention, or does a text develop itself? Why do certain works keep on saying something else? Pierre Macheray says in *A Theory of Literary Production*: "The work has its beginnings in a break from usual ways of speaking and writing — a break which sets it apart from all other ideological expression." (TP 52) Roman Jakobson says in "Dialogue On Time In Language and Literature": "One of the essential differences between spoken and written language can be seen clearly. The former has a purely temporal character,

while the latter connects time and space. While the sounds we hear dis-
appear, when we read we usually have immobile letters before us and
the time of the written flow of words is reversible." (VAST 20) Gertrude
Stein says in "Patriarchal Poetry": "They said they said. / They said they
said when they said men. / Many men many how many many many
many men men men said many here." (YS 123) Emily Dickinson writes
to her sister-in-law Susan Gilbert Dickinson: "Moving on in the Dark
like Loaded Boats at Night, though there is no Course, there is Bound-
lessness — ." (L 871)

Strange translucencies; letters, phonemes, syllables, rhymes, short-
hand segments, alliteration, assonance, meter, form a ladder to an out-
side state outside of States. Rungs between escape and enclosure are
confusing and compelling.

Brother Crackbone's Wife:
> My spirit was fiery so to burn all I had, and hence prayed Lord
> would send fire of word, baptize me with fire. And since the Lord
> hath set my heart at liberty. (C 141)

*   *   *   *   *

> I am a poet writing near the close of the 20th Century. Me with my
> hour at the ragged edge of letters.

Little by little sound grew to be meaning. I cross an invisible line spo-
ken in the first word "Then." Every prescriptive grasp assertion was
once a hero reading Samson. There and here I encounter one vagabond
formula another pure Idea. To such a land. Yet has haunts. The heart of
its falls must be crossed and re-crossed. October strips off cover and
quiet conscience.

New England is the place I am. Listening to the clock and the sun
whirl dry leaves along. Distinguishing first age from set hour. The eter-
nal and spirit in them.

A poem can prevent onrushing light going out. Narrow path in the
teeth of proof. Fire of words will try us. Grace given to few. Coming
home though bent and bias for the sake of why so. Awkward as I am.
Here and there invincible things as they are.

I write quietly to her. She is a figure of other as thin as paper.

Sorrow for the uproar and wrongs of this world. You covenant to love

*   *   *   *   *

Emily Dickinson:
> Master.
> If you saw a bullet

hit a Bird — and he told you
he was'nt shot — you might weep
at his courtesy, but you would
certainly doubt his word. (MLED 32)

If history is a record of survivors, Poetry shelters other voices.

Dickinson, Melville, Thoreau, and Hawthorne guided me back to
what I once thought was the *distant* 17th century. Now I know that the
arena in which scripture battles raged among New Englanders with
originary fury is part of our present American system and events, history
and structure.

Goodwife Willows:
Questioned all that ever the Lord had wrought, I'll never leave thee. I
could now apprehend that yet desired the Lord not to leave me nor
forsake me and afterward I thought I was now discovered. Yet hear-
ing he would not hide his face forever, was encouraged to seek. But I
felt my heart rebellious and loathe to submit unto Him. (C 151)

In a new world morphologies are triggered off. An English relation of
conversion related at the territorial heart of New England, is deterritori-
alized and deterred by the anxiety crucial to Puritan piety. I sense the
sound of something unbegotten, looming over assurance and sanctifica-
tion, over soil subsoil sea the sky.

*   *   *   *   *

Under the hammer of God's word. (W I:92)

During the 1630's and 40's, a mother tongue (English) had to find
ways to accommodate new representations of reality. Insecurity and suf-
fering caused by agrarian revolution in England, and changing econom-
ic structures all across Europe, pushed members of various classes and
backgrounds into new collectivities. English Protestant sects were united
in a struggle against Parliament, the Jacobean and Stuart Courts, the
Anglican Church and Archbishop Laud. Collective resistance to politi-
cal and religious persecution pushed some groups to a radical separa-
tism. Members of a fragment broke loose from the European continent.
Their hope was to ride out the cry and accusation of kingdoms of Satan
until God would be "all in all."

Thomas Shepard:
And so, seeing I had been tossed from the south to the north of
England and could go no farther, I began to listen to a call to New
England. (GP 56)

Schismatic children of Adam thought they were leaving the "wilderness of the world" to find a haven free of institutional structures they had united *against*. They were unprepared for the variability of directional change the wilderness they reached represented. Even John Winthrop complained of "unexpected troubles and difficulties" in this "strange land where we met with many adversities." (NQ H361)

A Bible, recently translated into the vernacular, was owned by nearly every member of the Bay Colony. It spoke to readers and non-readers and signified the repossession of the word by English. The Old and New Testaments, in English, were indispensable fictive realities connecting the emigrants to a familiar State-form, and home. Though they crossed a wide ocean, Scripture encompassed them.

From the first, Divinity was knotted in Place. If the place was found wanting, and it was by many, a rhetoric had to be double-knotted to hold perishing absolutism safe. First generation leaders of this hegira to New England tied themselves and their followers to a dialectical construction of the American land as a virgin garden pre-established for them by the Author and Finisher of creation.

"Come to me and you shall find rest unto your souls."

To be released from bonds, absorbed into catastrophe of pure change. *Here* is unappropriated autonomy. Uncounted occupied space. Heavy pressure of finding no content. Openness of the breach.

"The gospel is a glass to show men the face of God in Christ. The law is that glass that showeth a man his own face, and what he himself is. Now if this glass be taken away . . ." (W I:74)

Pilgrims sheltered inside God's Plot and looked out.

Widow Arrington:
> And hearing Dr. Jemison, Lamentations 3 — let us search and turn to the Lord — which struck my heart as an arrow. And it came as a light unto me and the more text was opened more I saw my heart. And hearing that something was lost when God came for searching. And when I came I durst not tell my husband fearing he would loath me if he knew me. And I resolved that none should know nor would I tell . . . and I wished I had a place in wilderness to mourn. (C 186)

*   *   *   *   *

On 3 October, 1635, Thomas Shepard and his family arrived in Boston Harbor on the ship *Defense*. "Oh, the depths of God's grace here," he later wrote, "that when [man] deserves nothing else but separation from God, and to be driven up and down the world as a vagabond or as dried leaves, fallen from our God — ." (GP 14)

There is a direct relation between sound and meaning.

Early spiritual autobiographies in America often mean to say that a soul has found love in what the Lord has done. "O, that when so many come near to mercy, and fall short of it, yet me to be let in!" (W II:229) Words sound other ways. I hear short-circuited conviction. Truth is stones not bread. The reins are still in the hands of God. He has set an order but He is not tied to that order. Sounds touch every coast and corner. He will pick out the vilest worthy never to be beloved. There is no love. I am not in the world where I am.

In his Journal Mr. Shepard wrote: "To heal this wound, which was but skinned over before, of secret atheism and unbelief." (GP 135)

*   *   *   *   *

Finding is the First Act (MBED 1043)

After the beaver population in New England had been decimated by human greed, when roads were cut through unopened countryside, the roadbuilders often crossed streams on abandoned beaver dams, instead of taking time to construct wooden bridges. When other beaver dams collapsed from neglect, they left in their wake, many years' accumulation of dead bark, leaves, twigs, and silt. Ponds they formed disappeared with the dams, leaving rich soil newly open to the sun. These old pond bottoms, often many acres wide, provided fertile agricultural land. Here grass grew as high as a person's shoulder. Without these natural meadows many settlements could not have been established as soon as they were.

Early narratives of conversion, and first captivity narratives in New England, are often narrated by women. A woman, afraid of not speaking well, tells her story to a man who writes it down. The participant reporters follow and fly out of Scripture and each other. All testimonies are bereft, brief, hungry, pious, *authorized*.

Shock of God's voice speaking English.

Sound moves over the chaos of place in people. In this hungry world anyone may be eaten. With a nest and litter. A wolf lies coiled in the lamb.

Silence becomes a Self. Open your mouth.

In such silenced women were talking. Undifferentiated powerlessness swallowed them. When did the break at this degree of distance happen?

Silence calls me himself. Open your mouth.

During a later Age of Reason 18th century Protestant gentlemen signed the Constitution in the city of Philadelphia. These first narratives from wide open places re-place later genial totalities.

During the 1850's, when the Republic was breaking apart, newly exposed soil from abandoned narratives was as rich and fresh as a natural meadow.

Emily Dickinson and Herman Melville are bridge builders. Their writing vaults the streams. They lead me in nomad spaces. They sieve cipherings, hesitations, watchings, survivals of sound-meaning associations: the hound and cry, track and call. So much strangeness from God. What is saved to be said?

Once dams, the narratives are bridges.

In 1850, when Melville wrote about American literary expression, he called the essay "Hawthorne and His Mosses," and chose a fragment from Hawthorne's story of Puritan doubt.

> 'Faith!' shouted Goodman Brown, in a voice of agony and desperation; and the echoes of the forest mocked him, crying — 'Faith! Faith!' as if bewildered wretches were seeking her, all through the wilderness. (PT 251)

*   *   *   *   *

Thomas Shepard:

> *Ans.* A mighty prince is absent from a traitor; he sends his herald with a letter of love, he gives it to him to read; how can he receive the love of the prince when absent? *Ans.* He sees his love in a letter, he knows it came from him, and so at a distance closeth with him by this means; so here, he that was dead, but now is alive, writes, sends to thee: O, receive his love here in his word; this is receiving "him by faith." Acts ii.37,38. (W II:599-600)

In Europe, Protestant tradition since Luther had maintained that no-one could fully express her sins. In New England, for some reason hard to determine, Protestant strictures against public confession were reversed. Now the minister's scribal hand copied down an applicant for church membership's narrative of Mortification and Illumination.

Caldwell points out that during the 1630's, in the Bay Colony, a disclaimer about worthlessness and verbal inadequacy had to be followed by a verbal performance strong enough to convince the congregation of the speaker's sincerity.

New England's first ministers must have wrestled with many conflicting impulses and influences. Rage against authority and rage for order; desire for union with the Father and the guilty knowledge they had abandoned their own mothers and fathers. In 1636 the Antinomian Controversy erupted among this group of "Believers, gathered and ordained by Christ's rule alone . . . all seeking the same End, viz. the Honor and Glory of God in his worship." (VS 73)

The Antinomian Controversy circled around a woman, Anne

Hutchinson, and what was seen to be: "the Flewentness of her Tonge and her Willingness to open herselfe and to divulge her Opinions and to sowe her seed in us that are but highway side and Strayngers to her." (AC 353) Thomas Shepard made this accusation. Paradoxically he was one of the few ministers who required women to recite their confessions of faith publicly, before the gathered congregation; and his standards for admission to the Cambridge First Church were far freer than most.

Thomas Prince lectured Anne Hutchinson in court: "You have stept out of your place. *You have rather bine a Husband than a Wife and a Preacher than a Hearer; and a Magistrate than a Subject,* and soe you have thought to carry all Thinges in Church and Commonwealth, as you would, and have not been humbled for this." (AC 383)

Prince, Cotton, Winthrop, Mather, Shepard, and other men, had stepped out of their Places when they left England. In Europe they were Subjects. In New England they were Magistrates and Preachers. They sought to carry all things in Church and Commonwealth. She was humbled by them for their Transgression. Anne Hutchinson was the community scapegoat.

Kenneth Burke says in *A Grammar of Motives*, "Dialectic of the Scapegoat": "When the attacker chooses for himself the object of attack, it is usually his blood brother; the debunker is much closer to the debunked than others are. Ahab was pursued by the white whale he was pursuing." (GM 407)

I say that the "Scapegoat Dialectic" is peculiarly open to violence when the attacker is male, his blood brother female. Kenneth Burke dissects grammars in a realm of discourse structured, articulated, and repeated by men.

Thomas Shepard:
> We are all in Adam, as a whole country in a parliament man; the whole country doth what he doth. And though we made no particular choice of Adam to stand for us, yet the Lord made it for us. (W I:24)

*   *   *   *   *

The Sound Believer
> MATT. xviii.ll — "I came to save that which was lost." (W II:111)

Thomas Shepard:
> And I considered how unfit I was to go to such a good land with such an unmortified, hard, dark, formal, hypocritical heart. (GP 61)

Thomas Shepard was an evangelical preacher who comforted and converted many people. Edward Johnson called him "that gracious sweet Heavenly minded Minister . . . in whose soul the Lord hath shed abroad his love so abundantly, that thousands of Souls have cause to bless God for him." (W I:77) Thomas Prince said he "scarce ever preached a sermon but someone or other of his congregation was struck in great distress and cried out in agony, *'What shall I do to be saved?'*" (GP 8) Jonathan Mitchell remembered Shepard's ministry: *"Unless it had been four years living in heaven, I know not how I should have more cause to bless God with wonder."* (C 13) Mitchell also remembered a day when, "Mr. Shepard preached most profitably. That night I was followed with serious thoughts of my inexpressible misery, wherein I go on, from Sabbath to Sabbath, without God and without redemption." (W I:cxxxi) Mr. Shepard called his longest spoken literary production, unpublished in his lifetime, *The Parable of the Ten Virgins Open and Applied.* The earnest persecutor of Anne Hutchinson and repudiator of "erroneous Antinomian doctrines" confided to his *Journal*: "I have seen a God by reason and never been amazed at God. I have seen God himself and have been ravished to behold him." (GP 136) The author of *The Sound Believer* also told his diary: "On lecture morning this came into my thoughts, the greatest part of a Christian's grace lies in mourning for the want of it." (GP 198) A note appended to the conclusion of the Autobiography he titled "My Birth and Life" is enigmatic. "A Roman, being asked how he lived so long, answered, *Intus melle, foris oleo. Quid loquacius vanitate, ait Augustinus."* (GP 77) [on the inside, honey; on the outside, oil. Which babbled more of vanity? said Augustine.]

Edward Johnson pictured the minister of the Cambridge church as a "poor, weak, pale-complexioned man, whose physical powers were feeble, but spent to the full." (GP 8) He wept while composing his sermons, and went up to the pulpit "as if he expected there to give up his stewardship." (W I:lclxxix)

Thomas Shepard died after a short illness, 25 August 1649. He was forty-three. Some of his last words were: "Lord, I am vile, but thou art righteous." (GP 237)

Cotton Mather described his ordinary conversation as "a trembling walk with God." (GP 7)

*   *   *   *   *

Thomas Shepard:

> I never went out to meditate in the fields but I did find the Lord teaching me somewhat of myself or himself or the vanity of the world I never saw before. And hence I took out a little book I

have every day into the fields and writ down what God taught me
lest I should forget them. (GP 42)

*   *   *   *   *

Emily Dickinson:
      Little Cousins
         Called back. (L 1046)

Between 1637 and 1640, Thomas Shepard transcribed into a leather-
bound pocket-notebook the testimonies of faith given in his church by
fifty-one people who were applying for church membership. He said of
1637, that God in that year alone "delivered the country from war with
the Indians and Familists, who rose and fell together." (W I:cxxvi)

The applicants during this tumultuous time, when it seemed dangerous
to speak at all, especially to express spiritual enthusiasm, were from a wide
social spectrum. A third of them could read or write. Almost half of them
were women. The speakers included four servants, two Harvard gradu-
ates, traders, weavers, carpenters, coopers, glovers, and one sailor. Most
were concerned with farming and with the acquisition of property. Most
applicants were in their thirties and forties. Most were starting to raise
families. Each one knew that reception into church fellowship was neces-
sary in order to gain economic and social advantage in the community.
Some later became rich; some are untraceable now through genealogical
records. Both male servants gained financial and political freedom.

Two women were servants. Two were widows who managed their
own estates. The rest generally spent their days cleaning, sewing, mar-
keting, farming, and giving birth to, then caring for, children. Some lat-
er died in childbirth. Although women were subservient to their hus-
bands and fathers in worldly matters, in matters of the spirit, and in
Shepard's theology of conversion, they were relatively independent.
Most of their narratives reflect this autonomy. They are as long or
longer than those spoken by men.

Each confession of faith in Shepard's book has its own carefully de-
marcated space among the rest. Each has the narrator's name for a
chapter heading. Husband's names cover or obscure the names of
wives. The recitals seem to have been copied down quickly. Shepard
uses a form of shorthand in places. His nearly microscopic chirography
is difficult to decipher. Often the minister surrounds a confessor's name
with ink-scrawls and flourishes. Subsequent editors have subtracted, de-
leted, interpreted, and normalized his odd symbols and abbreviated
signals. This is a pity because much of Shepard's originary eccentricity
has been muffled.

Often the Narrator-Scribe-Listener-Confessor-Reporter-Author changes
person, character, and gender in mid-sentence. Present slides into past
and comes back. He She I Thou join voices now. No bonds

Thomas Shepard:

> when the time of calling comes . . . the Lord Christ from heaven
> speaks, takes the written word in his own lips . . . and thereby
> pierceth through the ears, to the heart, through all the noise of
> fears, sorrows, objections against believing, and makes it to be
> heard as his voice . . . speaks and calls, and makes the soul under-
> stand his voice: so that this call is not a mean business, because the
> Lord Jesus himself now speaks, whose voice is glorious. (W I:221)

   *   *   *   *   *

Went forth to meet the Bridegroom (W II:111)

Old Goodwife Cutter:

> And Lord brought us through many sad troubles by sea and when
> I was here the Lord rejoiced my heart.
> But when come I had lost all and no comfort and hearing from
>   foolish virgins
> those that sprinkled with Christ's blood were unloved.(C 145)

Brother Winship's Wife:

> Hearing — 2 Jeremiah — two evils broken cisterns —
> I was often convinced by Mr. Hooker my condition was miserable
> and took all threatenings to myself . . .
> Hearing — say to them that be fearful in heart, behold He comes —
> Mr. Wells — pull off thy soles off thy feet for ground is holy.
> And hearing Exodus 34, forgiving iniquity . . .
> Hearing whether ready for Christ at his appearing had fears,
> city of refuge.
> Hearing — oppressed undertake for me — eased. (C 147-9)

Hannah Brewer:

> And I heard that promise proclaimed — Lord, Lord merciful and
>   gracious etc.
> — but could apply nothing. (C 141)

Brother Winship's Wife:

> Hearing of Thomas' unbelief, he showed trust in Lord forever for
> there is everlasting trust and stayed. (C 149)

Goodwife Usher:

> And I heard — come to me you that be weary — and Lord turn me
> and I shall be turned —

and so when I desired to come hither and found a discontented
    heart
and mother dead and my heart overwhelmed.
And I heard of a promise — fear not I'll be with thee.
And in this town I could not understand anything that was said,
I was so blind and heart estranged from people. (C 183)

John Sill His Wife:
    Oft troubled since she came hither, her heart went after the world
    and vanities and the Lord absented Himself from her
    so that she thought God had bought her hither on purpose
    to discover her. (C 51)

Mrs. Sparhawk:
    And then that place fury is not in me, let Him take hold of my
        strength.
    Saw that there was but two ways either to stand out or to take hold,
    and saw the promise and her own insufficiency so to do. (C 68-9)

Alice Stedman:
    Hearing Mr. Cotton out of Revelation — Christ with a rainbow on
        his head,
    Revelation 10 — I thought there was nothing for me,
    I thought I was like the poor man at the pool. (C 105)

Goodwife Grizzell:
    Hearing Mr. Davenport on sea — he that hardened himself against
        the Lord
    could not prosper — and I thought I had done so.
    I considered I had a principle against faith
    yet a kingdom divided cannot stand. (C 189)

Brother Jackson's Maid:
    When Christ was to depart nothing broke their heart so much as
        then. (C 121)

*   *   *   *   *

Billy Budd, Sailor (An Inside Narrative); Herman Melville's anachronistic
testament or final signal wasn't published in his lifetime.

"God bless Captain Vere!" (BB 123)

At sea long ago, a conventional felon's syllables of untamed thought
are benediction and salute to the Commander who could have been his
Father.

These first North American Inside Narratives cross the wide current
of Scripture. I meet them in the fields. They show me what rigor. I dare
not pity.

When they went to meet the Bridegroom it was too early. Then there is nothing to believe. Sorrows in our country call.

Reason will trample on a force-field of passionate enunciation.

Assurances, questions, citations, dams, figments, echolaic slivers, are emblazoned ciphers of Inspiration.

I am pulling representation from the irrational dimension love and knowledge must reach.

"All adrift to go." (BB 129)

*　　　　　*　　　　　*　　　　　*　　　　　*

Thomas Shepard:
> Yet we could not go back when we had gone so far. And the Lord saw it good to chastise us for rushing onward too soon and hazarding ourselves in that manner, and I had many fears and much darkness (I remember) overspread my soul, doubting of our way, yet I say we could not now go back. Only I learnt from that time never to go about a sad business in the dark, unless God's call within as well as that without be very strong and clear and comfortable. (GP 57)

Brother Crackbone's Wife:
> Yet heard I was under wings of Christ, one of them yet not under both. (C 140)

DISCUSSION

SUSAN HOWE: The whole problem with writing this piece for me is to write it in a way that *is* the thing I am talking about at the same time I am anchoring it down with certain facts. I think there is a continuous peculiar and particular voice in American literature. First I thought it originated with Cotton and Increase Mather, then with early Captivity Narratives, most specifically Mary Rowlandson's, but I kept being pulled farther and farther back. Now I see you can trace this voice as far back as 1637 when the Great Migration was occurring and so many emigrants were arriving in New England. Patricia Caldwell's book shows that there is a profound difference between English conversion narratives and American ones of that period. The difference was there from the beginning and I think this difference is still with us. I am only speaking of American English here and of course by now many other languages have been added to the mix. I happen to be concerned with a particular time and place. New England in the 17th century. I think it is here and now.

Around 1637 in England, the Puritans were uniting against the king. The Revolution that was about to happen there was caused by many forces — many radical religious sects, political groups, etc. Separate factions were increasingly united against the Monarchy. When splinter sects broke off from the European continent and arrived on the North American one, suddenly there was nothing to unite *against* any more: there was no more state. Statelessness must have represented freedom and fright. All the settlers, some would say invaders, now had to connect them to home, familiarity, and family was the Bible. They had a text. Almost all colonialists could read and if they couldn't they were used to hearing the written words spoken. They knew the structure of the sound of the words in the Bible. The Bible in English was a very recent invention. The translation of the Bible from Latin into the vernacular had caused bloodshed and tremendous upheaval hardly 100 years earlier. Men and women had only recently died on the scaffold over the issue of translation. Now another generation, and a variety of economic and social classes arrived in this completely unfamiliar place, after a long ocean voyage that was often hellish. Somewhere on the passage they had to convince themselves that the land was holy and that they were on a mission from God as laid down in the Old Testament. These emigrants saw the land through a book. A sacred book. Divinity was tangled in place. *They* were a new typology. They were inside the story, like Jonah in the whale. One reason perhaps why Jonah is an omnipresent figure in the narratives. But Jonah wanted to get out of the whale. In these narratives there is a terrible conflict over what is inside or outside. It is as if the narrators enveloped themselves inside God's Plot to survive the threat of openness. Something quite new there might be *no* words for. Here is a kind of desperate dependency on biblical quotations. The quotations become a second voice. Often a paternal and contradictory one. The syntax is choppy and nervous.

ALAN DAVIES: Why do you think the conversion narratives, at least the ones you recounted, were so harsh? They talked about being pierced by an arrow in their heart, being ravaged or being stricken. Terms like that. It didn't seem like it was a happy experience. It seemed like a rape.

HOWE: Many of these narratives are grief-stricken. Before Conversion the Soul is supposed to be in a state of doubt and pain — that *was* the tradition — but here, after the narrator has seen the light, the voice trails off. Back in England the Presbyterian churches (the Congregational Church was an offshoot) were very upset that American ministers were allowing members of the congregation to stand up and speak in church. Normally in a Puritan church and most separatist churches you would tell your conversion to a select group of elders, always male of course, you would not tell it to the assembled congregation. Public narratives represented a democratic expression and allowed a kind of open-endedness of discussion among a mixed group of people. This was something new. How would the story go? Could it be controlled? Such lack of order upset even quite radical and rebellious English Non-Conformists. It didn't last long in New England. The colony leaders soon put a stop to it. But at first they tolerated and defended it in print. Caldwell says that it is possible that the depression and anxiety among first generation colonists was so pervasive it forced public expression of spiritual doubt. Such intense anxiety and desolation had to be released into words.

Remember that most of these peoples' lives had been thrown into confusion by the chaotic changes in England while Feudalism was being crushed by commercialism and the new market economy. The Enclosure laws had thrown thousands and thousands off common land they had farmed for centuries. Many of the emigrants were traumatized before they got here. Massive economic forces swept them away. On some level the migration might have been seen as a vanishing. American education teaches us a certain mythology about origins. Religious persecution caused the Pilgrims to sail in the Mayflower etc. On one level it's true. Among other things what gets left out is that vast economic changes on some level caused the religious change. But beyond both categories, religious and economic, in history individuals get lost. Particularly women as we well know by now, but not only women — individuals. The individual voice tends to get erased. Singularities are surrounded and erased by factions. This is also true in the editing of a text. What gradually gets edited out in a narrative is singularity. René Thom, the mathematician who writes about catastrophe theory, shows just how necessary singularities are. On a whole other level maybe, but sometimes mathematicians and poets try to understand similar problems. I think Thom's ideas, on some level, perfectly apply in this situation. A singularity is the point where chaos might break out or in.

Alan Davies says the conversion experience in these narratives seems like an arrow in the heart, a rape. Often saints and mystics use similar imagery. A poet like Cranshaw, and other English metaphysical poets of the period, dwell at length on the wounds of Christ, the tears of the Virgin, the body as meat, etc. The early American poet, Edward Taylor, loved George Herbert's poetry and imitated it, took lines and titles from Herbert, etc. But in Taylor, Herbert's meter and meaning have become harsh and fractured. It is the harshness of biblical language spoken in English and now cut away from the Island of England and the continent of Europe. Perhaps on a subliminal level native American languages have influenced Taylor's choice of words for his poems. This is a new voice in poetry that seems (sounds) stilted and wild at once. Shepard's narratives have this same sound and syntax. Both Mathers carry it to incredible degrees. Dickinson and Melville inherit it. I think Anne Bradstreet remains an English poet in her diction. But then I don't think of her primarily as a religious poet.

ROGER HORROCKS: I wonder if you see any parallel to your close readings of early conversion narratives with the recent and very controversial wave of popular culture studies of, for example, soap operas, which have been closely tied up with trying to reconstruct the history of women by looking at popular culture of particular interest to women — as a means of exploring women's discourse. I wondered if you had any thoughts about that kind of contemporary parallel, whether you felt comfortable with that, or whether you felt what you were describing was very much a specific historical moment that has passed?

HOWE: Well in the first place conversion narratives weren't only given by women — captivity narratives were told by women in the majority of cases and they soon became similar on some level I suppose to soap operas. But I am really hesitant to connect any early narratives with *The Guiding Light* or *As the World Turns*. Strangely the titles of these soap operas have a vaguely holy ring. Not so strange because the United States remains a Puritanical nation the minute you get away from the larger cities. I am absolutely sure that Westerns are direct descendants of Captivity Narratives. It's a fascinating area. The difference here is that soap operas are controlled by a capitalist economy — how well do they sell soap? These narratives were written down in a very brief period before any sort of government control was possible.

I hope women who are historians don't dwell for too long on the subject of soap operas, because it seems to me simplistic. Insulting to the real achievement of women. I am a poet. I work in the tradition of other poets who have inspired me; poets in the 20th century most of whom are men. Why are there so few women (until just recently) in this tradition? This tradition that I hope I am part of has involved a breaking of boundaries of all sorts. It involves a fracturing of discourse, a stammering even. Interruption and hesitation used as a force. A recognition that there is an other voice, an attempt to hear and speak it. Its this brokenness that interests me. I see a contemporary American practice that isn't what necessarily gets into the canon and has trouble getting published. It is an echo of an undervoice that was speaking from the beginning and is peculiarly American. This voice keep on speaking *against* the grain.

Yet even here when the history of this sub sub group gets written even *here* women get shut up or out. This seems more important to explore than the subject matter of soap operas. Yes they may represent a voice of women but there are other women's voices also. I can't pretend that I don't think there is a sort of pantheon of poets. Poets that have been great influences on me, whose poems I love. I am interested in getting women in that pantheon and keeping them there. I am not interested in putting women down with soap operas to study them because I really do believe that is *down*.

HORROCKS: The point that was interesting to me was that on one hand you are talking about poetry in what in orthodox terms is called high culture; on the other hand, you were talking about the local church — which looks like a standarized form of popular culture — but inside it you found an underground poetry.

HOWE: The Bible crosses and contains high and low culture. The local church is different again from the non-local soap opera. A soap opera is disposable. The Old and New Testaments are not disposable. They are infinitely original, mysterious, and anonymous. The same words from certain psalms that comfort and inspire Wallace Stevens, T. S. Eliot, and Emily Dickinson also comfort and inspire Jane or John Doe. Mind you I feel that the Bible is gradually being watered down for a mass market. When I speak of the Bible I am speaking of the King James version. The Puritans were using the Geneva Bible in 1637. That would have been the Bible Shakespeare knew, that and Tyndale's. Probably Shakespeare and Thomas Shepard would have disliked the King James version.

I think of a poet as being a receptor of many voices. A mixture of cultures and voices. But each poet is one voice — a singularity. I guess I want to know what the singular voice consists of. To find what the idea means. A search for origins in some sense. One of the problems of the soap opera image you raise is that once a soap opera gets on television there is a kind of individualism that got erased. The search for majority approval — ratings, etc. — mows down the eccentric.

STEPHEN LOWY: That's a voice in captivity as well.

FIONA TEMPLETON: Have you looked into the similarity between the phenomena you're describing and other literatures or cultures of exile as well as of colonialism, which is an exile without you yourself moving, where your culture [is put in exile]? What [I'm struck by] as a non-native-American is an American rage to self-historicize [without reference to how other cultural situations produce otherness].

HOWE: I don't know if it's a rage. But I do think it originates in the sense that here there was a Beginning. Not that many centuries ago. The past of Europe or Asia or Africa goes back and back. So does the past of America. There were cultures here, this was not a wilderness, cultures were thriving here, before the Europeans arrived. Nevertheless, there was a sense to the keepers of records that this was a continent that had been invisible and suddenly was visible. Of course other cultures produce otherness. But I am in this culture and trying to understand this culture. It certainly isn't easy to understand. I guess I am guilty of the rage you speak of and you are probably right that it is self-centered.

DAVIES: I was wondering, Susan, you know you constructed a very deliberate talk, fragmentary or not, consisting maybe half of your own words and half of other people's words. After that, you know, you paused, stepped back and said something like: I just wanted to show that by 1720 there was a mistaken picture, or words to that effect. I wonder if that very fact of the way you deal with this information doesn't suggest to you that the interpretation or the opinion is entirely separate from even the evidence of what happened, and therefore even more enormously separate from any idea about "what really happened." Somebody used the term "real event." I never really encountered one myself [laughter]. I wonder, in other words, if the very fact of the way you work doesn't demonstrate that we can't be more — live in kind of, in the evidence as it is, and you can bring back from it certain things but you never are in both of those places at the same time.

HOWE: Of course I can't *really* bring back a particular time. That's true. Or it's true if you think of time as moving in a particular direction — forward you say. But what if then *is* now. I hope my work here and elsewhere demonstrates something about the mystery of time. And I do not believe you never encountered a *real* event. Come on. That sounds so theoretical! Have you ever been really hungry? Did the dentist ever hit a nerve when he was giving you a filling? Have you ever had someone you love die? Did the Holocaust never *really* happen? Did we never *really* drop an atomic bomb on Hiroshima?

I found that when I tried to explain one poem of Emily Dickinson's it was a work of the imagination I was trying to decipher but embedded in the work were traces of *real* events. There was no end to the traces. I had to practically go back to Adam and Eve. Perhaps not a real event but you know what I mean. To try to understand one chapter of *Moby Dick* let alone the book, I was led away nearly forever . . . disaster [laughter]. That was when I got mired in British colonialism, enclosure laws in England, etc. All through Melville use of the word "Delight." On the other hand, maybe those people (in Shepard's church around 1637) pulled *me* in. I didn't mean to find them they somehow found me as they find others. Shepard came to a place. A geographical spot. I came to a poem then a novel. (I don't know if you can really call *Moby Dick* a novel.) Shepard and his followers hoped they would find rest. What they found was open. A book couldn't keep it in.

CHARLES BERNSTEIN: Do you see it as a political role of a poet doing historical and textual inquiries in the way that you do?

HOWE: I wouldn't want to decree what the political role of any poet should be. Who am I to say? For a long time I thought it was my political purpose to find some truth that had been edited out of our history. For example, I thought it was urgent that I bring Mary Rowlandson's narrative back into our consciousness. I love words. I hope they are allowed to suggest all meanings possible. I hope that language will always be an undiscovered country. All poetry that sets words free is political. The irony is that "political poetry," poetry with a specific political agenda for improvement, tends to imprison knowledge. But words will always escape into their own mystery. At least I hope they will.

SOURCES

Burke, Kenneth. *A Grammar of Motives*. New York: George Braziller, 1955. Abbreviated in the text as *GM*.

Caldwell, Patricia. *The Puritan Conversion Narrative: The Beginnings of American Expression*. Cambridge & London: Cambridge University Press, 1983.

Derrida, Jacques. *Dissemination*. Trans. with an intro. by Barbara Johnson, Chicago, London: University of Chicago Press, 1985. Abbreviated as *D*.

Dickinson, Emily. *The Letters of Emily Dickinson*. Edit. by Thomas H. Johnson and Theodora Ward, Cambridge and London: Harvard University Press, 1958. Abbreviated as *L*.

Dickinson, Emily. *The Manuscript Books of Emily Dickinson*. Edit. by Ralph Franklin, Cambridge and London: Harvard University Press, 1981. Abbreviated as *MBED*.

Dickinson, Emily. *The Master Letters of Emily Dickinson*. Edit. by Ralph Franklin, Amherst: Amherst College Press, 1986. Abbreviated as *MLED*.

Hall, David D. *The Antinomian Controversy, 1636-1638: A Documentary History*. Edit. with intro. by David D. Hall, Middletown CT: Wesleyan University Press, 1968. Abbreviated as *AC*.

Heimert, Alan. "Puritanism: The Wilderness and the Frontier." *New England Quarterly* (September 1953): 361-82.

Jakobson, Roman. *Verbal Art, Verbal Sign, Verbal Time*. Edit. by Krystyna Pomorska and Stephen Rudy, Minneapolis: University of Minnesota Press, 1985. Abbreviated as *VAST*.

Macheray, Pierre. *A Theory of Literary Production*. Trans. Geoffrey Wall. London: Routledge & Kegan Paul, 1978. Abbreviated as *TP*.

Melville, Herman. *Billy Budd, Sailor (An Inside Narrative)*. Edit. by Harrison Hayford and Merton Sealts, Chicago and London: University of Chicago Press, 1962. Abbreviated as *BB*.

Melville, Herman. *The Piazza Tales, and Other Prose Pieces 1839-1860*. Evanston and Chicago: Northwestern University Press and the Newberry Library, 1987. Abbreviated as *PT*.

Nuttal, Geoffrey F. *Visible Saints: The Congregational Way, 1640-1669*. Oxford: Blackwell, 1957. Abbreviated as *VS*.

Shepard, Thomas. *God's Plot: The Paradoxes of Puritan Piety, Being the Autobiography & Journal of Thomas Shepard*. Edit. with an intro. by Michael McGiffert, Amherst: University of Massachusetts Press, 1972. Abbreviated as *GP*.

Shepard, Thomas. *Thomas Shepard's "Confessions."* Edit. by George Selement and Bruce C. Woolley. Collections of the Colonial Society of Massachusetts, vol. 58. Boston: The Society, 1981. Abbreviated as *C*.

Shepard, Thomas. *The Works of Thomas Shepard*. Edit. by John A. Albro, 3 vols. Boston, 1853; reprint ed., New York: AMS, 1967. Abbreviated as *W*.

Stein, Gertrude. "Patriarchal Poetry" in *The Yale Gertrude Stein*. Edit. by Richard Kostelanetz, New Haven and London: Yale University Press, 1980. Abbreviated as *YS*.

Notes for an Oppositional Poetics

Erica Hunt

I developed the title and theme of this talk — "The Possibility of Oppositional Poetics" — in the Spring of 1988, while reading monographs on human rights and Elaine Scarry's book, *The Body in Pain*, a philosophical treatment of pain, social and personal attitudes towards pain, and as an instrument of state power. Some time later, I came across the two books I will discuss later, *Beloved*, by Toni Morrison and *Survival in Auschwitz* by Primo Levi, two works of what I call oppositional writing. After I gave this talk in the following Fall, I was influenced by several articles, a few of which actually furthered the critical thinking here, and others which added special urgency to the task, if only for their obdurately blind point of view.

One article in particular provides a starting place: I happened to find it in the kind of magazine you read in airports while waiting for a connection. For that reason, I have no author to cite, and in fact it doesn't really matter since it has the stamp of popular wisdom, delivered daily on the evening news. The article was written to celebrate the 50th anniversary of the beginning of World War Two. In passing it observed that Europe in 1945 ended a cycle of violence lasting many centuries — that the post-war period marks the longest interval of peace in several hundred years.

What the article omitted is the fact of a New War, its violence dispersed in dozens of places throughout the world. It is a war that, according to *The State of the World Atlas* includes 26 million armed forces and 52 million who stand ready to supply it. In the constant and global New War, there are six times as many military personnel as medical personnel, consuming 40% more of all government spending than health care. In 1985, the New War had displaced 14 million refugees fleeing ethnic and political persecution, a number that no doubt has grown in the last four years. Fifty-seven out of the world's 125 states participate in this New War, the era of official peace, employing exceptional methods of social control: execution, terror, torture and disappearance. What feels like peace to the western world is for a good portion of the rest protracted violence in which 24% of the world is hungry, while one "developed" country, in this case Germany, consumes more income than half the world's population.

The point is that the industrialized countries have managed to create the illusion of a world at peace — with the exception of a few remote places. The effects of this displacement of violence, outside the borders of the west, are not easily conjured away. The violence of the New War doesn't just occur in the Third World, that other planet, but erupts internally and scabrous in exhausted cities and nerve-dead rural areas, seeping into the lives of the nominally less marginal.

In America, one of the seats of power that has brought such "peace," the majority are complicit, often unconsciously, with the New War, and as the borders of countries dissolve and nations become more interdependent, the violence spreads and entangles.

The conjunctions multiply between the nations at "peace" and those in a state of war. The most devastated populations of South America grow the drugs consumed by the most devastated populations of our cities, smuggled in through the same paths on which our country sends its guns. Americans lose jobs that pay "family" income to overseas subsistence wage workers in US government supported authoritarian states. Agricultural chemicals banned in this country are exported to poorer countries where they are used on the produce shipped back to American supermarkets.

If the negative character of the exchange between the west and the rest is abundant and abundantly repressed; its positive character is equally hidden. The levels of systemic warfare conceal the price that most of us pay beyond taxes. What is stunning is the brimming void in which visionary culture confronts power.

In recognition of the scope of the submerged, disconnected and violent character of contemporary life I renamed this talk "Notes for an Oppositional Poetics". Oppositional poetics and cultures form a field of related projects which have moved beyond the speculation of skepticism to a critically active stance against forms of domination. By oppositional, I intend, generously, dissident cultures as well as "marginalized" cultures, cutting across class, race and gender.

Poetics is derived from philosophical and structuralist studies of literature, descriptive of the way sounds, words, phrases and sentences form literary units. Poetics distinguishes between genres, typically by identifying the literary norms of writing and reading along rationalized lines of authority, from poem to essay. Prestige is crucial to the division of genre; forms rise to the top or sink, subtly redefining the rigid distinctions of genre. Essays ascend through ornament or logic, shifting with the era; an objectivist poetry reproduces the architecture of fact, a strain of fiction studies the double bind of the entirely lived imaginary; the advances often attributed to the mastery of a particular writer or group of writers is severed from its social origins.

But conventional poetics might also be construed as the way ideology, "master narratives", are threaded into the text, in content and in genre: fiction and nonfiction, objective and subjective voice, definite and indefinite register. The affinities and subordination are familiar — and familial — linked traceably to the way the social body is organized. Notions of character as a predictable and consistent identity, of plot as a problem of credibility, and theme as an elaboration of a controlling idea: all these mirror official ideology's predilection for finding and supplying, if necessary, the appropriate authority. Social life is reduced once again to a few great men or a narrow set of perceptions and strategies stripping the innovative of its power.

In an expanded sense of poetics, a more fluid typology would favor plural strategies to remove the distance between writing and experience, at least as it is socially maintained by the binarism of fact and fiction, of identity and nonidentity. So that plots are or can be historical or hysterical, revised or translated, manufactured plausibly or incredibly, ludicrous or cold eyed, bewildering or conspiratorial. Or character might be singular, plural, inexplicable, composite, evolving, non-human or found. And theme might consist of a surface, a tone, a didacticism; be latent or disjunct. All this is to suggest that narrative invention stems from multiple levels of perception and experience that literary standards conceived as ceiling tend to raze.

Dominant modes of discourse, the language of ordinary life or of rationality, of moral management, of the science of the state, the hectoring threats of the press and media, use convention and label to bind and organize us.

The convenience of these labels serves social control. The languages used to preserve domination are complex and sometimes contradictory. Much of how they operate to anesthetize desire and resistance is invisible; they are wedded to our common sense; they are formulaic without being intrusive, entirely natural — "no marks on the body at all".

These languages contain us, and we are simultaneously bearers of the

codes of containment. Whatever damage or distortion the codes inflict
on our subjectively elastic conception of ourselves, socially we act in an
echo chamber of the features ascribed to us, Black woman, daughter,
mother, writer, worker and so on. And the social roles and the appro-
priate actions are similarly inscribed, dwell with us as statistical likeli-
hoods, cast us as queen or servant, heroic or silent, doer or done unto.

The codes and mediations that sustain the status quo abbreviate the
human in order to fit us into structures of production. There is a place
for everyone, even the subordinate, if they know their place. It is con-
sciousness of the subtractive quality of the primary vehicles of socia-
lization that fuels the first intuition, the first sentiment of opposition.

In general, for a person of color, a woman, a member of the working
class, school is first place where she is encouraged to exchange the rich-
ness of her experience and the values of her community for standards
that run directly counter to her sense of solidarity. Even a child knows
the terms of the exchange are unjust.

In communities of color, oppositional frames of reference are the
borders critical to survival. Long treatment as an undifferentiated mass
of other by the dominant class fosters collective identity and forms of re-
sistance. In a sense, then, oppositional groupings, be they based on
class, race, gender or critical outlook, have traditionally been depen-
dent, in part, on external definition by the dominant group — the per-
ceived hostility of the dominant class shapes the bonds of opposition.
And that quasidependent quality extends even further: we get stuck
with the old codes even as we try to negate them. We experience acute
difference: autonomy without self-determination and group identity
without group empowerment.

The effect of this can be sensed in the feeling of captivity we have be-
fore there is a psychic or social advance, the state of alienation we reside
in: somehow the codes fit and do not fit us, somehow we are the agents
of the prescribed predicates and not the agents. The simple negations
that form the borders of opposition, the residues of old encounters be-
tween dominant and subordinate stand as prison walls as much as they
suggest shelter, collapsing from obsolescence or repeated attacks, con-
straining the new languages that must be made for resistance.

Inside what is rich about the wonder of having survived at all, of be-
ing a people or group still on its feet are also the values that make us sus-
picious of variations from tradition. We judge then as we have been
judged, sanctioning the differences that are our common property. We

reiterate codes that negate our humanity by denying human differences among us. The white woman who engages images with scientific and erotic intensity; the Korean woman who pleasures combatively, the Black man who yields feeling cerebrally is doubly, sometimes triply, exceptionalized in social life.

Water closing over the surface where the rock plunges in. Our recovered histories are filled with tales of the wounded, of marginalization, involuntary silence, mental and physical illness and death. They are the metonymic correlates of the wounded social body; the fractured desires of opposition and subordinated groups spell out caution.

Projects of historical reconstruction are common to all contemporary oppositional intellectuals in America. This follows from the erasure of "other" from dominant historical accounts; if it said by those who deny us now that we have no past, then we have to insist we have a past as deeply as we have a present.

The goal of these reconstructions, traditionally, is to find orientation, example and value with which to fuel present resistance. The positive aspects of these projects were:

*The discovery that history could be reconfigured.

*Attention drawn to the fact of erasure and to the continuity of the expressive impulse for liberation,

*Reflexivity: the contemplation of the past could be a critical reflection on the present.

But there was a downside to these projects as well:

*Conservatism: nostalgia for a lost unity or richness of culture: e.g., goddess culture, the African motherland, the poet as prophet.

*Insularity: an inability to acknowledge or find value in the synthetic texture of present culture, or in syncretism, and a rejection of the nonorganic or nonindigenous.

*Cooptation: the reinscription by dominant discourse on conceptual advances made by oppositional groups into the terms, values and structures of dominant ideology.

Two examples of the last come to mind: When I was a child Black people rarely appeared on television as socially complete human beings. When there was a Black person on television, the person was usually male, very very accomplished and distinguished, and my mother would call all of us into the room to hear what he, as a representative of the race, would say in this brief window of public space. We held to that screen, bound in aura of unity, done proud by association, fixed on the

few words he could say in 20 seconds; an oracular experience objective-
ly disproportionate to his fragmented electronic presence. In his decon-
textualized state, he served as the Black place holder of sorts between
the loop of recitals of dominant power. But his telecast also reiterated
the authority of the medium: he held the appearance of an autonomous
hero without a community, a man of merit throwing the rest of us onto
ambiguous ground. A role model from outer space.

Another example is the feminist project to understand and reshape
the boundary between public and private. The goal of this project was
to show that forms of private life are a matter of public policy, a notion
which tremendously advances strategic intervention in the way that
codes have organized family and personal life.

Feminists traced the multiple patterns of a woman's life and family
life in history, showing that contemporary middle class norms were not
the triumphant restoration of an ideal, but related to patterns of pro-
duction, reproduction and consumption. Their value informed critique
commented directly on capitalist as well as liberal, socialist and other
left theories of society.

Feminism had a popular component, drew responses from many
women and men who felt they were living truncated lives. It ignited
public debate and catalyzed a social movement, awakening in many
women the desire to engage the public realm.

Despite these accomplishments, two subtle transformations of this
conceptual advance occurred: the first was to transform women's de-
mands for greater public roles into tokenism, granting exceptional sta-
tus to women willing to battle for the right to labor for a wage on terms
identical to men's dehumanized conditions of work. The second trans-
formation was the counterdemand that the values of private life, intima-
cy and cooperation (to name two), be abandoned as the price of entry
into the public sphere.

The principle of cooptation is this: that dominant culture will transfer
its own partiality onto the opposition it tries to suppress. It will always
maintain that it holds the complete world view, despite the fissures. Op-
position is alternately demonized or accommodated through partial con-
cessions without a meaningful alteration of dominant culture's own terms.
The opposition is characterized as destructive to the entire social body
and to itself. State power in dominant culture depends upon its reducing
social and political problems into pathologies requiring the police. It is a
small step from that point to reducing world politics to individual aberra-
tion and to gaining our consent to maintain a world-wide police.

Literary cooptation generally doesn't require a police, the economics of literary production usually effect sufficient control. From the financial insecurity that seems to be an inescapable occupational hazard to the difficulties of getting into print and the narrow range of options for literary presentation, it has not been difficult to limit oppositional writing. Moreover, literature in this culture appears a fragmented professional specialty; oppositional writing tends to be the object of the practices it protests, its social demands illegible in print.

In literature — a highly stratified cultural domain — oppositional projects replicate the stratification of the culture at large. There are oppositional projects that engage language as social artifact, as art material, as powerfully transformative, which view themselves as distinct from projects that have as their explicit goal the use of language as a vehicle for the consciousness and liberation of oppressed communities. In general, the various communities, speculative and liberatory, do not think of each other as having much in common, or having much to show each other. In practice, each of their language use is radically different — not in the clichéd sense of one being more open-ended than the other, but in the levels of rhetoric they employ. More interesting is the limitations they share — limitations of the society as a whole which they reproduce, even as they resist. To articulate these intuitions, by no means mine alone, is to go down to the deepest roots of official culture and the state's role in preserving the status quo, and find how oppositional culture is both a wedge against domination, opening free space, and a object/material, absorbed by dominant culture.

It is worthwhile to note that many oppositional writers of color, feminist writers and speculative writers' consciousness has been shaped in powerful ways by social movements. In America, social movements fulfill part of the role that opposition parties play in other countries: channeling the expression of mass resistance and the demand for social transformation. (Think of the American writers who were formed out of the abolitionist, pacifist and antiwar, populist, labor, suffrage and women's and civil rights movements as these movements pursued change in areas critical to creating genuine democracy.) This is not to reduce writing to its social voice, but only to extend the usual critical focus to beyond the psychology of individual writers.

It is no coincidence then that writers who use words to produce critical views in language as a social and intellectual activity, or to liberate a richness of expression, frequently think of their writing in oppositional terms. Like race, class, gender, and affectional freedom, insights based on language as a mediation of consciousness have a central position in

developing visionary culture. But as a strata of movement, they too suf-
fer from a kind of poor visibility, marginalization as a "special interest"
group dependent on a self-justifying chain of the avant-garde and view-
ed as destructive more than constructive.

Speculative projects are not exempt from the cul de sacs that contain
other oppositional writing. For instance, there is nothing inherent in
language centered projects that gives them immunity from a partiality
that reproduces the controlling ideas of dominant culture. When such
projects produce claims of exclusive centrality, they are bound to be dis-
turbing to allies who have experienced social subordination. There are
also serious shortcomings in any opposition that asserts its technical
victories and removes itself from other oppositional projects on the
grounds of pursuing new possibilities of consciousness. The fetishization
of the new is well advanced in our society, and borrows from dominant
culture that culture's authority: it feeds our collective amnesia.

One troubling aspect of privileging language as the primary site to
torque new meaning and possibility is that it is severed from the politi-
cal question of for whom new meaning is produced. The ideal reader is
an endangered species, the committed reader has an ideological agenda
both open and closed, flawed and acute, that we do not address directly.
On one level the lack of address is a problem of the dispersed character
of the social movements in this country at present; on another level is
the general difficulty of looking squarely at the roles we play as writers in
forming social consciousness. It runs directly across the grain of some
sense of writing as a private act done in dialog with one's materials, with
the art body, an art public. But rather than simply negate that threshold
sense of writing as an autonomous specialized art form, I would suggest
that it is important to think how writing can begin to develop among
oppositional groups, how writing can begin to have social existence in a
world where authority has become highly mobile, based less on identity
and on barely discerned or discussed relationships.

While all critical projects begin with simple negation, all advance
when any of them advances. Each new movement of understanding
yields twofold benefits: they show us where there is solid ground and
shadow; and they show us that interconnections proliferate; that change
for those with the least status pulls everyone forward or back. Thus the
civil rights movement accomplished more than gaining the franchise for
African Americans: most immediately, it removed pathological racists
from the open and delegitimized the worst aspects of Jim Crow. More-
over, it proved the efficacy of mass mobilization and organization, it fed
expectations of a political and economic democracy, and it reopened

the space for dissent.

Contiguity, as a textual and social practice, provides the occasion to look beyond the customary categories of domestic and international, politics, history, aesthetics, philosophy, psychology, sociology and so on. As a social practice it acknowledges that the relationships among groups who share an interest in changing the antidemocratic character of the social order is not as oblique as their individual rhetoric would represent. As a reading and writing practice, it suggests new synthesis that move out of the sphere of a monoculture of denial; syntheses that would begin to consider the variance between clusters of oppositional writing strategies with respect for what has been achieved by each and a sense of the ground that holds it in place.

Its in this context that I've been thinking about the two books I mentioned earlier, *Beloved* by Toni Morrison and *Survival in Auschwitz* by Primo Levi, which have in common protagonists who survive an extraordinary level of legally sanctioned violence. *Beloved* is a work of fiction, in fact a gothic, and *Survival* is a memoir — and of course there are crucial differences that follow from the recollected and the imagined. Levi is quite candid about his partiality, he doesn't propose as Morrison, a conventional novelist, does the total world of a piece of fiction. He wrote *Survival* to frame the recollections that he subsequently reframed in later books, for example, *The Reawakening* and *The Drowned and the Saved*. Morrison imagined a true event with the purpose of "creating a monument" to African American slaves. The common bond these works share, beyond their self-evident critique of dominant culture, is that they show that violence is not exceptional, that majorities can be inoculated to tolerate growing levels of targeted violence.

Someone gave me *Beloved* shortly after my daughter was born. It didn't take me four pages to realize that it was about infanticide and the abyss of powerless parenthood. I put it aside until I had evolved my own version of motherhood.

The book concerns an escaped slave, Sethe, and her only remaining child, a daughter, Denver, who live in Ohio. They live in a house animated by the emotional energy of Sethe's murdered child — Beloved, called Beloved because that is the only word that Sethe could afford to have engraved on the child's tombstone. The story of Beloved's murder is told from multiple points of view through flashbacks, stimulated by the arrival of an old friend, a fellow ex-slave, Paul, who Sethe has not seen in 18 years. They were to have escaped together, along with her husband, children and the other men, but the plan was detected. Only Sethe was able to escape with her three children. The account of Sethe's flight in the fifth month of pregnancy with three young children provides some of the book's most harrowing enactments, reiterating, in an oblique way, the escape of Eliza in *Uncle Tom's Cabin*, but with significant differences. What was suppressed in the *Cabin*, is the ground explored by *Beloved* — the particular concentration of the effects of racial, economic and sexual oppression. It is Sethe's fleeting triumph that she was able to bring all her children with her out of slavery, an extremely rare feat. In this act, she negated the logic of slave culture to whom the ownership of Black women meant the ownership of reproductive capacity — children and potential fertility and the perpetuation of slave culture.

Sethe is, as far as she knows, the only one among her compatriots to have successfully escaped. Her husband, who planned to accompany her, disappears on the night of her departure. She reaches her mother-in-law in Ohio, recovers from having given birth prematurely during her flight, settles for a brief period into a new emancipated life. For reasons that Morrison seems to attribute to community apathy or envy, local Black people fail to tell Sethe or her mother-in-law that white strangers have arrived in their hamlet. At the last moment, Sethe sees the figures in the distance, recognizes her former master by the shape of his hat, and sweeps her children into a shed. There, in a daze of remembered pain, she slits each of their throats, killing one of them, determined not to return them — or herself — back into slavery. The posse enters the shed, recoil and realize that as property Sethe is worthless to them, having shown her radical refusal of reproductive use.

Sethe is jailed, then released through the intervention of sympathetic abolitionists: but her three remaining children are afraid of her: they understand that she has a love that can kill. Only one child stays, the girl, Denver; the two boys leave as soon as they are able. Denver stays behind in a mixture of resentment and paralysis induced by her mother's act. For Denver, the choices for an independent life are limited: she knows only the world Sethe inhabits, a world where no self-possession is possible for women.

The second movement of the book concerns the tentative relationship between Paul, the ex-slave with whom much of Sethe's story is exchanged with tales of his own miserable sojourn. The relationship's development is interrupted by the appearance of a young Black woman, about 18 years old, apparently a victim of trauma, with no memory of her own. Sethe nurses the strange woman back to health, who as she grows stronger literally assumes — that is absorbs — the identity of the murdered child Beloved. The open end of the book is that the minor and sometimes violent disturbances in the house, attributed to Beloved's ghost, disappear as the strange woman takes on the person of *Beloved*.

The book is a lineal descendant of the slave narrative. In that respect it shares the hesitations, the selectiveness, the vivid accounts of dehumanization and brutality recounted by former slaves, though very few slave narratives were written by women. It views slavery from the sign of the mother situated in the context of ownership, in the plantation owners possession of other human beings, in a mother's ownership of her body, and in the manner in which the logic of ownership is enacted on her children. In *Beloved*, every woman has lost at least one child — at the auction block or sometimes because the mothers made similar though less dramatic choices to that of Sethe, refusing to nurse a child they were forced to conceive through rape. It is probably here that we can see the origin of her community's failure to warn Sethe of the posse — for she alone of all the local women had all her children in emancipation.

The book achieves its contemporary and plural edge through a reading of it as a statement of problem in African American and feminist thought. Both movements lack an analytic that weaves insight about the qualitative and connecting conditions of sex, race and class oppression. Both until very recently tended to characterize oppression within their own singular terms. And there is insufficient language to articulate the connective tissue that joins their critiques.

Beloved begins this task by linking the battle for control of Sethe's reproductive capacity to the dispersed and wounded kinship she has with her people. When she murders her child she radically undermines her worth as an object of slavery. When she murders her child she emotionally mutilates herself and her community. The men in town avoid contact afterwards: Paul is chased off for a while when someone gossips the entire story to him.

The novel also illuminates the relative privilege of a Black woman who has all her children with her. Sethe through the patronizing charity of her previous owners was allowed to choose her husband. She chose him, because of all the men where she lived, he alone used his days of rest, Sundays, to hire himself out so as to purchase his mother's freedom and send her to Ohio. When Sethe arrived at her mother-in-law, she alone of the fugitives had an established place to stay. Her mother-in-law, a respected spiritual leader in the community, made a party for all her neighbors on an eve following Sethe's complete recovery, a party in which the abundance of victuals and pies expressed a kind of victory. And it was the next day the posse came for its unfinished business.

Morrison's strategy of a gothic narrative suggests that even the ghosts must be recovered within the bounds of fictive kinship, e.g., humanity.

On another level, the use of supernatural approximates white Americans' conventional disbelief, even obliviousness to the most rudimentary accounts of slavery and its legacy, including, up until recently, the fact that 20 million Africans died in the slave trade during the Middle Passage.

Survival in Auschwitz is an autobiographical work by Primo Levi, an Italian Jew who spent ten months in Auschwitz from 1944-1945. A chemist by training, he joined the Italian resistance only to be caught very early on, and then deported by the Nazis with about 600 other Italians.

Two grim accidents begin and end this volume of his memoirs. In the first he is asked during his initial interrogation what he was doing out of the prescribed area after curfew. In a quick and critical decision, he identifies himself as Jewish, with the mistaken belief that it might lead to less suffering than if he admits to being a political.

The second turn comes at the end of Levi's memoir, he describes surviving against all odds the methodical and monotonous routines of the death camp. He succumbs to scarlet fever about a month before the Russian advance on the Polish front. Sick internees were expected to die: minimal provision was made for their care in the infirmary. In his severely weakened state, depleted and cold, perpetually hungry, he has no reason to believe that he will survive his fever. Yet, as it turns out, as the Russians draw near, the Germans evacuate everyone in the camp able to walk. Virtually none of the evacuated survived the march. The only survivors of his section of Auschwitz are those confined to the infirmary.

Within this context of choice and accident, Levi's tone is clear and dispassionate — that is, he employs a level method of address more commonly associated with the writing of natural scientists, in detailing the forms of men he finds in a social organization driven by ideological supremacy, deprivation and mass murder.

The bureaucratic rationalism of death stamps the camp into a hierarchical and rigid order: those who look "fit" live, those that do not die. Jewish women and children are killed almost immediately; Jewish men as long as they are not yet ill, live. The SS inspect, disinfect, shave and number and discipline. The interns are divided into the green triangles — criminals, red triangles — politicals; and red and green triangles — the Jews. The criminals are in charge of dispensing the rations and are surrogates for the SS, enforcing obedience. The high numbers are recent arrivals: Levi is 174517. There are very few low numbers, the few who live at Levi's arrival are the survivors of the Warsaw ghetto. There are about 30,000 people in the camp during the course of the memoir. Only 800 survived.

The prohibitions are innumerable and the rites profuse and senseless.

In this order, ubiquitous signs admonish hygiene and ethics. One message heads all the corridors: *Arbeit Macht Frei* — Work Gives Freedom.

The number of different languages, and the numbing depression that is the unshakeable companion of the inmates makes organized resistance difficult. Resistance is manifest in its most shrunken form — the muffled will not to die. Eventually, Levi learns how to make himself understood. Communication and imitation permit Levi to operate as an "organizer", camp slang for someone who knows how to use the breaches in the system to survive. Although Levi uses the word organizer, it is probably more descriptive to say counter-organizer. He organizes against and despite the order that conspires his death.

The longer he stays the more he becomes acquainted with how to work accident to his advantage, which is the essence of an organizer. By theft, exchange, trade or skill, the organizers are able to get extra rations or amenities without which life would be unsupportable. The organizer is one who escapes the snares of his illusions about his condition, who manipulates the order to look the other way from him when he is obtaining the forbidden means of survival.

The language of the first part of the Levi's account uses the first person almost exclusively, reflecting the degree to which social cohesion has been reduced. While there are individual bonds, these bonds are the atrophied connection between fellows in a state of misery waiting for death. But as the signs of liberation mount (Russian and English bombing draws closer to the camp), Levi begins to use the word "we" consistently, eventually using the word "you", correlating to the change from victim to witness. Although the account is a chronological one, it is also structured by topic. There is, too, another sense in which time has been pressured from its usual linear representations; the book is an act of retrospection, yet the language — particularly its progressively differentiated use of pronouns that correspond to the approach of liberation, suggests the continuous present.

The dispassionate tone of Levi's memoir validates lucidity as an emblem of his prevailing and of triumph. In the preface to his book of essays, *The Drowned and the Saved* (translated by Raymond Rosenthal), Levi says:

> Almost all of the survivors, orally or in their written memoirs remember a dream which frequently recurred during the nights of imprisonment, varied in detail but uniform in its substance: they had just returned home and with passion and relief were describing their past sufferings, addressing themselves to a loved one, and were not believed, indeed were not even listened to. In the most typical (and cruelest) form, the interlocutor turned and left in silence.

This account of the dream bears a morphological resemblance to the description of torture given by Elaine Scarry in *The Body in Pain*:

> Torture . . . consists of a primary physical act, the infliction of pain, and the primary verbal act, the interrogation. The verbal act, in turn, consists of two parts, the 'question' and the 'answer', each with conventional connotations that wholly falsify it. The question is mistakenly understood to be the motive; the answer is mistakenly understood to be the betrayal. The first mistake credits the torturer, providing him with a justification, his cruelty with an explanation. The second discredits the prisoner, making him rather than the torturer, his voice rather than his pain, the cause of his loss of self and the world.

The dream Levi speaks of seems to bear a close relation to the social and moral world of pre-war Europe, and the power of European anti-Semitism and the Nazis in defining the social world, even the affective world. Substitute for loved ones, in Levi's comment, one's country or one's neighbors, and the nightmare's content about the reversal of moral responsibility becomes clear.

By contrast to the tone of *Survival*, Levi's sequel, *The Reawakening*, is teeming with language and story. *The Reawakening* traces his liberation through his travel through Europe back home to Turin, a period of six months. The liberation represents a kind of potential utopic chaos. Episodes are picaresque, society is classless. Every character regains the power of telling, a power almost obliterated by the cataclysm of fascism. Levi's sense of solidarity is boundless, there is no state, only personalities. Thus even the process of getting enough food to eat, keeping warm, etc., deliriously emancipated from the mean and obsessive regulation of the camp, is based on a principle of restored humanity — a free association.

In the discourse of conventional literature, Levi's and Morrison's works are the literatures of two "special interest groups," victims that won't stop whining, or alternatively, who are invested with special moral authority that eliminates the need to rigorously take positions in the present. To say they are of special interest pronominalizes them, fractures them, blunting their critiques, severing them from the contemporary crisis in human rights.

"It is only the prisoner's steadily shrinking ground that wins the torturer his swelling sense of territory" (Scarry).

Both *Survival* and *Beloved* do aspire to be monuments, to commemorate through telling that which has been suppressed or might be construed as betrayal. The monument achieves its effects through moves that occupy space, by recovering lost territory, that is the body, and the domestic. It is said that civil war monuments in this country face south if in the north or face north if in the south. These monuments face in two directions simultaneously as well, addressing the past (and making the most of its pained voice) and attempting to form the bases of current critical thought.

"Intense pain is language destroying — as the content of one's world disintegrates, so the contents of one's language disintegrates" (Scarry).

Both works are written in variations of normative, linear prose. Their linear appearance is a deliberate contrast to the experience of involuntarily induced dissociation. The linearity is there for self preservation, as such it suppresses other meaning, past humiliation — of that which it is too painful to speak. Despite the superficial linearity, they both eschew chronological treatment of time, they jump around in the continuous present and repeat incidents as a kind of parallel of spoken recollection. The use of internalized time structure has some implication for the official historical time it is their goal to supplant. Bidirectionality gives this linear quality a spin as well: each book's central character has a partially corroborating witness, someone who shares their destiny but not their fate.

"Time is precisely the impossibility of an identity fixed by space" (Michel de Certeau, translated by Brian Massumi, *Heterologies*).

The use of internalized time structure has some implication for the official historical time it is its goal to supplant. Causality is occluded: both Levi and Morrison tell a story about the "last man". In *Survival*, the last man is hung shortly before the liberation. He is being hanged for plotting among the prisoners — mutiny against the SS. The SS assembles the entire sector to watch the hanging in the course of which, the man cries out "I am the last man." Levi writes that with this final shout he knew that the program of extermination had extinguished the last shred of resistance in himself and the prisoners. Morrison continually identifies Paul as the "last man" at Sweet Home (the plantation); he alone survives the serial traumas of the fugitive existence and the ritual bestialization by the laws of slave society.

I have chosen writing derived from extremely violent conditions to take a look at how such writing renders negation, and the strategies for resistance in the world and the text. The means for rendering oppression are limited. The two works that are at the center of my talk are aimed at creating opinion and critique to supply a multiple focus and means of opposition. They beg the question of what function writing in the present can perform in dispersing a domination that monopolizes public and private life and ignores the violence that it leaves in its wake. Certainly writing itself cannot enlarge the body of opposition to the New Wars, it only enhances our capacity to strategically read our condition more critically and creatively in order to interrupt and to join.

Language and Politics

Jackson Mac Low

The topic of language and politics is so vast and the prospect of attempting to deal with it is so daunting that I'm doubtful of being able to say anything meaningful on it in the short time available tonight. I must take the plunge. However, taking the plunge, any plunge, is even more dismaying to me than contemplating the topic.

Am I to say that my work with language is motivated either wholly or in part by political concerns? Even that vague formulation is already too pat, too simple. I doubt that my most basic workings with language have been significantly motivated by political views. Outside of my directly political writing in verse and prose — which usually deals unequivocally with topical themes, even when composed by systematic-chance methods — the main places where I see clear political concerns and implications are in my verbal-musical performance works, for which I've long used the general term "Simultaneities," not only for group realizations but even for solos, since both consciously incorporate environmental sounds, etc., as well as those deliberately produced by performers. (We're going to have to deal with a bit of history; so let's get on with it.)

I began composing works for multiple voices in 1955. In my first Simultaneity, "21.21.29.,the 5th biblical poem(for 3 simultaneous voices) the 1st biblical play" (written 27 January 1955 — despite the title it's not really a play), silences are indicated by boxes, each of which stands for a silence as long as the time in which each reader might say any word she chooses. Each line ending is indicated by a nonvocal sound chosen by the individual reader, who makes the same sound after each line before the last one in each stanza, and a different one after each stanza ending. (Each reader may utilize a different pair of sounds, or all may use the same two.) Tempo, loudness, etc., are chosen and varied freely during performances.

In various other texts composed before 1960, numbers are printed, usually at the ends of lines and stanzas, to indicate durations of silence: performers are given the options of measuring silences either by clock seconds or half-seconds or by slow counts; in the latter case the slow counts are sure to differ both from clock seconds and from each other, reflecting both differences between performers and between the inner states of each performer at different times. In some written before and during 1960, tempo and loudness are generally regulated by indications such as "fast" and "slow," "loud" and "soft," each freely interpreted by the individual performer.

By 1960 many of these works also included musical sounds and/or noises. Their texts were chance-generated: each resulted from a system of chance operations which drew the verbal contents from one or more source texts and determined the structure, usually a kind of verse of which the metrical unit was the "event" (word, phrase, or other string or, as in the "5 biblical poems," a duration of silence) rather than the foot, syllable, or stress (i.e., each line comprises a certain number of events). The silences cued by numbers or boxes are perceptibly longer than the pauses customarily occasioned by punctuation marks and stanza and section breaks in the reading of most verse and prose.

By 1960 some Simultaneities included musical sounds and/or noises, and by late 1960, prolonged and/or repeated speech sounds. The delivery of some texts was regulated by in-performance chance operations, often quite elaborate. For instance, in the simultaneous-performance version of *Stanzas for Iris Lezak* (first performed in a program of avant-garde music at The Living Theatre, then at 14th Street and 6th Avenue in New York, in August 1960) the performance text consists of a very large number of 5"-x-8" filing cards on which are typed the separated stanzas of the verse poems and the separated paragraphs of the prose pieces, constituting this collection, written May-October 1960 and published in 1972 (Barton, Vt.: Something Else Press).

At the beginning of a performance, the text cards are shuffled and distributed equally among the performers, who read from them in their shuffled order. To regulate delivery each performer is also given a pack of playing cards and a group of cards on both sides of which numbers are written. A different playing card determines the speed and loudness of delivery of the words on each text card. The number cards give durations of silences and (by virtue of numbers being odd or even) cue production or nonproduction of musical sounds or noises at the ends of lines and/or stanzas and of prose paragraphs.

However, the *interpretation* of the playing cards and numbers involves a significant degree of choice on the part of the performers. The *suits* of the cards determine the *loudness* of the delivery of each of the texts: diamonds call for loud speech; hearts, moderately loud; clubs, moderately soft; and spades, soft. Similarly, the *denominations* of the playing cards determine the *tempo* of speech, ranging from very slow (aces) to very fast (kings). But in both cases the individual performers have to determine what these general categories of reading speed mean to them at each moment of the performance. Though the texts read and the general categories of loudness and tempo are determined by chance (i.e., by the three kinds of cards), the *specification* of the loudness and tempo of delivery is the work of each individual performer.

Even the rules governing the interpretation of the number cards give the performers some leeway, some degree of choice, for though the numbers stand for numbers of seconds, and the performers are given the option of measuring the durations of silences with watches, they are also given the alternative of measuring them by thinking "a-thousand-and-one, a-thousand-and-two," etc. The (putative) seconds measured by the latter method are sure to differ both from clock seconds and from each other in accordance with performers' idiosyncrasies if not their deliberate choices. The nonverbal sounds are chosen freely by the performers.

In 1960-61 I wrote 501 numbered "Asymmetries" (nonstanzaic poems): about half were published in *Asymmetries 1-260* (New York: Printed Editions, 1980). Readings and simultaneous performances of them are regulated by the spacing of words on the page (empty spaces indicate silence), their character formats, and their punctuation. They may be performed as speech and/or musical sounds, with or without silences. Performances of groups of "Matched Asymmetries" (all in each group are "about one subject"), written later in the 60s, include only speech and silences (see *21 Matched Asymmetries* — London: Aloes Books, 1978).

At the end of 1960 I also began producing scores in which the scope of performers' choices widened significantly. In "Thanks, a simultaneity for people," each performer chooses any utterance, ranging from a short vocal sound, such as that corresponding to a single letter, to a whole paragraph. The performer makes this utterance once, or repeats it any number of times, and then falls silent for any desired duration; after that, the performer chooses another utterance, delivers it once or any number of times, again falls silent, and so on throughout a performance, which comprises simultaneous sequences of such individually chosen utterances and silences.

The score of "A Piece for Sari Dienes," also written late in 1960, is a drawing produced by rubbing a pencil over the holes of a punched IBM card placed over one third of the back of a folded flyer for a 1955 exhibit of Dienes's works at the Betty Parsons Gallery on 57th Street in New York. Performers are asked to make a sound, any sound (vocal or nonvocal, verbal or nonverbal), for each of the marks on the drawing. Their freedom of interpretation is limited only by the number of marks on the drawing, though the grouping of the marks strongly suggests a similar grouping of sounds.

In early 1961, I began composing "Gathas," performance pieces whose texts are hand-lettered in the squares of sheets of quadrille ("graph") paper. The earlier of these comprise chance-generated configurations of repeated transliterated mantras, each repetition usually lettered vertically. Only one mantra appears in each Gatha, repeated whatever number of times the generative chance system dictated. I called these scores "Gathas" because most of the mantras in them are Buddhist and the term "Gathas" denotes versified portions of Buddhist sutras and also (in the books of Dr. Daisetz Teitaro Suzuki) short poems that Zen masters and their students recite to each other or write (sometimes on walls), often as manifestations of enlightenment.

I first composed nonmantric Gathas in 1973: more than twenty of them, made up of English words drawn by chance operations from a decidely nonreligious text by Kathy Acker (the third mailed-out fascicle of *The Childlike Life of the Black Tarantula*). Subsequently, I composed several "Vocabulary Gathas," each comprising words spelled solely with the letters of a friend's name (no letter being repeated in any word more times than in the whole name), and in 1980 I began making "Free Gathas" (ones composed without using chance operations), of which the words were chosen spontaneously and intuitively as I made the scores, though rules guided their placement.

In performing Gathas, participants follow freely chosen "paths," usually from one square or group of squares to adjacent squares, but sometimes skipping to nonadjacent squares, speaking or singing letter sounds, letter names, syllables or other letter-group sounds, words (including ones fortuitously made up of letters in adjacent squares), or groups of words (including phrases, sentences, or complete mantras). In addition, letter-to-tone-class "translation" rules specific to each Gatha make it possible for musicians to realize Gathas on instruments: letters that are pitch-class names are translated accordingly (e.g., an "A" may be played as an A natural in any octave); various pitch classes are assigned, partially by chance, to letters that aren't pitch-class names (e.g., in some Gathas, an "M" may be played as any G natural).

At every point the individual not only chooses how to move from one square or group of squares to another, but also whether and how to group letters in adjacent squares, to render the letters as speech or song or instrumental sounds, and to interact with the sounds produced by the other performers and ambient sounds (those occurring in the environment of the performance). Very many parameters are fully under the performers' control and subject to their deliberate or spontaneous choices, limited only by the configurations of letters in the squares and by the very general rules of procedure.

My "Vocabularies" are Simultaneity scores made in 1968 and from 1972 through 1979 (the Vocabulary Gathas mentioned before are hybrids of Gathas and Vocabularies). Each Vocabulary is a drawing made up solely of words constituting partial anagrams of one particular name (with no letter repeated in any word more times than in the whole name). Performers move freely from one word to any other, saying them singly, grouping them into phrases or sentences, or translating them into sequences or aggregates (intervals, chords, clusters) of instrumental tones. The main limitation is that performers (unlike those of Gathas) should *never* break words up into syllables, phonemes, or other fragments. The other limitations (as with Gathas) are that performers should only say or play words included in the drawing and/or structure words (articles, prepositions, pronouns, linking verbs) that are also partial anagrams of the name, that they should follow the simple procedural rules, and that they should listen closely and interact with both each other's sounds and those in the environment.

My "Word Events" are similar to the Vocabularies and Gathas, but they have no scores. The source of each Word Event is a particular name, word, or string (phrase, sentence, etc.). Any speech sound (phoneme) included in that name, etc., and any syllables, other phoneme strings, words, or word strings that may be produced by combining those speech sounds may be brought freely into a performance as speech or song. Instrumentalists may either "translate" the letters of the source name, etc., into pitch classes, following consistent systems of their own devising, and improvise upon them, or they may improvise freely, interacting with the vocalists and ambient sounds. The only limitations upon the participants are that they bring into the performance only speech sounds found in the source name, etc., linguistic units composed by combining those speech sounds, or (if they choose "translation" methods) instrumental sounds including only tones in the pitch classes corresponding (according to the particular instrumentalist's system) to letters in the source name, and that they listen closely to, and interact with, each other and ambient sounds.

(In most Word Event performances, though vocalists have followed the given procedure, instrumentalists have improvised freely without using a translation system.)

While performing these works, as well as other Simultaneities composed between 1955 and the present by using chance operations; by following specific acrostic, diastic, anagrammatical, or other types of rules; or (as often recently) intuitively — or by various combinations of these ways — a strong political dimension gradually became apparent to me. By 1964 I had realized that these performances constitute analogical models of the types of utopian societies usually called "anarchist" ("lacking a coercive state apparatus") and "libertarian" ("maximizing individual liberty").

(Some professed libertarians are not anarchists, notably, in the United States, those connected with the Libertarian Party, who favor a "minimal government" that would protect property rights. My own "ultimate" politics are anarchist, libertarian, and pacifist: "ultimate," since in day-to-day politics I favor participating in electoral politics, supporting candidates and policies that seem more nearly consonant with or likely to further my "ultimate" goals — but doing so without illusions — and within clearly defined limits, I may support what seems a lesser evil to hinder or help avoid what seems to be, or apt to lead to, a greater one. However, my pacifism is uncompromising.)

Although a few of the Simultaneities, such as "Thanks" and "A Piece for Sari Dienes," have very few and simple rules, some (e.g., the Stanzas and Asymmetries) are governed by many rules, some complex. All these rules encourage individual performers to choose freely in many areas. They are asked always to listen closely and make their choices both in a state of choiceless awareness (see below) and in relation with other performers' and ambient sounds.

Most of the arrays of verbal and musical materials utilized in Simultaneities have been produced by systematic chance operations involving a minimum of choice on the part of the author-composer. Such methods are used mainly to evade the ego (at least partially) in order to present concrete words, etc., relatively unburdened by the composer's emotions, taste, and predilections, and to encourage in the composer, performers, and audiences an attitude of "bare attention" or "choiceless awareness." My motivations for using such methods stem directly from Buddhism, especially Zen, and I was strongly encouraged to carry out chance operations with verbal and other materials by John Cage's musical compositions of the early 1950s, composed by means of I Ching chance operations (which I've seldom used), and by Cage's brilliant advocacy of chance and indeterminacy in art.

However, non-chance-operational rules of composition and intuitive choices have also figured in the genesis of my work in varying degrees, the latter more and more through the 1970s and '80s. One might say, then, that my compositional practices since 1954 have entailed a dialectic between choice and chance (the "given"), while the performance practices of those realizing my Simultaneities entail a similar dialectic between choice and the given, the latter including the compositions' materials and rules (which sometimes require in-performance chance operations).

Interpreting each Simultaneity, performers are asked to produce — following the rules but otherwise freely, spontaneously, and coopera- tively — a total situation (comprising language and/or "musical" and/or other sounds, and sometimes projections of slides, films, videotapes, or computer graphics — some of which may themselves be used as scores) in which they are both choicelessly aware and making choices that help maximize its value to each of them. This epitomizes a basic Buddhist and anarchist paradox: that one may make meaningful choices while being choicelessly aware and fully respecting others' choices.

If such performances are utopian analogies, the procedural rules, texts, scores, and other given materials are analogs of the circumstances given by nature and historical development that would confront indi- viduals in *any* society. Freedom, spontaneity, and intuition are confron- ted by necessity — the given — and this opposition may be "dialecti- cally overcome" or "transcended" in the course of performances. Such "sublimations" are not results of the *author-composer's* "playing with op- posites" but of the independent (though cooperative) activities of both composer and performers.

But can it be that this confrontation is merely a life-sapping contradic- tion rather than a life-enhancing dialectic? I cannot reach a firm conclu- sion about this. Certainly vitality and what might be called "beauty" (despite the term's archaic associations and the predominant attitude of choiceless awareness) have been manifested during more than a few Si- multaneity performances. But do these situations truly embody and serve freedom? Sometimes I think so. But sometimes I think the politi- cal analogies I have drawn are illusory — that these works subsist solely in the realm of the aesthetic.

Now what the devil does *that* mean? Does *anything* subsist in only one realm, and is there indeed a realm of the aesthetic? Isn't aesthetics itself a relatively recent invention (initiated in the mid-eighteenth century by Alexander Baumgarten)? Perhaps what is more important is that these, like other works of art, express meanings significantly different in kind

from the political, and inexpressible otherwise than by the works them-
selves as realized in performances (I don't mean that the *author-composer*
is expressing these meanings but that the *performances* do so quite aside
from anyone's intentions) and that they may sometimes induce some
measure of choiceless awareness in performers and audiences.

Nevertheless, I believe the political dimension of these works is genu-
ine, even though it may constitute neither the major motivation for their
production and performance nor the only source either of their value or
of their effects on audiences and performers. The peculiar dialectic of
freedom and necessity inherent in their realization embodies basic po-
litical and existential truths and encourages an attitude of choiceless
awareness even toward making choices. When they're realized by fully
committed participants, audiences and performers may live for a time
in a climate close to utopia.

FORUM:
Inman, Weiner, Sherry, Piombino

One To One

P. Inman

A personal name delineates one's space from that of the others'. My name marks my spot on the assembly line off from yours, though our jobs may well be interchangeable. "Each individual has his own place; and each place its individual. Avoid distribution in groups; break up collective dispositions . . ." (Foucault, *Discipline and Punish*).[1] To be delivered a subpoena the subpoena'd must have an address. To be drafted, or inundated with credit card bills, the billed must have a name. Linnean classification begets the mailing list.

Althusser: "Every human, that is to say social individual, cannot be the agent of a practice unless he takes the form of a subject. The subject form is in fact the form that the historical existence of every individual, every agent of social practices, takes; for the relations of production and reproduction necessarily involve, as the integrating element, what Lenin called "ideological social relations," which in order to function, imposes on every individual agent the form of a subject.[2]

Craving for faces. For facial imagery. Iconology. From your generalized Medieval Christ figure to the realistically depicted wart on the Dutch burgher's nose. My son bowled over by how realistic the graphics of a computer game are. His two buddies sitting next to him receding into a less & less vivid reality the more he gets into the game.

Defoe describing Crusoe's day-to-day routines. Accumulating minutiae & details. Building up the inventory of facts while Crusoe stock-piles goods. Narration as accounting.

Good old days. In precapitalist narrative forms the hero was generic.

Or at least not very specific. Capitalist narrative made a science of individualizing; describing facial tics. The movement from *Romance of the Rose* to Fielding to Henry James. Greater & greater psychological resolution. Now all that's been assimilated. We don't have to work as hard at it. Psychology need just be hinted at before the plot proceeds.

Hierarchical pyramid. Sentence/paragraph/story. Emblematic of the same old top/down society we've been living in. It all flows up to the top, gets digested, then excreted back down. I like thinking of *Pere Goriot* (or "Miami Vice") as plumbing.

Ideology constructs the subject. Singularizing, it suppresses all collectivity. The individual lives as if it were a subject not subjected.

In *Discipline and Punish* Foucault shows that alongside the maturation of the capitalist system of production the scientific location & elucidation of "the individual" (preeminently through the psy- and medical sciences) becomes an increasingly effective means of control & repression. Keeping tabs. The body is acted on by a barrage of knowledges & disciplines. Defined, analyzed &, most importantly, located and fixed. The individual as part of a taxonomy. The body as a map of the terrain. Formulate a category: female hysteria. Describe it, validate it "scientifically". Use it as a means of abnormalizing women who are dissatisfied with their second-class social status. Anna O. & the woman's suffrage movement.

Kids prefer watching TV videos of Guns & Roses to hearing G&R songs over the radio. They can see the haircuts & costumes behind the music. Are they dolts or merely the next wave of reality effect junkies?

Lit crit's notion that behind the allusions & in-group imagery stands the genius of Wallace Stevens. The persona of the poet who, even if you don't understand what the hell he's saying, represents what's best in our culture, our human spirit. The poem not so much a unit of meaning as an emblem of it. The real story that of the artist as super individual. The sensibility before you punch in on the time-clock. The promise that it'll be there when you come home from another day at the office.

Marx had thought that the factory as gathering place would socialize the workforce. He hadn't anticipated a late capitalism mobilized against such an effect. Home & school as decontamination chambers. Media opium replacing religion. The brain police & the other kind.

Medicine, psychology, criminology, sociology. Which treat bodies as machinery (passim Descartes, the "father" of our Western subject). Developing alongside the dirty sciences. Industrialization, Taylorization, automation.

Narrative & its strategic mode: realism.

Narrative implicates the subject through its insertion of s/he into the action. Stories must end up somewhere. They must be told to *someone*. What this presentation lacks is an audience. Subject as terminus. The story's protagonist acts as a duplication of that someone, the reader. Why else all the effort realist texts expend on rendering their characters true-to-life, believably like their readers, if not for the purposes of effecting an identification?

Narrative triumphs precisely through the consolidation of isolate detail, fragmented experience. It solidifies. Things all come together at the end of the episode, denying social atomization by the production of a kind of aesthetic afterlife where things will be made whole again. Its closure indicates not only that of the unitary subject's, but the possibility of closure itself. Case closed. I peeked at the end of the book before I got there.

No mere play on words to couple "viewing point" with "point of view".

Once constituted as a name, once disposed toward its options, once "profiled", it becomes clear in what ways the constructed subject is supposed to behave. As a free agent. There are precedents, so many years of them. The mock-up is assigned its own motives. It has no one to blame but itself — or other selves. "It doesn't surprise me that she turned out that way." There is no societally stacked deck.

Perspective painting develops a visual representation in which the viewed is given to the eye as a unified, shrink-wrapped field, to be apprehended with the viewer as its hidden point of reference. Unlike preceding spaces, perspectival space acts as an information funnel whose only possible endpoint could be the merchant, or emergent banker's, eye.

Perspective produces the subject as viewing point. Omega eye. It reminds the viewer where s/he is. That this is not natural, as is sometimes suggested, becomes evident when other modes of art are examined. Chinese, cave, all-over. Surface line, sans illusionistic depth. No visual cue as to where I should position myself relative to the scene before me. Viewer is not incorporated, before the fact, into the picture.

Realism is still the heavy. Graphic violence as an index of "the public's" need for junk. Not a need to know, but a need to see: CBS news. Real blood, sex, in between bullet holes. Increase the dosage of verisimilitude.

Subject-as-construct. Perception socially constructed (i.e., ideological). Or how we use the tools, the biological hard-wiring, channelled. A menu on the computer terminal.

Subject disruption #1: Hannah Weiner's *Clairvoyant Journal*, which through the development of several interpenetrating narrative lines, the push & pull of its alternative voices, frustrates an homogenized reading of the text. A viable identification of its author.

Subjecthood is not an essence preceding social existence. It's not what's left over once the dross has been drained away. It is the dross. It is a convergence of practices, a point of production. A product, not a producer.

Subject disruption #2: Charles Bernstein's stylistic indeterminacy. A constant defusion of the idea of "voice". Style becoming, not a matter of authorial signature, not even a style, but a tactic, a strategy to get into the text.

Subjectivity — once the sole privilege of the boss (who alone is important enough to merit a personal history, a bio note) — gradually democratized. Awarded to the anonymous masses at the bottom of the heap: lumpen, women, peasants, loonies. While this is supposedly a function of egalitarianism, in reality such democratization is used as a means of supervision. Building up a file.

Subject disruption #3: Tina Darragh's entangling of biographical revelation with procedural operations on the dictionary & other found texts. A graphic materialization of the anecdotal. The author made of definitions. The subject produced by geometric patterns mapped out on a page.

Suppose no viewing funnel. No hierarchy of picture planes, no visual pyramid pointing back to the viewer's eye. You don't have to stand in this spot if you don't want to. Suppose no buyer/patron generating the occasion for the picture in the first place. No patriarch pictures on the dollar bills.

Syntax represents a closure itself. A unifying structure. A grammatical identity with the closed boundaries of the reading subject. It guarantees order, mirroring psychic order. To use Greenberg's metaphor (viz. the painting canvas), syntax cuts out a space for the spectator. Through its regularity the narrative line's forward motion, it's arrival on time at its destination, is assured.

The subject is a channelling device. It fixes one's view on her/his own life. On her family history, on his career, on their strategies for self-improvement (jogging, bigger bucks, EST). All the while obfuscating the social forces that have put them where they are. That have produced their personality makeup score.

Through the unified reading subject all the typical narrative shifts in time, location, points of view, are tied together. It is because the narrative's loose ends must be tied together that such a subject can be constructed. The text produces the reader as a non-contradictory subject, always there to receive the story's impulse. It positions him/her as the unified source of its message (Stephen Heath) while circularly validating that source's existence with its own.[3] As such a subject becomes progressively entrenched the story line can give it more slack. The contemporary image can streamline, move faster, accommodate more. MTV montage as grapeshot.

Various individuals, via the social contract, voluntary association, or whatever, don't constitute society. The network of social formations & practices constitute them. "He" or "she" being the name of those social forces' intersection. Their pseudonym.

What are case histories if not narratives?

Writing is inescapably political. It doesn't illustrate the bleakness of late capitalism. It can't get outside itself. It is, rather, amidst itself, made out of the societal world around it.

Notes

1. Michel Foucault, *Discipline and Punish*, tr. Graham Lock (New York: Vintage, 1979), p. 143.

2. Louis Althusser, "Response to John Lewis" in *Essays in Self Criticism*, tr. Alan Sheridan (London: New Left Books, 1976), p. 95; as cited in Alex Callinicos, *Althusser's Marxism* (London: Pluto Press, 1976), p. 70.

3. Stephen Heath, *Questions of Cinema* (Bloomington: University of Indiana, 1981), pp. 43-54.

Hannah Weiner

I think that disjunctive and non-sequential writing can change states of consciousness, awakening the reader to reality, and thus the need for political change.

I think it does this by forcing an aberration in the left brain language centers. I have seen examples of writing in *Scientific American* (September 1979) of people with diseases of the left hemisphere and they read like disjunctive and non-sequential writing.

Disjunctive and non-sequential poetry thus forces a cross to the right hemisphere. This cross can take place only at alpha brain wave levels, when the hemispheres meet (according to Robert Orenstein in *The Psychology of Consciousness* [New York: Viking Press, 1972]). This alpha state is a raised level of consciousness akin to the meditative state as shown by bio-feedback machines.

This is not, however, a state of bliss, which is supposedly registered by theta brain wave levels.

Further confirmation of disjunctive and non-sequential writing directly affecting the brain is found in an essay by Alan Davies and Nick Piombino in $L=A=N=G=U=A=G=E$ (Volume 4, 1981), which discusses the production of the N400 brain wave in response to subjects' coping with "nonsense." Davies and Piombino quote a *New York Times* (March 11, 1980) report on this research: "This N400 wave seems to be tapping into a higher mental process."

CHARLES BERNSTEIN: In responding to Hannah Weiner's comments, I want to point to a related, if opposing, comment made by Paul Sprecher at the same New School session (following my talk). Sprecher pointed to the relation between certain forms of "disjunctive" poetry and glossolalia (speaking in tongues) as practiced by certain charismatic Christian sects. What if glossolalia produced the same detectable brain wave alteration as discussed by Weiner? In the case of glossolalia, any "measurable" heightened consciousness is co-opted (or absorbed) by the social circumstance in which the physiological/cerebral event is experienced. The political issue can never be the cerebral event in isolation but rather must include the social context in which the event is interpreted or in which it functions, uninterpreted. In this respect, it is worth noting that the new formalists, who advocate a return to strongly metered traditional verse, have, at least in one instance, justified their position by arguing that such verse exercises the right brain in sharp contrast to unmetered, including disjunctive, poetry which appeals only to the left brain. Indeed, this raises a fundamental flaw in reductivist left brain/right brain dualism: distinctions like intuitive versus analytic are social not biological distinctions, reflecting, for example, class, education, and gender. For me, the political question concerns the *mind in action*, in context, not the brain as receptor.

WEINER: Glossolalia is a result of heightened states of consciousness and is non-political, like other effects of heightened consciousness such as telepathy, out of body travel, clairvoyance, healing. The work is to make the consciousness political. At heightened states of consciousness, both sides of the brain are energized, thus making the mind in action more effective because it has more power and knows more.

The Boundaries of Poetry

(from *Our Nuclear Heritage*: "Muslims in Soho")

James Sherry

As a result of the international communication facilities technology breakthrough, the Ayatollah Khomeini's message condemning Salman Rushdie to death was heard round the world, penetrating national and geographic boundaries as if they were the paper walls of a zen retreat. As a result of this communication mechanism, the borders of ideas and of nations have a different composition than they did 50 years ago.

The content of the Ayatollah's proclamation is radioactive in the same sense as the electronic advertising and political slogans discharged via TV and radio. Content proclaimed using individual media such as books or short-range media such as public speaking establishes meaning within the boundaries of a discipline or context and expands slowly, mechanically, meeting other content at agreed upon cultural borders.

Content proclaimed using these radioactive mechanisms establishes a nucleus of meaning at critical mass. Once this critical mass is reached, the content begins to contaminate all the meanings surrounding it at nearly light speed and over a much larger area than the voice or the written word.

Not only is the meaning heard around the world, but every non-inert meaning around the individual binds with this meaning for as long as the word continues to be heard. The meanings bind with one another and create a meaning static that is heard along with, often overriding, the intended meaning.

This electromagnetic (meaning) pulse (EMP) renders all meaning-oriented communications chaotic, that is, unpredictable. Hearing a violent proclamation from such a great distance has this side effect of shutting down meaningful communications. The half-life of the Ayatollah's proclamation is the limit of anxiety. And certain kinds of rhetoric have this effect regardless of the mode of communication.

228

Even the word "hearing" in the sense I have been using it means something other than sound waves entering the ear. Hearing now presents an extended text to the hearer every time a concept related to the hearing is presented. And it is true for seeing, speaking, and reading as well.

The Ayatollah engages the West in a battle between correctness and freedom. In the Ayatollah's view people should be treated in accordance with the precepts of Islam. In Western eyes people should be treated in accordance with the laws and constitutions of nations. The Ayatollah's proclamation reveals the weakness of the national boundaries and of the muscle-bound nation states themselves in the age of world-wide radioactive language.

Only a world-wide monoculture can decide such moral issues for everyone and I along with most Western intellectuals lean against that. . . . Certainly in most local disputes today I would side with the rights of the individual and the minority, and when I think of who is promulgating the rationalist international position today — corporations, Republicans, Western supremacist groups, Zionist Israel, South Africa, Japanese corporations. . . .

As the boundaries of the state are breached by international radio forces, the boundaries of the poem, the line, the word, the text are extended beyond any individual tongue to all discourse, even non-human discourse. We no longer speak and write English without reference to the community of human tongues and translations of world-concepts into our national languages.

Dialectical formation and destruction takes place at every level in the poem as a political agenda, committed by the parasites of preconception. Do we rest in English because we speak it? Do we conform to a prosody in order to be able to express ourselves? Yet we cannot reinvent all of language and poetry every time we write. There are aspects of the poem that can be redefined and aspects which are borrowed.

Appropriation in art and the use of modes of discourse not native to the writer in poetry pass through the border of the disciplines of art as if they had no mass. And yet they are visible everywhere in the interaction between the reader/viewer and the word. Rauchenberg painting on an image of Rembrandt brings into question the assumption that the limits of art are individual expression.

When I, in a genre other than poetry, question the notion of literary invention as well as literary convention. Not only is authorship questioned but property as well. When Baudelaire writes poetry in a prose format, that attachment of poetry to verse is severed. The way Silliman leaves a space between sentences throws the onus of the writing from the writer to the reader.

The state sponsored poetry of borders — line, meter, or simplified prosody which simply redefines the borders — operates within the striated space created by the state and mirrors its bureaucracy as the structure of the atom mirrors the social structure. Alternative strategies such as I have just described are now being established as primary poetics and interpolated into the canon.

Anapests, "poetic" emotions, and cabinet bureaus furnish a cultural-political domicile populated by self-congratulatory bureaucrats. Modernism produced an alternative structure that recognized the limits of traditional prosody. Where Modernism failed was in its description of the essentially social nature of language with aestheticized nature-oriented prosody. Modernism put political content in the poem where it was canonized and coopted.

In the post-Mallarméan field poetry, space is defined on the page in heterogeneous smooth space. Bruce Andrews' "elusive continent" where "hinges / ride / lava" (*Getting Ready to Have Been Frightened*, pp. 36 and 110) bodes ill for the linear metrics of the Greeks and English. Length and stress are both mutated in an open area where language mobilizes a network of meaning using the open space as a kind of time divided by an unquantified movement of the eye and breath while reading.

The utopia of this approach tantalizes the reader. It idealizes a society where there is no pull between what we want and what we have to do, no conflict between the citizen and the legislator. It postulates an unalienated alternative. It may do so as a critique of contemporary society or it may do so as a sincere proposal, but to date it can only do so as the art of one person or a collaboration among a few.

Yet a continuous appeal goes out to all minorities, disenfranchised, terrorists, sub-language groups: "This is your poetry. Join the network to discover new ways of making meaning. Do not fixate on poem, voice, other striated and arbitrary meaning formations. We offer a processual, unbounded methodology that can be applied to any language and can include all languages."

Like the mathematics of chaos, poetry shows that the world is composed primarily of complex systems and that even the simplest of these do not have simple dynamic properties. Avoiding facility in art to define a thing is easy. To define an interaction, a polity, is difficult, because all differences are taken into account. "Slow and rapid are not quantitative degrees of movement, but two types of qualified motion" (Deleuze and Guattari, *Nomadology: The War Machine*, tr. Brian Massumi).

Poetry resides in an objective zone of fluctuation contiguous to reality.

Sensitive and sensible evaluations pose more problems than they solve. Even problematics is only one mode. And the heterogeneous open field is itself bounded by definitions of states of being experimental or avant-garde.

In contrast state poetry organizes around axioms of prosody, metrics defined by categories. This is the rigor against which one tests oneself not by seeing how far away from it one can go, but without going back at all. What Webern described as "not returning to the keynote." Pierre Boulez distinguishes between two types of time in music. Striated time broken up by measures which can be regular or irregular but is always assignable, and smooth space in which the partition "can be effected by the will" (*Boulez on Music*, tr. Susan Bradshaw, p. 85).

But the catch. The advertising agencies and the newspaper headlines utilize language strategies unbounded by grammar which the new poetry has introduced. The advertisers limit the variation of grammar and change the instrumentality from ways of creating meaning to ways of getting people to buy product, but the effect is to undermine the divisions of grammar. By calling the non-systematic and/or redefined language of goal-oriented problem solving to come to the aid of the state without the exigencies and martial law of wartime, the state brings a fifth column into its central definitions manufactory.

And the computers which run it, as I have noted elsewhere, use a language that is not hierarchical, in which every part of speech and punctuation is as vital to the functioning of the whole as any other. The dictation of the subject-verb-object sentence is overwhelmed by a language of units moving across a surface determined not by the end of the instruction set but by the velocity with which a continuing loop of transactions are performed. IBM computers have no executive although they execute, only a fifo queue for executions and an incremental. The executioner is merely an ordering principle.

Cultivate Your Own Wilderness

Nick Piombino

It would be difficult to deny that the 20th Century has been a period of exceptionally forceful competition among social paradigms. An unending plethora of conceptions of social reality have ripened and ultimately fallen from the contemporary tree of knowledge into a veritable cornucopia of desperate experiments and wildly hopeful fantasies, charismatic leaders, tragic swindles, some silly and some ghastly utopias and some impressive advances. Some of these advances are already showing signs of wear and tear but have attained a degree of historical importance. Others, such as the civil rights movement, the women's movement, the mental health movement (to name a few) have left an invaluable inheritance and an example of growth and change towards healthier ways of living. Other attempts left many people with a lot of physical and emotional baggage they don't need.

Like all forms of human endeavor, poetry lives and thrives, matures and finally fades away in importance and relevance, in part according to social conditions. As a result, as with other forms of essentially individual behavior, there is a dynamic relationship between the social responses to poetry and the meaning of this effect on the actual practitioner's purposes and aims. The social fact, for example, that poetry has learned how to survive and even flourish, in ways, in a vacuum, as it does in the United States, illustrates amply the paradoxical relationship between the actual powers of poetry and its apparent social reception. As illustrated by the biographies of many great poets, poetry can germinate and grow quite excellently in the arid desert of practically no response whatever. Emily Dickinson and Charles Baudelaire may serve as bright examples.

There are poets who can make the rain fall in the desert. I think of Allen Ginsberg. When he sings to hex the government, I don't hear the music of the spheres. But when he envisions, like his soulmate Walt Whitman, the individual's *relationship* to government, world, mind, cosmos, I wonder if everyone hasn't been transformed.

If we are to speak of the "social" as poets I think it would be most valuable to visualize it as a largely internal entity, part reality and part fantasy no matter what happens on television. If a poet feels the need to address the whole society, I think it would be more effective to do so as if she were talking to someone else (which includes, of course, partly talking into the void). Perhaps we ought to image the social as if it were a person, and in the United States, not a very well or at times very coherent person, and then, even as a kind of other person within that person, partly unknown to the person — to me this would approximate the "social" as it may be seen from a poet's viewpoint. In psychoanalysis this is called the superego, which once I called the supraego to underline those aspects of the conscience over which the individual has little power or influence. Having, in fact, very little real power to reshape society by force, at least for very long, the poet learns, like any other individual, to adapt externally. But the *internal* adaptation that takes place simultaneously is not like the external one, and is different in some essential way from that of the average person. The poet must learn to rebel in a certain sense internally whether or not he or she rebels externally. Without this small rebellion, staged within the self again and again, there, in fact, would be no poem. With groups the story is different. The fact that a very large group of people came together to protest the war in Vietnam (and who would not think of Allen Ginsberg in this context) did not alter much the overall and pervasive feeling of powerlessness among individuals in our society. So what is the power of the poet under such conditions to effect the social policy? To me the answer lies in the fact that poetry carves out a place for the social to exist in some freer way inside the individual human being. Denise Levertov once said that the language poets take a private space on the public beach. My response to this is that it takes a private place within for the individual to find any comfort or freedom at all on the public beach — which, in fact, is the only beach for most of us. Poetry attempts to redefine the whole of experience by confronting it with its own language, creating a self-transformative loop between language and experience, helping externalize what is too often regarded as a public province internally by the individual.

We live in a time when most individual experience is reduced to an obscene version of social homogeneity. It is abundantly clear to most people in the United States by now that if you conform in your thoughts you will fit in. A ready sense of humor will protect us from any real reaction to a departure in the usual expressions. The unconscious wish to suppress all idiosyncrasy is an obsessive trait which belongs to a primitive form of tribal self-protection. In this sense we might say that the individual has "come a long way" but the individual as group or the group as individual is still largely infantile — particularly (as babies are) when it doesn't get its own way with what it regards as "the individual." Under such circumstances *poetry only survives in hidden forms*. This means *really* secret, not just esoteric or obscure, but simply inscrutable. In this way it protects its ageless loyalty to real experience, and real human needs. As long as extreme social hypocrisy remains, poetry will turn to extreme means to protect itself like this, and will discover its power in guarding the ancient truths and nothing will publicize it to the detriment of this function, no matter how energetic the broadcasting — to whatever extent the gulf between the poet and the public continues to be an externalization of the gulf between the truly valued and the unquestionably phoney. Such things cannot be changed quickly or easily because the situation has little to do with the "social" in the reportorial sense but more to do with the group conception of the internal human being and the group's beliefs about the conditions under which its importance is actually realized (which *is* in a certain sense known, but unconsciously denied, for the same reasons that so many other ideals are lost somewhere between their acknowledgement and their actual application). Here and now the poet struggles to transgress not so much the external laws and norms which are unjust but the group continues to declare just, as obnoxious and limiting and vicious as these can be — but the far more insidious, cancerous and pervasive subliminally imposed internal ones. In this arena the powers and means of the poet differ from that of most other people though they partake of the universal spirit in the individual experience, or strive to. The poet is best equipped to intelligently transgress certain extremely important, actually crucial internal entities from a cultural viewpoint, crucial particularly to the inner needs of the productive individual within the culture. The poet's sensitivity is able to creatively transgress certain internal boundaries in order to help define their continued existence from the point of view of overall consciousness, and sometimes to even help redefine them. Sometimes poetry does the latter by helping the conception of the internal person to rid itself of boundaries which are already probably in a rotted condition and are ready to go. It is because of this that poets become expert revolutionaries, though they should take care not to obsessively apply their expertise in this area, which results from purposes which are not precisely the same as those of full-time political revolutionaries. Suffice it to say that the ordinary "peacetime" activities that each are generally attracted to are not consistently the same. The poet has special skills in creatively transgressing internal boundaries because of the wish to make a contribution to what is out there in here.

In closing I'd like to turn around that famous dictum of Gertrude Stein: we are all a found generation.

Comedy and the Poetics of Political Form

Charles Bernstein

> For if a swan could sing we would not know what she was insisting. But we
> are not, or few of us, swans, and have no excuse.
>
> — Flo Amber

> *The Crooked shall be made Straight and the Straight sundered into a thousand*
> *Shards.*
>
> — Ezekial Horn

1.

No swan song will serenade this series to its close, only further compli-
cations to abet what has preceded, add some chiaroscuro to the dozing
points of light; plug up some holes and drill some more, calling the
leaks poetry, the clogs excess.

My theses have taken me some strange places, beyond Moorish inte-
riors to an inlet inside a dome. An insistence whose luster is so much
scotch-guard against spoilage, whose dethronements dissolve into vale-
dictory reprise.

There's another way of saying it, of putting the cork back on the boat,
the wheel around the spin: I mean to see the formal dynamics of a
poem as communicative exchanges, as socially addressed, and as ideo-
logically explicit. And, squinting to bring that into view, focus on the
sometimes competing, sometimes reinforcing realms of convention and
authority, persuasion and rhetoric, sincerity and conviction. For many a
person has been convicted thanks to too much sincerity and not enough
rhetoric, too much persuasion and not enough authority.

Conventions are made to be broken in that they are provisional rath-
er than absolute, temporal rather than eternal. Differing conventions
mark not only different times but also different classes and ethnicities.
As we consider the conventions of writing, we are entering into the poli-
tics of language.

235

Writing conventions play a fundamental role in the legitimation of communicative acts. They determine what is allowed into a particular specific discourse: what is accepted as sensible or appropriate or within the bounds of morality.

Yet dominant conventions are hardly the only conventions with authority and refusing the authority of particular conventions does not, in any sense, put one outside conventionality. Conventions are not identical to social norms or standards, although this distinction is purposely blurred in the legitimation process. Inflexible standardization is the arteriosclerosis of language. The shared counterconventions that may develop — whether among small constituencies of poets or political groupings or scientists or regional communities — are often a means of enhancing communication and articulation, in many cases because certain details (palpable material or social facts) are not articulable through prevailing linguistic conventions. Indeed, in its counterconventional investigations, poetry engages *public* language as its roots, in that it tests the limits of conventionality while forging alternate conventions (which, however, need not seek to replace other conventions in quest of becoming the new standard). Moreover, the contained scale of such poetic engagements allows for a more comprehensive understanding of the formation of public space: *of polis*.

Problems of authority emerge from counter-establishment conventions as much as from established conventions. The poetic authority to challenge dominant societal values, including conventional manners of communication, is a model for the individual political participation of each citizen. The peculiar act of exercising this authority has implications for the public sphere insofar as such independent exercise of authority is not legitimated within a political context that fosters passivity. What seems to be discouraged in American politics is any active participation in the designation and description of public policy issues — a ceding of authority that politicians, journalists, and the public are forced to accept if they are to play the conventional political roles to which they seem to have been assigned. The poll remains the most conspicuous example of this disenfranchising process, for polls elicit binary reactions to always-already articulated policies — a stark contrast to proactive political participation that entails involvement in formulating these policies — *including formulating the way they are represented*.

This, in turn, suggests that authority must not be conflated into a single ambivalent figure; we must constantly be on guard to differentiate realms and degrees of authority, specifically in terms of the type of control that is exerted: the power of persuasion versus the coercion of physical force;

vatic, perhaps even fatuous, poetic authority versus the psychological
and behavioral manipulation of advertising or behavioral engineering;
the authority of a school system versus that of an army, the authority of
money versus aesthetic innovation.

Convention is a central means by which authority is made credible.
As a result, convention can neutralize substantive conflicts: Tweedle-
dum & Tweedledee may say the opposite things but this becomes a
technicality within the context of their identical form.

> "If you think we're wax-works," [Tweedledee] said, "you ought
> to pay, you know. Wax-works weren't made to be looked at for
> nothing." . . .
> "I know what you're thinking about," said Tweedledum; "but it
> isn't so, nohow."
> "Contrawise," continued Tweedledee, "if it was so, it might be;
> and if it were so, it would be; but as it isn't, it ain't. That's logic."[1]

This is the logic of standardized form, the axiomatizing of difference,
so that our opposition is so much waxwork, for which we are to be paid
a penny a word. — "They've got a laser printer, we'd better get a laser
printer — lest our message will lack credibility."

I am not suggesting switching from an uptight business suit into sin-
cere jeans, as if to re-enact the fallacy of Romantic authenticity; but rath-
er acting out, in dialectical play, the insincerity of form as much as con-
tent. Such poetic play does not open into a neat opposition of dry high
irony and wet lyric expressiveness but, in contrast, collapses into a more
ambivolent, destabilizing field of pathos, the ludicrous, schtick, sarcasm;
a multidimensional textual field that is congenitally unable to maintain
an evenness of surface tension or a flatness of affect, where linguistic
shards of histrionic inappropriateness pierce the momentary calm of an
obscure twist of phrase, before cantoring into the next available trope;
less a shield than a probe.

The nonsincere, antiauthentic use of form is both antiformalist and,
insofar as New Critical and Greenbergian formalism provides a conven-
tional, highly partial, reading of modernism, un-"Modern": though
very much part of the radical modernist traditions. Both the formalist
and new critical maps of modernism tend to treat stylistic developments
as a series of autonomous technical "advances" within an art medium
and without recourse to sociohistorical "explanation": a "canonical"
strategy that underwrites the teaching of literature in most university set-
tings, as Ron Silliman noted in his presentation.

The project of particularizing, historicizing, and ideologizing the in-
terpretation of poetry must especially, even primarily, address itself to

the stylistic features of the work. That means refusing to interpret formal dynamics as divorced from the historical and theatrical arena in which they are situated. In this context, Jerome McGann provides a useful model for reading Byron's formal strategies, specifically proposing Byron's direct confrontation with his audience, his inclusion of ungeneralizable and often savage personal details, and his blatant use of dissimulation as a refusal of the Romantic poetics of sincerity. By Romantic sincerity, I mean the poet's lyric address to the human-eternal, to the Imagination, that seems to allow the poem to appear to transcend the partiality of its origin. Thus the poet is able to speak for the "human" by refusing markers that would pull against the universality of "his" address — a strategy that enables us to misread Wordsworth as speaking as directly to us in 1988 as to his contemporaries. Indeed, Romantic sincerity engenders the idea of autonomy in New Critical and formalist approaches to twentieth century art.

Historicizing a poem's deployment of artifice specifically brackets the canonical, teleological approach to stylistic innovation, which graphs particular innovations onto a master narrative of the medium's history. For one thing, these master narratives need to be partialized as specific historical projections for particular ideological purposes. Innovation "itself" may be thought of in social and not just structural terms (*equally* structural and social). That is, the rupturing of patriarchal discourse may be read in terms of sexual and racial politics as well as in terms of structural innovation in the abstract. At the same time, normative discursive practices need to be read in terms of the political meaning of their formal strategies.

On the one hand, this means considering how conventional writing — with and without oppositional content — participates in a legitimating process. On the other hand, this suggests the sort of penetrating analysis provided by Nathaniel Mackey on the social meaning of stuttering/limping in Jean Toomer, Ralph Ellison, and William Carlos Williams (a device that might also be interpreted, for example, in terms of cubist fracturing);[2] or Nicole Brossard's framing of her poetry in terms of the attempt to write without recourse to phallocratic grammar (a project that might also be understood in terms of its relation, for one example, to the new narrative strategies of writers such as Alan Robbe-Grillet.) Likewise, the innovations of white, male, heterosexual artists are not "purely" stylistic — and perhaps the harshness or bumpiness of the anticonventionality of Bruce Andrews or myself needs to be read in terms of male sexual poetics as much as we read Brossard or Mackey, at least in part, in terms of ethnic or sexual identity.[3]

2.

I do not think that all conventions are pernicious or that all authority is corrupt. But I do think it is essential to trace how some uses of convention and authority can hide the fact that both are historical constructions rather than sovereign principles. For convention and authority can, and ought, serve at the will of the polis and not by the Divine right of kings or the economic might of Capital. In this sense, I would speak of a phallocratic voice of truth and sincerity as one that hides its partiality by insisting on its centrality, objectivity, or neutrality — its claim to mainstream values; a voice that opts for expedience at the expense of depth, narrative continuity at the expense of detail, persuasion at the expense of conviction. This is a constantly self-proclaimed public voice, implicitly if not explicitly deriding the inarticulations, stutterings, inaudibilities, eccentricities, and linguistic deviance of specifically marked "special interest" groups. The legitimating markers of persuasion and conviction in our society are intimately tied in to what can usefully be stigmatized as a male heterosexual form of discourse, one that I think "men" writers, given their specific vantage of being identified with this discourse, can also rupture, cut-up, break apart in order to expose and defuse and reform.

Earlier in this series, Erica Hunt spoke, in part in terms of her experiences as a black woman, of feeling constrained by the private, fragmented, or subjective (subjugated) voices authorized for her and of her desire for, yet suspicion about, a "public voice", understood as one that carries the power and legitimacy of more conventional narrative discursive practices. In contrast, I felt my initiation into such a "public" voice was the product of a profound humiliation and degradation that I had but little choice to undergo: a private-school hazing into Grammar, that once Mastered I cannot unlearn, but which, like many men, I am perennially suspicious of even as it continues to inform the expression of my (most well-founded) beliefs and convictions: the artifice of my authenticity.

So, again, I do not propose some private voice, some vatic image of sincerity or the absolute value of innovation, as an alternative to the limitations of the voices of authority I can never completely shake off. For I am a ventriloquist, happy as a raven to preach with blinding fervour of the corruptions of public life in a voice of pained honesty that is as much a conceit as the most formal legal brief for which my early education would seem to have prepared me. If my loops and short circuits, my love of elision, my Groucho Marxian refusal of irony is an effort to explode the authority of those conventions I wish to discredit (disinherit), it constantly offers the consoling self-justification of being Art, as if I could escape the partiality of my condition by my investigation of it. But my art is just empty words on a page if it is does not, indeed, persuade, if it enters into the world as self-justification or self-flagellation or aesthetic ornamentation rather than as interaction, as conversation, as provocation (for myself and others).

My sense of evacuating or undermining the public voice does not mean that I am giving anything up, except if gain is conceived purely in terms of the accumulation of tokens that can be used to buy things exclusively at the company store. It is a sort of aspect blindness that measures communication in numbers of "contact hours" rather than in depth of exchange, in terms of exposure rather than the *company* that communicative exchange — human contact — can provide ("which [people] die miserably every day / for lack of / what is found there"[4]). The "in"articulate, the stutter or limp that Mackey sees in black writing and music, the stammering fragmentation that Susan Howe hears in the earliest recorded voices of North American women, the ludicrous or awkward or damaged or crooked or humiliated, all open up into the "syncopated, the polyrhythmical, the heterogeneous",[5] the offbeat. In contrast, the dominant public language of our society, to use a male metaphor, has been so emptied of specific, socially refractory content that it can be easily and widely disseminated; but this is a dissemination without seed. It is not communicative action but communication behavior: for one speaks less to particular individuals than to those aspects of their consciousness that have been programmed to receive the already digested scenes or commentaries provided.

The bent appears so only by dint of the refraction of the social medium that we see it through: so many straight sticks broken by an effect of light through water. & the straight is no less an auditory illusion (contrived elocution), unmasked in its collusions as a tortuously circuitous distance between two points, the result of a kind of grammatical red-lining or gerrymandering, yet stoically insistent on its own rectitude and irreducible economy.

Politics as opposed to what? For this begins to sketch the politics of a poetic form in the negative sense: what keeps the lid on; not only the straight but also the smug, the self-righteous, the certain, the sanctimonious, the arrogant, the correct, the paternalistic, the patrician, the policing, the colonizing, the standardizing, and those structures, styles, tropes, methods of transition, that connote or mime or project (rather than confront or expose or redress) these approaches to the world.

Don't get me wrong: I know it's almost a joke to speak of poetry and national affairs. Yet in *The Social Contract*, Jean-Jacques Rousseau writes that since our conventions are provisional, the public may choose to reconvene in order to withdraw authority from those conventions which no longer serve our purposes. & poetry is one of the few areas where this right of reconvening is exercised.

But what if the social body has spoken and one finds oneself outside the "mainstream values" that it ratifies. For majority rule can mean forcing inhospitable conventions on unwilling subjects. An ominous example of this problem is the recent election, by a majority of voters, of an ACLU-baiting candidate for U.S. president. Equally disturbing, and instructive for this discussion, is the success of the English First movement. Democracy, without individual and sectarian liberty, is a mockery of justice. So it is necessary to insist that any social contract has independent clauses that not only protect but also foster dissident forms of life, manners of speaking, ways of thinking.

Poetry and Public Policy. The two have rarely seemed, surely long have seemed, so far apart. As distant perhaps as conventions are from the authority that once gave them life and now have deserted them like so many ancient tumuli, monuments to what was a merciless Sovereignty but now is a vestigial software system that we call the standard English of the living dead. One of the more remarkable insights of the late sociologist Erving Goffman was that every interpersonal interaction should be read as an institutional and ideological event; indeed, that conventions, which are enacted at every level, can best be understood institutionally. This microcosmic view of public space suggests an arena for poetry that shortcircuits those near-moronic voices who each month, it seems, moan about the loss of celebrity status or mass audience for the "serious" writer. This repeated misapprehension, both of the history of the reception of poetry in the United States or Britain and of the meaning of "public", is a clinically precise instance of a particular picture holding one captive, in Wittgenstein's phrase, and so forcing the same conclusion again and again.

What is to be regretted is not the lack of mass audience for any particular poet but the lack of poetic thinking as an activated potential for all people. In a time of ecological catastrophe like ours, we say that wilderness areas must not only be preserved but also expanded regardless of how many people park their cars within two miles of the site. That the effect these wilderness areas have is not measurable by audience but in terms of the regeneration of the earth that benefits all of us who live on it — and for the good of our collective unconscious and much as our collective consciousness. I've never been to Alaska but it makes a difference to me that it's *there*. Poets don't have to be read, any more than trees have to be sat under, to transform poisonous societal emissions into something that can be breathed. As a poet, you affect the public sphere with each reader, with the fact of the poem, and by exercising your prerogative to choose what collective forms you will legitimate. The political power of poetry is not measured in numbers; it instructs us to count differently.

3.

Adorno writes in his *Aesthetic Theory* that "truth is the antithesis of existing society".[6] This statement suggests that the authority of our conventions is bogus, that only by negating the positive values that legitimate existing societies can we find truth. Yet this statement is a logical paradox which, like the paradigmatic example "This sentence is false", appears to contradict itself. If truth is the antithesis of existing society, then falsity is the thesis of existing society, including Adorno's statement; or perhaps truth pertains only to nonexisting societies and once a socius actually exists only false-consciousness is possible (including mistaken views about the inevitability, or nature, of the Dark). I might wish to revise Adorno's remark by saying that truth is the synthesis of existing societies, but that would be to substitute my own poetic pragmatism for Adorno's more rhetorically scathing insight, as if I didn't get the joke. There is a range of attitudes one can have toward the truth or falsity of existing societies that allows neither for total negation or total affirmation; this is why irony, in the narrowest sense of suggesting a binary model of assertion/rejection, is formally inadequate to allow for what a mix of comic, bathetic, and objective modes might: an intercutting that undercuts the centrality of a governing narrative or prosodic strategy.

Anything that departs from the sincere or serious enters into the comic, but the comic is anything but a unitary phenomenon, and the range of comic attitudes goes from the good-humored to the vicious, from clubby endorsement of the existing social reign to total rejection of all existing human communities: Poet as confidence "man", deploying hypocrisy in order to shatter the formal autonomy of the poem and its surface of detachment; the sincere and the comic as interfused figure, not either/or but *both and*. For our sincerity is always comic, always questionable, always open to mocking. We are pathetic and heroic simultaneously, one by virtue of the other, a vision of human being that is the basis of the work of the other Williams, Tennessee.

By insisting that stylistic innovations be recognized not only as alternative aesthetic conventions but also as alternative social formations, I am asking that we bring devices back from a purely structural interpretive hermeneutics. In order to fully develop the meaning of a formal rupture or extension, we need a synoptic, multilevel, interactive response that accounts, in hopefully unconventional antiauthoritative ways, for sexual, class, local-historical, biographical, prosodic, and structural dimensions of a poem. This would mean reading all writing, but especially official or dominant forms of writing, as, in part, "minority" discourse in order to partialize those cultural and stylistic elements that are hegemonic and to put all writing practices on equal terms from a social point of view. At the same time, it would give a greater emphasis to the stylistic features and structural innovations of so-called marginal writings than is often now the case. For every aspect of writing reflects its society's politics and aesthetics; indeed the aesthetic and the political make an inseparable *poetics*.

Poetry can bring to awareness questions of authority and conventionality, not to overthrow them, as in a certain reading of destructive intent, but to reconfigure: a necessary defiguration as prerequisite for refiguration, for the regeneration of the ability to figure — count — think figuratively, tropically. That poetry of which I speak is multidirectional and multivectoral; for while some vectors are undermining others just keep on mining.

The interpretive and compositional model I am proposing, then, can be understood as a synthesis of the three Marxes (Chico, Karl, Groucho) and the four Williamses (Raymond, William Carlos, Tennessee, and Esther).

4.

When convention and authority clash you can hear the noise for miles. And this social noise is a sound that poetry can not only make but echo and resound. And while this convention of the permanent committees on the politics of poetic form is over, there is one last directive to pass on: Hold your own hearings.

Notes

1. Lewis Carroll, "Tweedledum and Tweedledee", chapter 4, *Through the Looking Glass*, in *The Annotated Alice* (Cleveland: World Publishing, 1963), pp. 229-31.

2. See pp. 91-2, above: ". . . the phantom limb is a felt recovery, a felt advance beyond severance and limitation which contends with and questions conventional reality, that it's a feeling for what's not there which reaches beyond as it calls into question what is. . . . The phantom limb haunts or critiques a condition in which feeling, consciousness itself, would seem to have been cut off. It's this condition, the non-objective character of reality, to which Michael Taussig applies the expression 'phantom objectivity,' by which he means the veil by way of which

a social order renders its role in the construction of reality invisible. . . ."

The stutter is a striking example of what I call an antiabsorptive or disruptive device in *Artifice of Absorption* (Philadelphia: *Paper Air*, 1987). In an article on the video work of Jean-Luc Godard, David Levi Strauss cites an interview with Gilles Deleuze in which he "characterizes Godard's method of 'turning aside,' of diversion and interruption as a 'creative stutter' ": "In a way, it's all about stuttering: not the literal speech impediment, but that halting use of language itself. Generally speaking, you can only be a foreigner in a language other than your own. Here's it's a case of being a foreigner in one's own language." [Levi Strauss, "Oh Socrates: Visible Crisis in the Video & Television Work of Jean-Luc Godard and Anne-Marie Miéville," in *Artscribe* 74 (1989), p. 29; Deleuze is quoted from an interview in *Afterimage* No. 7 (1978).] — But, as I argue in "Time Out of Motion: Looking Ahead to see Backward" [in *American Poetry* 4:1 (1986)], much of the most radical American poetry is the writing of nonnative speakers: a nonnativeness that can range from a social given to a cultural invention. For the poet, like the Jew in Edmond Jabès's sense, is in exile, even in her own language.

3. Rosmarie Waldrop, in her presentation, suggests that the conception of poetry as quasilegislative — certainly an aspect of my investigation — may be a particularly male aspiration.

4. "Asphodel, That Greeny Flower", in *The Collected Poems of William Carlos Williams, Vol. II: 1939-1962*, ed. Christopher MacGowan (New York: New Directions, 1988).

5. Mackey, p. 100.

6. Theodor W. Adorno, *Aesthetic Theory*, tr. C. Lenhardt, ed. Gretel Adorno and Rolf Tiedemann (London: Verso, 1984) p. 279. Cited by Anne Mack and Jay Rome in "Clark Coolidge's Poetry: Truth in the Body of Falsehood", *Parnassus* 15:1 (1989), p. 279. Mack and Rome pair this quote with another from *Aesthetic Theory* (p. 472) that suggests that art's function is "the determinate negation of the status quo."

Contributors

Jerome Rothenberg is author of *Khurbn & Other Poems* and *New Selected Poems* from New Directions. His landmark *Technicians of the Sacred* has been reissued by University of California Press. He is a professor at University of California at San Diego.

Bruce Andrews coedited $L=A=N=G=U=A=G=E$ and *The $L=A=N=G=U=A=G=E$ Book* (Southern Illinois University Press). His books include *Give Em Enough Rope* (Sun & Moon Press), *Getting Ready to Have Been Frightened* (Roof Books). He teaches political economy at Fordham University and is at work on a study of American intervention in Vietnam, *Surplus Security*.

Rosmarie Waldrop is co-editor of Burning Deck Press of Providence, Rhode Island. Her collections of poetry include *Reproduction of Profiles*, from New Directions, and *Streets Enough to Welcome Snow* from Station Hill. She is the distinguished translator of Edmond Jabès, Paul Celan, and others.

Nicole Brossard is one of Quebec's most celebrated writers and author of many volumes of poetry, most of which have been translated into English and published by Coach House Press. She was a founding editor of the influential Montreal magazine *La Nouvelle Barre du Jour*. She lives in Montreal.

Nathaniel Mackey is editor of *Hambone* magazine. His books include *Eroding Witness* (University of Illinois Press, 1985; National Poetry Series volume, selected by Michael Harper) and *Bedouin Hornbook* (Callaloo Press). He is associate professor of literature at University of California, Santa Cruz.

Jerome McGann is Commonwealth Professor of English at the University of Virginia and author of *The Romantic Ideology*, *The Beauty of Inflections*, and, most recently, *Social Values and Poetic Acts* (Harvard University Press). He is editor of the Oxford Byron.

Ron Silliman's essays are collected in *The New Sentence* (Roof). He has published over a dozen books of poetry, including *What* and *Tjanting* from The Figures. Silliman, who lives in the San Francisco Bay area, is a former editor of *The Socialist Review* and edited the anthology *In The American Tree*.

Susan Howe is author of *My Emily Dickinson*. A number of collections of her poetry have been published, including *Articulation of Sound Forms in Time* (Awede Press), *Europe of Trusts* (Sun & Moon), and *A Bibliography of the King's Book or, Eikon Basilike* (Paradigm Press). She lives in Guilford, Connecticut.

Erica Hunt's poetry has been published in *boundary 2*, *Hambone*, and the anthology *In the American Tree*. She is a program officer at the New World Foundation, which funds civil rights and community organizing programs.

Jackson Mac Low's books include *Representive Works: 1938-1985* (Roof), *Pieces of Six* (Sun & Moon), and *Bloomsday* (Station Hill).

P. Inman is author of *Think of One* (Potes and Poets) and *Red Shift* (Roof), among other collections of poetry. He lives in Greenbelt, Maryland.

Hannah Weiner's books include *Spoke* (Sun & Moon) and *Little Books/Indians* (Roof).

James Sherry edits Roof books and directs The Segue Foundation. His books include *Popular Fiction* (Roof) and *In Case* (Sun & Moon).

Nick Piombino is the author of *Poems* and the forthcoming *Boundary of Blur*, a collection of essays, both from Sun & Moon. He is a psychoanalyst in private practice.

Charles Bernstein coedited $L=A=N=G=U=A=G=E$ and has edited collections of contemporary poetry for *The Paris Review* and *boundary 2*. He is author of *Contents Dream: Essays 1975-1984*, *The Sophist*, and *Rough Trades*, all from Sun & Moon.